Genesis 1-2

a
Harmonised and Historical Reading

Peter Heavyside

My help comes from the Lord, who made heaven and earth

First Edition: 2018

Second Edition: 2022

ISBN: 978-1-3999-2906-6

Ascent Publications

www.lulu.com/ascentpublications

Use of alternative versions is based on analysis of the relevant Hebrew or Greek texts. 'AT' stands for 'author's translation'. Transliterations of the Hebrew are based on the consonantal text.

Cover Design: Anissa Pahlke

All proceeds from this book will go to The National Association for People Abused in Childhood (https://napac.org.uk/).

Dedication

This book is dedicated to the memory of my mother and father

My first tutors in the gospel

Both asleep in Christ and in the hope of the resurrection

Contents

Preface

I suppose from one perspective, this short book could have a limited shelf-life. As current fashions that endeavour to accommodate scripture's teaching about creation with evolutionary theory pass from the scene, as fashions tend to do, the claims of evolutionary creationism that are countered in the book could no longer be needed.

But it is my hope that this work will have more enduring value from a number of different but related perspectives.

- First, as a defence of scripture's integrity against liberal critical handling which claims to identify historical errors or failures of historical accuracy, inconsistencies and mythological genre within scripture – whatever the motivation for such handling, which is certainly not limited to an evolutionary creationist agenda. This is the book's principal purpose.

- Second, as a sound exposition of aspects of Genesis 1 and 2, exploring some of the eternal themes that God begins here.

- Third, as an illustration of how to deal with "problem" passages. Rather than running shy of such passages, I encourage you to embrace them in order to discover God's purpose by taking perceived problems in scripture as signposts for matters of deeper significance.

It is also my hope that, with God's blessings, this book will contribute to strengthening and restoring faith in God and his word so that we might join together with the psalmist and confess, "Our help is in the name of the LORD, who made heaven and earth" (Ps. 124:8).

A note for those who might have read a series of essays I had published in *Testimony* during 2016-2017. The content of this book includes that material but considerably expands upon it while also including refinements of the original exposition.

Peter Heavyside, Hong Kong, August 2018

Preface to the Second Edition

On several occasions in the First Edition, the point was made that scripture's quality as God's word is the only basis shared by special creationists and evolutionary creationists upon which discussion and debate can take place. It was stated that any rebuttal of the conclusions in this book must turn on demonstrating the interpretation of scripture presented in it is mistaken.

This invitation was taken up by *Christadelphian Origins Discussion* (COD) and across the period August 2019 to January 2020, COD published a series of critiques of some of the arguments laid out in the book. Replies to the critiques were posted to the COD site and can be viewed there (see Chapter A1 for details). Since then, some of my readers have urged me to incorporate the debate with COD in a Second Edition because they regard the outcome of the debate to be a further sound and detailed substantiation of the harmony and historicity of Genesis 1 and 2. This Second Edition answers that call and the substance of my Replies, with comprehensive referencing to COD's posts, are published in the Addendum.

I have taken the opportunity of some minor editing of the original material of the First Edition and of including a Scripture Index.

My hope continues that, with God's blessings, this book will contribute to strengthening and restoring faith in God and his word so that we might join together with the psalmist and confess, "Our help is in the name of the LORD, who made heaven and earth" (Ps. 124:8).

Peter Heavyside, Valencia, Spain, April 2022

1: Preliminary Remarks

From the earliest days of Darwinism, Christians of many hues have embraced evolutionary theory as describing God's creative methodology.[1] 'Theistic evolution' was coined to describe this accommodation of scripture's creation record with evolution. More recently, 'evolutionary creationism' has been employed, sometimes with the purpose of categorising a Christian embrace of evolution that sees God as more involved in the evolutionary process than was typical with theistic evolution. In this book 'evolutionary creationism' will be used to refer to both models since, to all intents and purposes, they are one and the same.[2] Since the early days, increasing numbers of Christian churches have adopted evolutionary creationism. An American anthropologist, writing in 2004, observed evolutionary creationism (or 'Theistic Evolutionism' as she expresses it) is 'taught at most mainline Protestant seminaries, and it is the official position of the Catholic church.'[3]

The emergence of comparative genomics in the late 20th century, which appeared on the surface to provide strong evidence for common descent, strengthened the impulse to accommodate the creation record with evolutionary theory, and this has resulted in still further penetration of evolutionary creationism into Christian denominations and sects.[4] A particular illustration of the significance of comparative genomics is the establishment of The BioLogos Foundation in 2007 by

---

[1] *BioLogos*, http://biologos.org/common-questions/christianity-and-science/christian-response-to-darwin [referenced January 9, 2017]; Denis Alexander, *Creation or Evolution: do we have to choose?* Monarch Books, Oxford, UK and Grand Rapids, Michigan, USA, 2nd edition, 201-205.

[2] Denis O Lamoureux, *Evolutionary Creation: A Christian Approach to Evolution*, https://biologos.org/uploads/projects/Lamoureux_Scholarly_Essay.pdf [referenced October 31, 2017]; Eugenie C Scott, *Evolution vs. Creationism: An Introduction*, Greenwood Press, 2004, 62-63.

[3] Eugenie C Scott, *Evolution vs. Creationism*, 64.

[4] Peter Enns, *The Evolution of Adam: What the Bible Does and Doesn't Say About Human Origins*, Brazos Press, 2012, ix.

Francis Collins, a former leader of the Human Genome Project, a serious Christian and an evolutionary creationist.[5]   The Foundation's stated purpose is to invite 'the church and the world to see the harmony between science and biblical faith as [they] present an evolutionary understanding of God's creation.'[6]

Tensions between evolutionary science and 'God-inspired' scripture[7]

A noteworthy feature of this more recent adoption of evolutionary creationism is its penetration into Christian evangelical communities. Illustrative of this is that *BioLogos*, for the most part, is an evangelical resource and a potent manifestation of such a trend. Yet, such evangelical communities have a heritage of defence of the integrity of scripture and of its verbal inspiration, including that the scriptures, also encompassing the creation record, are entirely inerrant. This is a matter on which they have stood apart from mainstream Christianity for more than 100 years.

It is no doubt with such a heritage of respect for scripture that evangelical evolutionary creationists attempt to reconcile evolutionary science with scripture. And it is this conflation – evolution plus a wholly inspired bible – that gives a new dynamic to the historical science-bible debates. They admit, however, that this is not an easy task. One such evolutionary creationist, Peter Enns, states unequivocally, 'Scientific and biblical models of human origins are, strictly speaking, incompatible' and, 'Evolution is a serious challenge... to the origin of humanity, of sin, and of death.'[8] So serious is the challenge, the same writer insists that evolutionary creationism cannot be an add-on to scripture but rather it demands synthesis that requires a willingness to rethink one's

---

[5] *BioLogos*, http://biologos.org/author/francis-collins/ [referenced October 31, 2017].

[6] *BioLogos*, http://biologos.org/ [cited January 9, 2017].

[7] 'God-inspired' is employed to represent the compound Greek expression used in 2 Timothy 3:16, *theopneustos*.

[8] Peter Enns, *The Evolution of Adam*, 138,147.

own convictions about the meaning of Genesis 1 and 2 in light of new data.[9]

Likewise, another evangelical evolutionary creationist, Denis Alexander, claims that only Genesis 2 to 4, being 'more historical' than Genesis 1, can hold a conversation with evolutionary science whereas Genesis 1 cannot.[10]

What these acknowledged tensions amount to is that, to achieve a harmonisation between scripture's creation record and evolutionary science, evolutionary creationists claim Genesis needs to be read in a new and very different way from the practice of the past. This is because, it is claimed, evolution affects how Genesis ought to be read.[11] It will be evident that such a shift in perspective is especially fundamental for Christian evangelical communities who have traditionally argued against a non-literal reading of Genesis 1 to 11. However, there is no new way of undertaking such a task and it is significant that evolutionary creationist apologists support their assertion about needing to read Genesis in a different way by drawing on 19th century liberal biblical criticism. This previously rejected 'higher criticism' is considered to be just one of three forces – alongside the forces of evolution and biblical archaeology – that demand Genesis is read differently from that which would be typical among conservative biblical critics. Indeed, Peter Enns avers that understanding the history of these three forces in the 19th century can ease evolution and Christianity toward meaningful dialogue.[12]

In case the point needs to be made more explicitly, this claim presumes that, alongside evolution and biblical archaeology, an approach that incorporates the conclusions and methods of liberal biblical criticism

---

[9] Peter Enns, *The Evolution of Adam*, 147-148.

[10] Denis Alexander, *Creation or Evolution*, 295. Peter Enns opposes this historical differentiation between Genesis 1 and 2; see Peter Enns, *The Evolution of Adam*, 52.

[11] Peter Enns, *The Evolution of Adam*, xix, xx, 3.

[12] Peter Enns, *The Evolution of Adam*, Chapter 1.

needs to be adopted in reading Genesis to harmonise scripture with evolution. This is a radical departure – of seismic proportions – for evangelical Christians who, for more than 100 years, have been leading proponents of conservative biblical criticism.[13]

Objections

While the forcefully articulated claims made for the evidence of common descent arising from genomic science must not be underestimated, fundamental to the argument of this book is that Christians ought to start with the authority of scripture and its revelation of a special creation[14] in Genesis 1 and 2. When mishandling of these chapters (and others) in order to sustain an evolutionary creationist reading is witnessed – often supported by the conclusions and methods of liberal biblical criticism – the conviction that Christians must first enquire at scripture's authority is fortified.

There are two clear, scriptural objections to evolutionary creationist philosophy. The first is this mishandling of scripture. The other objection relates to how evolutionary creationism impacts and destroys two fundamental aspects of the gospel and of God's revelation of his purpose in creation; matters which are seen most clearly as fundamental from the teaching and pen of the apostle Paul:

- the position of Adam and Eve as the sole ancestors of all men and women that have populated the earth since Genesis 1 and 2's creation; and

---

[13] Norman L. Geisler and Douglas E. Potter, *A Seismic Shift in the Inerrancy Debate*, 2018, available from www.academia.edu [referenced April 9, 2018].

[14] For a definition of 'special creationism' alongside that of competing models of human origins, see Eugenie C Scott, *Evolution vs. Creationism*, 51-52, 57-67. In terms of 'special creationism', the author's belief is that Genesis 1 and 2 record the creation of the heavens and earth described therein – "the world that then existed" (2 Pet. 3:6) – upon a previously existing planet earth and that these chapters have nothing to say about fossils found in the earth that pre-date that 'beginning'. For an illustrative interpretation of Genesis 1 and 2 along these lines, see Edward Whittaker, *For the Study and Defence of the Holy Scripture*, Testimony, Norwich, 1987, 65-75.

- the associated entrance into the world of sin and death through sin and the consequent necessity for redemption in Christ.

It has already been noted that evolutionary creationists acknowledge these scriptural teachings challenge and are incompatible with their own conclusions. Given the way evolutionary creationists handle, inter alia, Romans 5 and 1 Corinthians 15 to sustain their claims, this second issue also boils down to how one handles scripture. But the fundamental relationship of these things to and its detrimental impact upon scriptural teaching about salvation in Christ ought not to be overlooked. The apostle Paul's teaching regarding the entrance of sin and death into the world through the disobedience of Adam and regarding atonement being accomplished in Christ's victory over the same flesh and blood as fallen Adam, through his perfect life, death and resurrection, is clearly at the heart of God's gospel. And yet, as was earlier noted, evolutionary creationists recognise that, 'Evolution is a serious challenge... to the origin of humanity, of sin, and of death.'[15]

However, this book does not examine the destructive impact of evolutionary creationism on these fundamental aspects of the gospel. Rather, its purpose is to address just the first of the objections identified, the mishandling of scripture. Evolutionary creationist reading and treatment of Genesis 1 and 2 is taken as an illustration of such practice and as a foil throughout the core chapters of the book.

Evolutionary creationist reading of Genesis 1 and 2

The specific reading of Genesis 1 and 2 which is taken as a foil is found in a three-part blog titled *Israel's Two Creation Stories*, which is featured on the *BioLogos* website.[16] Here are some of the things asserted in that blog:

---

[15] Peter Enns, *The Evolution of Adam*, 138,147.

[16] Peter Enns, *Israel's Two Creation Stories*, http://biologos.org/blog/series/israels-two-creation-stories [referenced October 25, 2016]. For further comment on the claim that scripture presents two distinct creation stories, see also Peter Enns, *The Evolution of Adam*, 68.

- The author, Peter Enns, proposes that, with the discovery of ancient Near Eastern (ANE) creation stories, there is 'clear
  evidence to support a nonliteral reading of the Genesis texts.'[17]

- He adds that the two different perspectives on creation presented by Genesis 1 and 2 'suggest that... "recording history"
  is not the point'[18] and that this is 'clearly a very important point
  to ponder in the discussion between Christianity and evolution.'

- Furthermore, having dealt with one of several differences Peter
  Enns claims exist between Genesis 1 and 2, the author writes,
  'They cannot be harmonized – they were never intended to
  be.'[19]

Thus, this evolutionary creationist asserts that Genesis 1 and 2 are dis-
harmonious and non-historical; his claim that a non-literal reading of
the Genesis texts is required relates, as evidenced by his tight association of 'literal' and 'historical' in the blog, to his assertion that Genesis
1 and 2 are not historical.[20] In support of this argument, the author marshals eight differences which he claims exist between Genesis 1 and 2
and we shall consider each of these in separate chapters of this book.[21]
In a number of cases, the differences certainly exist but how these differences are read is crucial to determining if they truly support the dis-
harmonious and non-historical reading claimed by evolutionary creationists.

---

[17] See also Peter Enns, *The Evolution of Adam*, Chapter 3.

[18] See also Peter Enns, *The Evolution of Adam*, 40-41, 50-53.

[19] See also Peter Enns, *The Evolution of Adam*, 52.

[20] See Chapter 7 of this book.

[21] Writing at an earlier time, Peter Enns presents seven of these arguments not eight (Peter
Enns, *The Evolution of Adam*, 51). The eighth difference presented in the blog is one which the
author earlier rejected as significant – a claim about distinct literary styles between Genesis 1
and 2; on this see Chapter 6 of this book.

A range of views

As might be expected, there is a spectrum of evolutionary creationist opinion. In some respects, Peter Enns, the writer of the blog taken as a foil, could be regarded as representing a liberal extreme in his handling of scripture, albeit one who honestly faces up to the clear tensions he identifies between evolutionary science and scripture.[22] At appropriate points, consequently, reference will be made to another evolutionary creationist in order to demonstrate just how fundamental to evolutionary creationist thinking across the spectrum are the approaches to and handling of scripture against which this book argues. The second writer is Denis Alexander, an evangelical evolutionary creationist who displays a tendency for a more conservative treatment of scripture, albeit representing a position that tries to smudge the tensions between evolutionary science and scripture.

An illustration of Denis Alexander's more conservative approach is that, based on his conclusion, 'The general stance of Scripture is to view Adam as a real historical figure',[23] he endeavours to model for an historical Adam in his evolutionary creationist synthesis of evolution with scripture.[24] By way of contrast, Peter Enns does not, preferring to dismiss the historicity of Adam, including even from the apostle Paul's writings.[25]

Nevertheless, as will be evidenced throughout the book, even this more conservative evolutionary creationist manifests clear traits that resonate with Peter Enns' approach to scripture. An immediate illustration is that Denis Alexander writes, '[Genesis 1] cannot be history in any normal

---

[22] Some insight into Peter Enns' wrestling with these tensions can be seen here: Peter Enns, *The Evolution of Adam*, 123-126.

[23] Denis Alexander, *Creation or Evolution*, 302.

[24] Denis Alexander, *Creation or Evolution*, 288ff.

[25] Peter Enns, *The Evolution of Adam*, Chapter 7.

use of that term',[26] and while, as already noted, he confesses that scripture views Adam as a real historical figure, he claims Adam is not as historical as Abraham.[27]

The commonality of handling scripture this way by liberal and conservative evolutionary creationists demonstrates how such approaches to scripture are inevitably required to sustain an evolutionary creationist reading. And this illustrates that, in engaging with the specified *BioLogos* blog post as a foil, this book is not addressing fringe evolutionary creationist thinking; it is not targeting a 'straw man'.

Scripture's authority

It is important to note that in this book claims about differences between Genesis 1 and 2 are dealt with by examining the text closely rather than debating the general principles of the inspiration framework(s) lying behind evolutionary creationist's handling of Genesis 1 and 2.[28] This is to ensure the focus is on analysis of Genesis 1 and 2 and to demonstrate, thereby, it is entirely reasonable to read these chapters as being in complete harmony with one another and, importantly, with the rest of scripture. Alongside this analysis, it is shown that the historicity of Genesis 1 and 2 is entirely consistent with the way that the rest of scripture speaks of creation and with how these chapters are employed and interpreted by other prophets.

Getting on with the job of analysis of Genesis 1 and 2's meaning rather than, at the outset, getting bogged down in some detailed theoretical explanation of the pertinent inspiration framework and exegetical methods is judged to be the priority. Nevertheless, in the course of analysis of Genesis 1 and 2, the approach taken in exegesis of scripture will obviously be exhibited in practice. Furthermore, if the evolutionary creationist treatment of Genesis 1 and 2 is shown to be faulty in the

---

[26] Denis Alexander, *Creation or Evolution*, 180-188.

[27] Denis Alexander, *Creation or Evolution*, 293.

[28] For an illustration of evolutionary creationism being directly associated with competing inspirational models for scripture, see Peter Enns, *The Evolution of Adam*, 42, 93-95, 143-145.

following chapters, serious challenges are inevitably raised against their inspiration framework(s). Before concluding therefore, after analysis of Genesis 1 and 2 in some depth, some attention is briefly given to competing inspiration frameworks and associated exegetical methods.

However, even if there is disagreement with the model adopted in this book regarding scripture's inspiration, the exegesis of Genesis 1 and 2 and the associated conclusions about their harmony and historicity which are laid out in Chapters 2 to 11 remain and stand. It is crucial that this exegesis and its associated conclusions are, above all else, considered carefully. This is another reason for not being distracted by addressing inspiration framework(s) in detail at the outset.

Nevertheless, it is key to the approach adopted in the book to recognise a conviction about scripture's authority that is shared with evolutionary creationists, at least nominally. While there might be disagreement about inspiration models and related interpretive methods, evolutionary creationists nominally share a conviction that scripture is revelation from God through the work of the holy spirit in the prophets. This is especially the case for evolutionary creationists from evangelical Christian communities. Indeed, the fact that evolutionary creationists feel constrained to inject God and his creative activity into evolutionary science, thereby establishing the alternative category 'evolutionary creationism', is evidence of itself that the scriptures are accepted as authoritative in some manner. The approach in this book is to work on the basis of this shared view regarding scripture's authority: in the arguments laid out, scripture is presumed authoritatively to be God's word. From this perspective, the principal audience is those who likewise share a belief about the authoritative nature of the scriptures. The argument for creation over evolutionary science (as opposed to evolutionary creationism) is a different argument and would be a very different book.

Scripture's authority is something that arises from its origin and the qualities inherent to the scriptures that emerge from this. The apostle Paul wrote of its origin:

"All Scripture is breathed out by God" (2 Tim. 3:16)

Prophets are involved in this work, of course, but the apostle was une-quivocal regarding scripture's source: it is *from God* through his breathing out. As another apostle affirmed, scripture is *not* "by the will of man" (2 Pet. 1:21).

It is because scripture has such an origin that its qualities are superla-tive, as expressed in a variety of ways by the psalmist David – in fact, some of the psalmist's superlative expressions were purposefully picked up by the apostle Paul in the context of his explanation of scrip-ture's origin:[29]

> "The law of the Lord is *perfect*, reviving the soul; the testimony
> of the Lord is *sure*, making wise the simple; the precepts of the
> Lord are *right*, rejoicing the heart; the commandment of the
> Lord is *pure*, enlightening the eyes; the fear of the Lord is *clean*,
> enduring for ever; the rules of the Lord are *true*, and *righteous*
> altogether" (Ps. 19:7-9)

Key qualities for our present purposes are "sure [*'mn*]" (Ps. 19:7) and "true [*'mt*]" (Ps. 19:9[30]). The Hebrew word underlying 'sure' is the ex-pression transliterated in English bibles as 'Amen', an expression whose meaning is expounded by the apostolic writings to be "faithful and true" (Rev. 3:14). It is inescapable that such descriptions are right

---

[29] Note the following language picked up by the apostle; these points of contact are based on analysis of the relevant Hebrew and Greek:

Psalm 19	2 Timothy 3
"perfect" (Ps. 19:7)	"competent" (2 Tim. 3:17)
"sure" (Ps. 19:7)	"firmly believed" (2 Tim. 3:14)
"sure... true" (Ps. 19:7,9)	"truth... truth" (2 Tim. 3:7,8)
"making wise" (Ps. 19:7)	"to make you wise" (2 Tim. 3:15)
"righteous" (Ps. 19:9)	"righteousness" (2 Tim. 3:16)

[30] The same Hebrew word is employed about the Lord's law, his commandments and his word in Psalm 119:142,151,160.

about the scriptures given their origin is from God. This is because the Lord himself is identified and described by such terms multiple times; since God is 'sure' and 'true' then what he says through his word must likewise have the same qualities:

"Know therefore that the LORD your God is God, the faithful ['mn] God" (Deut. 7:9)

"he who takes an oath in the land shall swear by the God of truth ['mn]" (Isa. 65:16)

"you have redeemed me, O LORD, faithful ['mt] God" (Ps. 31:5)

"Blessed is he whose help is the God of Jacob ... who made heaven and earth, the sea, and all that is in them, who keeps faith ['mt] for ever" (Ps. 146:6)

"the LORD is the true ['mt] God" (Jer. 10:10)

It is noteworthy how some of these declarations are made in contexts in which God is described as creator:

- Creator of the heavens and the earth as portrayed in Genesis 1 and 2: note Ps. 146:6; Jer. 10:11-13.

- Creator of the new heavens and new earth: note Isa. 65:17.

Evidently, God's faithfulness and truth are as much bound up with his identity as creator of the heavens and the earth "in the beginning" (Gen. 1:1) as are these characteristics bound up with his promises about man's future as his new creation.

A word about terms employed

With this foundation regarding scripture's authority briefly laid out, a word about what is meant by 'harmonised' and 'historical' in the book's sub-title. While these terms are obviously set against evolution-ary creationist claims regarding the dis-harmonious and non-historical

11

nature of Genesis 1 and 2, it will be helpful to explain a little about the use of them in this book.

A 'harmonised' reading is an expectation brought to bear on handling of scripture that every part of the scriptures is in agreement with every other part to form a unified, while richly symphonic, message. In fact, scripture's ubiquitous harmony and inerrancy will be seen as fundamental to the exegetical methods employed. This expectation arises from the qualities of scripture which we have just considered, that scripture is 'sure' and 'true'. If God's word has these qualities, it is not possible that there could be dis-harmony between one part and another. If dis-harmony is detected it is because we have mis-interpreted one or both scriptures between which we have identified dis-harmony. Indeed, without such harmony one must question whether "truth", without which we cannot be freed (John 8:31-32) and without which we cannot be sanctified (John 17:17), is discernible at all, in which case these assurances of Christ would be worthless.

An 'historical' reading is one in which we fully accept that events which are portrayed in scripture, howsoever described, actually took place in accordance with what scripture says. This is not a claim that what scripture states about an historical event is the entirety of what took place. Rather, the things we are told about what occurred are those matters that God has deemed it necessary to communicate to us. But, when the witness to the events being recorded is God, we can be sure he picks out the most relevant aspects of all that was going on to place on record in scripture. It is also certain that, in a way that cannot be the case with man's historical writings, what God chooses to record and the manner of his recording are both accomplished with perfection; his record is inerrant in its entirety. It is important to note that a claim about the historicity of any specific scripture is not a suggestion that the fulness of that scripture's purpose is exhaustively described by recognising the events described as having really happened. As we shall see, scripture has deeper and more complex purposes than merely recording history and so scripture carries within it much more information than the historical events it describes. In this respect, scripture is not subordinate to history but history to scripture. In fact, this is one reason God will deem specific aspects of what took place, rather than their entirety, are those that it is necessary for him to communicate to us. It is also imperative to note this is not a statement that historical reference made by scripture has priority over its richly textured meaning. Rather, it is a claim that when scripture describes historical events as part of its richly textured meaning, then it necessarily follows from scripture's qualities and its origin that those events took place as described.

This full acceptance of the historicity of events that are portrayed in scripture, howsoever described, is something again that arises from the qualities of scripture that it is 'sure' and 'true'. If God's word has such qualities, it is not possible that an event described in scripture as having happened is something that did not occur. Given God is the author of scripture, we can be sure his historical records, properly interpreted, do not misrepresent what happened. It is evident also that it is scripture's qualities and its God-breathed origin that renders God's word capable of both accurately recording historical events (as witnessed and selectively portrayed by God) while also performing multiple other functions.

Finally, the point being made in the repeated, 'howsoever described', is that there must first be right interpretation of scriptures through discerning their various literary features. In the case of a metaphorical scripture, for example, the meaning of the metaphor must first be discerned before we are able to determine what the event is that is being described and which we are then obliged to take, since scripture is 'sure' and 'true', as having actually happened. Indeed, it is clear that both 'harmonised' and 'historical' turn on right interpretation of scripture. But this should not surprise us since, for example, the apostle Paul wrote of being approved before God by "rightly handling the word of truth" (2 Tim. 2:15). To be sure, rightly handling the word of truth is a major theme of this book.

These definitions regarding 'harmonious' and 'historical', founded upon what has been said about scripture's authority and its right interpretation, demand that any rebuttal of the conclusions in this book must turn on demonstrating the interpretation of scripture presented in it is mistaken.

An alternative reading

It is pertinent to ask of evolutionary creationists the question that Jesus posed to the Pharisees: "Have you not read that he who created them from the beginning made them male and female…?" (Mt. 19:4). Such a question provides a sound basis for evaluating the relevance and value of competing readings of Genesis 1 and 2. It is evident the Pharisees had certainly read this record of God's creation and that the point of Jesus' question is rhetorical – the Pharisees had read Genesis 1 and 2 but they had not read it properly.

When Jesus asked the lawyer, "What is written in the Law? How do you read it?" (Lk. 10:26), it is clear that the manner in which one reads scripture is about getting to the truth of its meaning. This is illustrated by Jesus' commendation of the lawyer's response in which he quoted Deuteronomy 6; the lawyer's reading evidenced he had perceived the real significance of the law – other readings, such as that by the Pharisees, were wrong and, worse, hypocritical.

In fact, 'have you not/never read?' is a common feature of Jesus' inter-action with the Jews and this repeated challenge expressed in such a manner further reinforces the weight of the matter (see Mt. 12:3,5; 19:4; 21:16,42; 22:31). Those to whom he addressed these questions had certainly read the relevant scriptures many times; the rhetoric of Jesus' repeated questions is that they had read God's word wrongly and therefore believed falsely. The number of times the Lord is recorded as exposing the hypocritical falsehoods of the Pharisees, chief priests, scribes, elders of the people and the Sadducees by challenging their reading of scripture is testimony to how crucial it is to perform right reading of scripture. It is obvious that, from Jesus' perspective, there is a right way of reading scripture and a wrong way of doing so and that the consequences of reading it wrongly can be dire.

Thus, it is crucial not to be misled into thinking 'a harmonised and his-torical reading' is just an alternatively valid reading to that of an evolutionary creationist who likewise accepts that scripture is inspired and revelation from God. It is equally important not to take the existence of different readings as evidence per se that:

- the text's meaning is uncertain; or that

- we must avoid certainty in our belief about the relevant scripture's meaning.

To do so would commit us, for example, to concluding the same about readings of the scriptures regarding the person of Christ from as diverse sources as Adoptionism, Socinianism, Arianism and Trinitarianism. As is the case regarding reading scripture to discover the truth about the person of Christ, so also how we read Genesis 1 and 2 can be a matter of truth or falsehood, integrity or deceit, uprightness or hypocrisy; it is about rightly handling the word of truth versus tampering with God's word. Such stark contrasts are strikingly highlighted by the Lord's repeated enquiry to the Jews about their reading of scripture.

Jesus' question to the Pharisees, "Have you not read that he who created them from the beginning made them male and female...?" (Mt. 19:4), invites us to examine how Jesus read these things, especially since there is no more masterful reading than his. Consequently, before examining each of the eight commonly deployed arguments for a disharmonious and non-historical evolutionary creationist reading of Genesis 1 and 2, we will consider his most important and unequalled reading of these chapters.

2: Jesus' Reading

Have you not read?

In posing this question to the Pharisees, Jesus referred to the creation of man and woman in order to substantiate his teaching that no man should put asunder what God has joined (Mt. 19:3-6; Mk. 10:2-9). In referring to man and woman's creation, Jesus drew on both Genesis 1 and 2 in a manner we shall examine in detail. The way Jesus quoted from Genesis illustrates clearly how he read the relationship of these two chapters and how he regarded their historicity. There are differences in the way Jesus' teaching is portrayed in Matthew and Mark, peculiar to each gospel's purpose, and these differences, when read together, coherently fill out the picture of Jesus' teaching and his discussion with the Pharisees. Both gospels also, through the differences in their portrayals, fill out our appreciation of Jesus' understanding of the harmonious correlation between Genesis 1 and 2 and of the historicity of these chapters.

Analysis of Jesus' use of Genesis 1 and 2

We first give our attention to considering how Jesus read the relationship between Genesis 1 and 2 and, specifically, whether he read these chapters as harmonious. The teaching narrated in each gospel is analysed against Genesis 1 and 2 in the following table, in which we note Jesus made multiple use of these early chapters of Genesis:

Mt. 19:4-5	Gen. 1 and 2	Mk. 10:6-8
"He who created them from the beginning"	"the beginning" in both gospel records is plainly a reference to Gen. 1:1. Matthew's expression "created them" is clearly taken from the final clause of Gen. 1:27	"from the beginning of creation"
"[he] made them male and female"	both gospel records include Jesus' reference to the final clause of Gen. 1:27	"God made them male and female"
"Therefore a man shall leave his father and his mother and hold fast to his wife, and they shall become one flesh"	both records include Jesus' reference to the words of Gen. 2:24	"Therefore a man shall leave his father and mother and hold fast to his wife, and they shall become one flesh"

It is clear from this tabulated analysis that Jesus employed two detailed aspects of Genesis 1 and one of Genesis 2 in order to establish his teaching about marriage. To evaluate Jesus' reading of the relationship between Genesis 1 and 2, and to draw conclusions about this, it is important that we consider two key features:

- The significance of "from the beginning", which is employed in both gospels (Mt. 19:4,8; Mk 10:6).

- How the two gospels record Jesus' association of parts of Genesis 1 with his use of the words of Genesis 2:24.

This is what we will now proceed to do.

From the beginning

When we turn our attention to Jesus' reading of the historicity of Genesis 1 and 2, we will witness that the principal significance of Jesus' use of 'from the beginning' is that it served to establish that God's revelation about marriage pre-dated the giving of the law and so takes precedence. The significant point about this expression upon which we focus now is that it is plain that everything that Jesus said about marriage in his employment of parts of Genesis 1 and 2:24 took place *at the beginning* of which he spoke. The making of male and female (Gen. 1:27) and the pronouncement about a man leaving his parents and holding fast to his wife (Gen. 2:24) both occurred at a time Jesus calls 'the beginning'.

It follows from this that, in Jesus' reading, Genesis1:27 and 2:24 took place during the same timeframe and, in this respect, they share a harmonised chronology.

We now turn to how the two gospels associate Jesus' use of parts of Genesis 1 with his use of the words of Genesis 2:24.

Associating Genesis 1 and 2

Matthew associates the making of male and female 'from the beginning' with Jesus' reference to Genesis 2:24 by use of the phrase "and he said [*kai eipen*]" (Mt. 19:5, AT). The first thing to note about this expression is that Jesus informed his audience that it was God who pronounced the words recorded in Genesis 2:24, something which Genesis does not make obvious.

Also, Jesus' revelation here highlights the prophetic role of Adam when he spoke the words of Genesis 2:23. Genesis records:

> "And *the man said*, 'This at last is bone of my bones and flesh of my flesh; she shall be called woman, because she was taken out of man. Therefore a man shall leave his father and his

mother and hold fast to his wife, and they shall become one flesh'" (Gen. 2:23-24, AT)

Alerted by Jesus' revelation that God spoke the words of Genesis 2:24, the following aspects reinforce that God spoke all the words uttered by Adam through him acting as his prophet:

- Genesis records that it was the man who spoke the words of Genesis 2:23-24.

- Adam could only know that the woman was bone of his bones and flesh of his flesh from God's revelation to him since, while the woman was made from his rib, he was in "a deep sleep" (Gen. 2:21).

- It is evident that the words of Genesis 2:23 are a prophetic utterance from the way the language of Adam's pronouncement is taken up by the apostle Paul in Ephesians 5:28-29, which the apostle moved on to describe as part of the profound mystery about these things referring to "Christ and the church" (Eph. 5:32).

We will consider the significance of these findings as we progress. For now, we should note that this conjunctive expression clearly connects what Jesus said afterwards with the same chronological locus that he established at the commencement of his response to the Pharisees. That is, as we have seen by considering Jesus' use of 'from the beginning', God's declaration in Genesis 2:24 (referenced in Mt. 19:5) took place at 'the beginning' when he made them male and female (Gen. 1:27; Mt. 19:4).

It is essential that we weigh the significance of this conclusion now reached twice: for Jesus, it was at the time of 'the beginning' when God "made male and female" (Gen. 1:27) that he also voiced the declaration recorded in Genesis 2:24. In Jesus' reading of Genesis 1 and 2, the two chapters coincide chronologically. This also evidences that, for Jesus, Genesis 1 and 2 are a *single story* of God's creation. Given Jesus' reading of Genesis 1 and 2 as this single story, it is evident he believed they are an integral and therefore harmonised record. This is a crucial aspect of Jesus' reading to which we shall return and whose relevance we shall evaluate as we progress.

The way that Mark associates Jesus' reference to aspects of Genesis 1 with his use of Genesis 2:24 differs from Matthew, but the substantive result is the same, even though it is a more involved route to that point.

Mark establishes a causal relationship between God's making male and female from the beginning and what he declares a man will do in Genesis 2:24: "for this cause" (Mk 10:7, AT). According to Jesus, the fact God made man "male and female" (Mk. 10:6; Gen. 1:27) *is the reason why* "a man shall leave his father and mother and hold fast to his wife" (Mk. 10:7; Gen. 2:24). But in Genesis 2, the causal relationship of God's declaration in verse 24 is with what the man stated in verse 23. The woman having been brought to the man by God so that he could name her (Gen. 2:22; cf. v. 19), the man pronounced: "This at last is bone of my bones and flesh of my flesh; she shall be called Woman, because she was taken out of Man" (Gen. 2:23). And it is this pronouncement that caused God's declaration in verse 24: "*Therefore* a man shall leave his father and his mother." According to the scripture in Genesis, the fact that man called the one who was brought to him "woman" – something arising from the manner of her creation (Gen. 2:23) – *is the reason why* "a man shall leave his father and mother and hold fast to his wife" (Gen. 2:24).

From these considerations it is clear that the reason given by Jesus for God's pronouncement in Genesis 2:24, that God made them 'male and female', coincides with the reason given in Genesis 2 for God's pronouncement, that is, that the man named her 'woman' because of the manner of her creation. The following table lays out these matters to establish this point with greater clarity:

Mk. 10:6-7	"God made them male and female"	*is the reason why*	"a man shall leave his father and mother"
Gen. 2:23-24	"she shall be called Woman, because she was taken out of Man"	*is the reason why*	"a man shall leave his father and mother"

This tabulation highlights that God's making man male and female (Mk. 10:6; Gen. 1:27) coincides with the woman's naming because she was taken out of man (Gen. 2:23). It follows from this that both these aspects of Genesis 1 and 2 are components of *the reason why* a man shall leave his father and his mother. Given the earlier findings, that both Genesis 1 and 2 both took place within the same timeframe, at 'the beginning', we know why this is so: the making of "female" (Gen. 1:27) is explained in more detail in Genesis 2 and summarised by Adam in his naming of her (Gen. 2:23). Thus, the making of "female" (Gen. 1:27) converges with the explanation of her having been "taken out of man" (Gen. 2:23); and it follows from this that Genesis 1:26,27 and 2:7,18-24 speak of the same creative event.

We also see in this reading of Jesus, that God's reasoning is portrayed as working together with man's response to God's revelation to Adam about the manner of Eve's creation. Drawing on the Genesis record, Jesus revealed an important aspect about why God made the pronouncement recorded in Genesis 2:24. This was God's plan from the beginning and the reason he made them male and female was so that the man might hold fast to his wife and become one flesh. On the other hand, Genesis tells us that God made his Genesis 2:24 pronouncement as a development of Adam's prophetic response that the woman was bone of his bones and flesh of his flesh. Thus, from the outset of mankind's creation, there is a work of fellowship between man and his God. Included in this work we see Adam exercising his mind on matters he has learned from and experienced with his creator – as mentioned earlier, given Adam was in a "deep sleep" when God built the woman from one of his ribs, Adam's pronouncement about her being "bone of [his] bones and flesh of [his] flesh" (Gen. 2:21,23) was evidently something about which he had received instruction from God. Both of these things, working in fellowship with God and exercising our minds on matters we learn from him is a behaviour to which each of us is called. It is clear also that these things function both to exhibit and to develop further in men and women the "image" and "likeness" of God (Gen. 1:26,27).

Again, we have evidenced for us that Jesus read Genesis 1 and 2 as a *single creation story*. Once more, it is evident Jesus believed these first two chapters of Genesis are an integral and therefore harmonised record. This is now seen not just in terms of chronology and events but also at the level of the way God's reasoning works in fellowship with the man.

Historical references

Having established that Jesus plainly regarded these chapters as harmonious, we now proceed to consider if he read them in a historical way. There are five aspects of the dialogue between Jesus and the Pharisees which indicate that the Lord regarded both Genesis 1 and 2 as historical and that specific events described in these chapters actually occurred. The first is the contrast set up by Jesus between what Moses wrote in Deuteronomy 24 and what is written in Genesis 2:24. The second is the theological conclusion which Jesus established on the basis of what Genesis says. The third aspect relates to the scope of Genesis 1 and 2 that is evidently included in Jesus' historical reading. The fourth is the manner in which Jesus referred to particular events within the creation narrative. The final aspect is the way Jesus independently testified himself that specific events happened when God created the heavens and the earth.

Regarding the first of these, both Matthew and Mark portray Jesus directing the Pharisees to an earlier time than Deuteronomy.[1] In Matthew 19:8 and Mark 10:6, Jesus' use of "from the beginning" occurs as part of a contrast he drew with the reference made by the Pharisees to the law of Deuteronomy 24. The thrust of Jesus' contrast is that God's revelation about the creation of male and female *and* marriage pre-dated the giving of the Deuteronomy law and so takes precedence. Note that, underlining earlier conclusions, for Jesus' argument to work, the creation of male and female *and* God's statement about marriage must have taken place at 'the beginning' since this is only the chronological locus employed by Jesus in establishing their precedence. From a historicity perspective, for this argument to be coherent, the record of God's creation of male and female and the declaration about becoming one flesh must be at least as historical as the giving of the law by Moses in Deuteronomy. This is so from two perspectives. First, the truth and weight of Jesus' argument rests on chronological precedence and, clearly, chronological ordering here is a function of history. Second, it would be incongruous for Jesus to have spoken of the historical law of Deuteronomy 24 while contrasting it with a non-historical thing from Genesis; such an argument would carry no weight.

---

[1] A tangential but related point regarding the handling of Genesis 1 and 2 is what Jesus' discussion with the Pharisees suggests about the Lord's view of who wrote these chapters. The way the dialogue runs in Mark 10 implies that Jesus' question to the Pharisees, "What did Moses command you?" (Mk. 10:3), expected them to consider the teaching of Genesis rather than Deuteronomy to which they made immediate reference. If this is so, then Jesus believed the things he mentions from Genesis 1 and 2 were written by Moses (without excluding Moses' use of earlier scriptural sources). Furthermore, Jesus explained that it was because of the hardness of the people's heart that Moses allowed them to divorce their wives (Mt 19:8; Mk. 10:5). Given this, it is probable that the people in Moses' time onwards were expected to see in Deuteronomy 24 an allowance for their hardness of hearts – that is the way God's justice is performed – and this indicates that the people in Moses' time must have known what was true from the beginning. This being probable, how would the people have known their heart would be judged as hard if they divorced their wives without availability of Genesis 2 or its precursor? Even if one is not persuaded by this consideration, the evidence of Matthew 19 and Mark 10 is that, according to Jesus' reading, it is historical fact that God declared what is recorded in Genesis 2:24 and that he performed the creation of male and female (Gen. 1:27) at the beginning. Given this, notwithstanding any posited late writing of Genesis 1 and 2, these chapters must be an accurate record of what took place.

The second aspect illustrating Jesus regarded Genesis 1 and 2 as historical is that his theological conclusion, "What therefore God has joined together, let not man separate" (Mt. 19:6; Mk. 10:9), rests on his use of the words of Genesis 2:24:

> "[God] said, 'Therefore a man shall leave his father and his mother and hold fast to his wife, and the two shall become one flesh'" (Mt. 19:5)

Either God said these words 'from the beginning' and their historical truth is a foundation for Jesus' theological conclusion about marriage or his father did not thus speak and the Lord's conclusion is without foundation.

We have seen that, during the course of his reasoning with the Pharisees, Jesus referred explicitly to Genesis 1:1; 1:27 and 2:24. In doing so, Jesus spanned the whole of the first two chapters of Genesis in order to establish the truth of what he was teaching. It would stretch credulity too much to be asked to accept that Jesus was merely selecting historical bits from generally non-historical stories. This third aspect points firmly to the fact that Jesus handled the entirety of Genesis 1 and 2 and the events referenced within these chapters as historical, so that every event described in them actually happened.

The fourth aspect of Jesus' historical reading of Genesis 1 and 2 is the manner in which he is portrayed as referring to specific events within these chapters. It is clear that Jesus did not just speak of God as creator of the heavens and the earth in some broad overview manner, leaving the specifics of how God performed his creative work for evolutionary science to discover and describe. Rather, he referred to highly specific features of the creation and handled these as historical and true. Not only did Jesus speak of God creating male and female – a clear reference to man's creation in Genesis 1:26-27 – but, by referencing God's pronouncement about marriage in Genesis 2:24, Jesus associated his teaching about marriage with the manner of Eve's creation out of Adam's rib such that she would be "bone of [Adam's] bones and flesh of [his] flesh" (Gen. 2:23). In these specific respects, Jesus read both Genesis 1 and 2 as historical so that it is these exact events which are described as having actually taken place. As will be seen, the creation of man in Genesis 1:26-27 and Eve's creation in Genesis 2:22 are two of three detailed aspects of the creation record which evolutionary creationists insist, if evolution is correct, cannot be accepted as historical.[2] Thus, evolutionary creationists find themselves directly and specifically in conflict with Jesus' reading.

Finally, it is evident that Jesus' reference to Genesis 1 and 2 in his dialogue with the Pharisees did not rely on the testimony of that scripture alone – the Lord did not rest his argument solely on saying something along the lines of, 'this is what Genesis 1 and 2 tell us' – though this is certainly one feature of what Jesus taught. Nor is Jesus' employment of the language of Genesis 1 and 2 a reference to the text of these chapters without any regard to the historicity of the events portrayed in them.[3] Rather, in this fifth aspect we witness Jesus himself testified certain things happened when God created the heavens and the earth. In this respect, Jesus acted as a second and independent witness alongside the testimony of Genesis 1 and 2. Certainly we witness Jesus

---

[2] See Chapters 5, 7, 8 and 10.

[3] This aspect distinguishes Jesus' reading of Genesis 1 and 2 from apostolic reference to the Hebrew scriptures in contexts where the writer mentioned things that emerge from the text but which are plainly not historical. This is exemplified in Hebrews 7:3, where the writer stated of Melchizedek, "He is without father or mother or genealogy, having neither beginning of days nor end of life, but resembling the Son of God he continues a priest for ever". It is plain that it is not historically accurate to say that Melchizedek was without parentage or that he was without beginning or end. Thus, in Hebrews 7 the writer referred to matters that arise from the Genesis 14 text and not, when he did so, to any history referenced by that text. This is different from other uses of the Hebrew scriptures where the prophet employs the text to refer to the same history to which the text originally refers; Jesus in Matthew 19 and Mark 10 exemplifies such a use of the scriptures. Regarding the usage in Hebrews 7, "without father or mother or genealogy, having neither beginning of days nor end of life" (Heb. 7:3) is a clear reference to a feature of the Genesis 14 text – Hebrews notes the absence of these things in the record. Thus, the focus is on the text and not on the history in this instance. Identification of this distinctive approach is also highlighted by recognising the writer to the Hebrews interpreted the meanings of Melchizedek's name and title (Heb. 7:2); in doing so, his focus was again on the text. Furthermore, it is in this context that the writer flagged the purpose in his distinctive approach when he said of Melchizedek, he is "made like unto the Son of God" (Heb. 7:3, ASV). Evidently, the writer, inter alia, surveyed features of the Genesis 14 text that are deliberately placed there by its author, God himself, as a prophetic similitude of the son of God. When the writer to the Hebrews referred to these features of the text that is just what he was doing, he was not employing the text to refer to the original history.

employing the language of Genesis but we also observe him doing so to refer back himself to the same historical events as originally referred to by that scripture. Mark's record includes a clear instance of this:

> "Jesus said... from the beginning of creation, 'God made them male and female'" (Mk. 10:5-6)

While Jesus here did employ the language of Genesis 1:27, this is also a clear declaration by Jesus of what happened; the gospel writer tells us that one of the things Jesus said is, 'God made them male and female'. Thus, Jesus himself asserted that God made them male and female, and he employed the language of Genesis to do so. This is independent testimony by Jesus of what God did, it is not only a reference to the language of Genesis 1. In a different way, Matthew's gospel also portrays the same kind of independent testimony alongside Genesis 1 and 2:

> "[Jesus] answered, "Have you not read that he who created them from the beginning made them male and female, *and said*, 'Therefore a man shall leave his father and his mother and hold fast to his wife, and the two shall become one flesh'?" (Mt. 19:4-5)

The key aspect of this record is that it is Jesus who told us *God said* the words that are recorded in Genesis 2:24 and which Jesus quoted in Matthew 19:5. It is noteworthy that Genesis does not inform us this is what happened; Jesus told us and in doing so he plainly referred back to the events of Genesis 2 to inform us about what took place. Thus again, Jesus independently asserted something about what God said, he did not merely refer to the text of Genesis 2. A final illustration of such independent testimony is seen in Jesus' explanation of the reason why God pronounced what he did in Genesis 2:24. It is Jesus who has testified to us that God's reason for declaring a man would hold fast to his wife and become one flesh was that he had created them male and female in the beginning. Again therefore, we see further independent witness from the mouth of the Lord Jesus about God's creative acts – and more than this, Jesus also informing us about God's reasoning – and this witness sits alongside the Genesis record itself.

These final two aspects of Jesus' historical reading of Genesis 1 and 2 are highly important from another perspective. Jesus' handling of detailed events of the creation record as historical, and his independent testimony to what God did, said and reasoned are features which are present many times throughout the scriptures. It is evident that God, through his prophets, pervasively repeats these things so that we are left in no doubt about what he did in Genesis 1 and 2. Plainly, God as creator of the heavens and the earth, as described in these chapters, is a crucial part of his identity that he reveals to us and which we are expected to believe. As we make progress in the remainder of the book, these two aspects of Jesus' historical reading will be highlighted when they feature in the writings of different prophets. At times, this might appear to be a little repetitive, but it is necessary so that there is no mistaking how extensively these things are testified about God's creative works.

Contrary to evolutionary creationist handling of Genesis 1 and 2 as non-historical, Jesus plainly read them as historical, so that Jesus handled the events referred to in these chapters as having actually occurred. This is evidenced in multiple ways and enjoys Jesus' own independent confirmation of the veracity of the creation record.

Conclusions: Jesus' reading

From the analysis we have undertaken of the reading of Genesis 1 and 2 by Jesus, we have seen the following matters:

- Jesus' reading establishes unequivocally that both Genesis 1 and 2 took place during the same timeframe, 'the beginning'.[4]

---

[4] This illustrates that Jesus' reading of Genesis 1 and 2 obviates a handling of Genesis 1:1 that sees the creation of the heavens and the earth "in the beginning" as an event which is chronologically earlier than the creative acts in verse 3 onwards. In Jesus' reading of Genesis 1 and 2, "the beginning" is a time that extends from Genesis 1:1 at least through to Genesis 2:24. But to avoid misunderstanding, this is not declaring a conviction that Genesis 1:1 speaks of the beginning of the physical universe and the earth within it. Rather, Genesis

- Jesus' reading confirms that the formation of Adam and then the making of Eve out of his side, as recorded in Genesis 2, is another portrayal of the creation of male and female of man in Genesis 1:26-27.

- Jesus regarded both Genesis 1 and 2 and the events described in these chapters as historically true across the entire span of their record, including at the level of detailed and specific events.

Given the perspective presented by this reading, Genesis 1 and 2 are records of the same creation; they are integral and in harmony because they are a *single story* of God's creative works. We have also seen from Jesus' reading that the way the record is laid out in Genesis 1 and 2 functions to show the man responding to God's revelation in fellowship with his God in the creation of the woman. This, of course, sets the scene for God's expectations of his people working with him in fellowship and having our minds exercised on matters we learn from him – all to progress and establish God's purpose in the earth.

These conclusions are not intended to dismiss evolutionary creationist observations about narrative differences between Genesis 1 and 2. Rather, they illustrate that any reading of these narrative differences needs to be directed at discovering scripture's didactic purposes in them. Furthermore, Jesus' reading requires a handling of these chapters that treats them as historical and as integral chapters that are in harmony. As we examine evolutionary creationist readings of Genesis 1 and 2, we need constantly to reflect on how such readings square with this most masterful of readings. This is because Jesus' reading requires that we handle Genesis 1 and 2 within a harmonised and historical framework, and this is on the authority of the one who said he spoke only those things he learned from his father because of which, in part, he was raised from the dead, the grave not being able to hold him.

1:1 speaks of the heavens and earth that were then brought into existence through God's creative words as recorded in Genesis 1 and 2 – this refers to the "the world that then existed" (2 Pet. 3:4-7).

3: How Long did it Take God?

In this chapter we examine the first of eight reasons, laid out in the *BioLogos* blog, *Israel's Two Creation Stories*,[1] for why we should not read Genesis 1 and 2 as harmonised in meaning or as historical descriptions.

It is asked how long it took God to accomplish his creation, with the assertion that Genesis 1 represents this as a six-day event while Genesis 2:4 signals that 'the second creation account happened either in one day or a continuous series of events not marked by the passing of days.'[2] We shall examine the spirit's purpose in Genesis 2:4 and discover that evolutionary creationist handling reads into this verse more than is there, whilst simultaneously not taking from it the great deal that is there.

Two creation stories?

But before addressing the evolutionary creationist assertions about disharmonies between Genesis 1 and 2 regarding creation's duration, we should first consider the claim about these chapters embedded in the blog title, *Israel's Two Creation Stories*. Are Genesis 1 and 2 'two creation stories',[3] an idea also central to source critical analysis of these

---

[1] Peter Enns, *Israel's Two Creation Stories*, http://biologos.org/blog/series/israels-two-creation-stories [referenced October 25, 2016]. See also Peter Enns, *The Evolution of Adam: What the Bible Does and Doesn't Say About Human Origins*, Brazos Press, 2012, 51.

[2] Peter Enns, *Israel's Two Creation Stories*. Denis Alexander also reads Genesis 2:4 "day" as referring to the entire creative work of Genesis 1; see Denis Alexander, *Creation or Evolution: do we have to choose?* Monarch Books, Oxford, UK and Grand Rapids, Michigan, USA, 2nd edition, 185, 194-195.

[3] For the claim that Genesis 1 and 2 are two creation stories see also Peter Enns, *The Evolution of Adam*, 50ff, 140ff.

two chapters,[4] or are these two chapters records of the same creation – are they a single creation story?[5] The unequivocal testimony of Jesus' reading – made evident in multiple ways – is that Genesis 1 and 2 are to be read as a single creation story.[6] Already then, and at a headline level, we see evolutionary creationism in conflict with the son of God. As we make progress, we will see the evidence build up – if any more is needed having seen the authoritative stance of the Lord – that Genesis 1 and 2 are a single creation story with the two chapters sharing a complementary presentation of God's creative works.

Marking days

Turning now to Peter Enns' first reason that he marshals to substantiate his position, we initially consider the second of the two assertions mentioned, that Genesis 2:4 introduces 'a continuous series of events not marked by the passing of days.'[7] Momentarily accepting this characterisation of Genesis 2 for the sake of analysis, would such a portrayal of things indicate that we have a creation record that is not in harmony with the six-day series of events of Genesis 1?

It is true that the absence of any mention of the passing of days in Genesis 2 makes this record different from Genesis 1. But the kind of difference identified here does not render these records either contrary or contradictory and therefore this is not evidence for them being disharmonious. For them to be contrary or contradictory would require, for example, Genesis 2 to state explicitly that creation did not take place across a number of days. Of course, Genesis 2 contains no such statement. Consequently, the claim that Genesis 1 and 2 'cannot be

---

[4] Pauline A Viviano, 'Source Criticism' in Eds. Steven L McKenzie and Stephen R Haynes, *To Each Its Own Meaning: An Introduction to Biblical Criticisms and their Application*, Westerville John Knox Press, 1999, 46-47 (available on Google Books)

[5] 'Whatever our opinion may be about whether the two accounts of Creation in chapters 1 and 2 originally belonged together, there is little doubt that as they are put together in the narrative before us, they are meant to be read as one account' (J H Sailhamer, *Genesis. The Expositor's Bible Commentary*, Edited by F E Gaebelein (Grand Rapids: Zondervan Publishing, 1990, 31.

[6] See Chapter 2, 'Associating Genesis 1 and 2'.

[7] Peter Enns, *Israel's Two Creation Stories*.

harmonized'[8] on the basis of this alternative is to posit a conclusion that has not been demonstrated. On the contrary, the characterisation of Genesis 2 considered here is sufficiently open in meaning to accommodate and harmonise with the testimony of Genesis 1.

In the day of making

Removing the second assertion naturally leads to a consideration of the first proposed alternative – that Genesis 2:4 speaks of the Genesis 1 creation record taking place in one day – since this would certainly set up conflict between the two records. The Hebrew lying behind the opening expression of "in the day that the LORD God made the earth and the heavens" (Gen. 2:4) is *bywm* ('in [the] day'), and it is on this basis that it is proposed that the record speaks of a single day.

There is no Hebrew for 'one' employed in Genesis 2:4 although, had scripture wished to emphasise such a sense, it could readily have done so.[9] Nevertheless, it is clear that "in [the] day [*bywm*]" could be read as speaking of a day – that is, is of one day. But the problem does not lie here; it resides in reading it this way in isolation from the rest of the verse. Closer examination of this verse reveals an internal chiastic structure,[10] partly evident in English versions (although they do simultaneously obscure part of the Hebrew chiasm). The following rendering

---

[8] Peter Enns, *Israel's Two Creation Stories*.

[9] Cf. "in one day [*bywm 'ḥd*]": Lev. 22:28; 1 Sam. 2:34; 1 Kgs. 20:29; 2 Chron. 28:6; Est. 3:13; 8:12; Isa. 10:17; 47:9; 66:8; Zech. 3:9.

[10] Recognising this chiastic structure depends, in part, on rejecting a structural analysis of the first two chapters of Genesis, based on source criticism, which sees the first chapter actually running from Genesis 1:1-2:4a, with the second chapter running from Genesis 2:4b-25 (see, for example, Pauline A Viviano, 'Source Criticism'). Such a structure separates Genesis 2:4 into two parts which denies any possibility of a chiasm within this verse. In place of such a structure, Genesis 1 and 2 are interpreted herein as follows:

- Genesis 1-2:1 covers the creation of the heavens and the earth in six days and marked by the inclusio "the heavens and the earth" (Gen. 1:1; 2:1).

- Genesis 2:2-3 introduces the seventh day of rest.

- Genesis 2:4-25 describes a sub-set of the events of day 6 with "the heavens and the earth" (Gen. 2:4) reprising the earlier inclusio to place what follows within the same semantic and chronological framework as Genesis 1:1-2:1. This indicates that Genesis 2:4-25 sits within the chronology of days 1-6 rather than

of Genesis 2:4 (AT), carefully following the Hebrew syntax, and shown alongside the transliterated Hebrew, illustrates this chiasm:[11]

> "these [are] [the] generations of the heavens and the earth"
>
> A
>
> *'lh twldwt hšmym wh'rs̱*
>
> > "in their creation"
> >
> > B
> >
> > *bhbr'm*
> >
> > "in [the] day of making"
> >
> > b
> >
> > *bywm 'ś́wt*
>
> "[by] the Lord God of earth and heavens"
>
> a
>
> *yhwh 'lhym 'rs̱ wšmym*

The opening and close of this chiasm,[12] highlighted by the repetition and inversion of 'the heavens and the earth' to 'earth and heavens',

---

being events subsequent to day 7. It is the content of Genesis 2:4-25 which places these events definitively in day 6.

With Genesis 2:4 now functioning as an integral verse, the chiasm becomes evident. The structure outlined above also serves to preserve a use of "These are the generations" (Gen. 2:4) which is consistent with its subsequent nine uses in Genesis (Gen. 6:9; 10:1; 11:10,27; 25:12,19; 36:1,9; 37:2). These nine uses all introduce the generations of men that follow in the narrative; with the structure employed herein, it introduces the generations of Adam – the creation of Adam and Eve – whereas the structural analysis which has been rejected requires it, uniquely, to refer backwards to Genesis 1.

[11] The infinitive construct forms of the Hebrew verbs 'to create [*br'*]' and 'to make [*'śh*]' at the centre of this chiasm are quite challenging to render in English. The translation offered should not be taken as a literal rendering of the Hebrew.

[12] Chiastic structure within Genesis 2:4 has been independently noticed by other writers. See C. John Collins, 'The wayyiqtol as "pluperfect": when and why' in *Tyndale Bulletin* 46.1 (1995), 117-140 (available at http://www.tyndalehouse.com/tynbul/library/Tyn-Bull_1995_46_1_08_Collins_WAYYIQTOL_Pluperfect.pdf), 138 and footnotes. But the structure identified in this chapter differs somewhat from these other analyses.

draws out a correspondence between 'generations' and 'the Lord God' – notably, when scripture historically for the first time refers to God by his name. This is a feature we will consider before concluding. There is also an obvious correspondence established, at the centre of the chiasm, between 'creation' and 'making', which picks up the creation context of Genesis 1 in a manner which we will shortly explore.

But the first aspect we should note and consider is how this chiastic structure highlights that the second part of the verse does not speak of 'in [the] day', but rather of 'in [the] day of making'. This is certainly how the phrase should be read, as is illustrated by the chiastic structure. This structure pairs 'in', which is employed in both central chiastic phrases, and 'creating' with 'making', which clearly correspond in meaning at some semantic level. The correspondence between 'in ... creating' and 'in ... making', with 'day' positioned between 'in' and 'making' in the second phrase, demonstrates that 'day' is part of the second literary unit. Thus, at the centre of this chiasm, 'in their creation' corresponds to 'in [the] day of making'. This finding substantiates that it is not legitimate to isolate 'in [the] day [bywm]' from the rest of the verse as though this carries the main sense of scripture here. Genesis 2:4 does not speak of the events of this chapter as happening 'in one day', it speaks of something being accomplished 'in [the] day of making'.

Such a reading is also confirmed by scripture's use elsewhere of the phrase 'in [the] day of making', a use which helps interpret the phrase's significance. With a couple of small variations,[13] the Hebrew of Genesis 2:4 for "in [the] day of making" is found in only one other place: Ezekiel 43:18. The topic there is the construction of the altar in the house which Ezekiel saw in vision. From Ezekiel 43:18 onwards the prophet's revelation turns to preparation for the altar's use. Barring miraculous intervention to shorten the time taken for construction, which

---

[13] These variations from Genesis 2:4 are as follows: (a) unlike Genesis, the infinitive construct of the verb 'to make [*śh*]' in Ezekiel has the definite article; (b) unlike Genesis, Ezekiel's infinitive construct carries the third-person-singular possessive pronoun. Since in both Genesis 2:4 and Ezekiel 43:18 the verb 'to make [*śh*]' is the infinitive construct form, we otherwise have an accurate syntactic and semantic relationship between these two phrases.

is no more required than it was in the making of the sanctuary's altar (Ex. 38:1-7), the making of Ezekiel's large altar would have taken several days. This points to 'in [the] day of making' speaking not of a single day being taken to construct the altar, but of 'the day' in which 'the making' (commenced several days earlier) was completed so that the altar could then be used. Indeed, Ezekiel's altar could not be used until it was completed, and it is of significance that it is its purification in readiness for employment for sacrifice that the narrative in Ezekiel 43:18ff proceeds to describe. Thus, the nature of the case requires a sense of completion: a half-finished altar could not serve an altar's purpose.

This indicates that in Genesis 2:4 the subject matter following "in [the] day of making" has to do with the completion of God's creative acts, the completion of his making. 'The day of making' of heavens and earth was not reached until this day. Prior to this day, God's creative work was incomplete; it was only on this day that the making was finished. The way that Genesis 2 moves on to say, "there was no man" (Gen. 2:5) pinpoints what was needed in God's creation to complete it. And the way that the chapter also moves on to say, "for Adam there was not found a helper fit for him" (Gen. 2:20) further indicates that, even having created the man, the day of making of heavens and earth was not yet fully accomplished – that is, God's creative acts were not finished until there was both man and woman. This informs us that Genesis 2:4ff is an expanded record of part of God's *day six* creative acts.

Creation and making

The pairing of 'creation' and 'making' in Genesis 2:4's chiastic structure reinforces this conclusion. Such a pairing serves to focus the narrative on the creation of man, male and female, on day six. This is seen to be so because prior to Genesis 2:4, other than in verse 3, which cannot currently occupy our attention, it is only in the context of the creation of man that 'creation' and 'making' have been employed together:

"Then God said, 'Let us *make* man in our image . . . So God *created* man in his own image, in the image of God *created* he him; male and female *created* he them" (Gen. 1:26-27).

Genesis 2:4's use of this 'creation' and 'making' pair now about "the heavens and the earth", scripture having previously used this pair of the creation of man, highlights that the principal purpose of all aspects of creation in Genesis 1, summarised inclusively by "the heavens and the earth" (Gen. 1:1; 2:1), was for man's habitation and dominion (Gen. 1:26,28). Thus Genesis 2:4 functions to show, inter alia, that the order of creation in Genesis 1 does not emphasise the principal role that man has to play in God's purpose. It is Genesis 2 which further ensures that we understand that man, although not first created, is the pinnacle and principal objective of God's creation and of his purpose in initiating this work. The Lord God now uses the language of man's creation and making about the summary of all that was created to position man at its centre. 'The heavens and the earth' are presented as being for man and in man.

The generations of the heavens and the earth

Having seen that one of the functions of Genesis 2:4 is to position man as the centrepiece of God's purpose in creation, we are led to consideration of how the chiastic structure of this verse draws out a correspondence between "generations" and "the LORD God". This is because, as we shall now see, this aspect of the chiasm relates closely to man's position. And such a consideration needs also to account for the fact that this is when scripture, historically for the first time ever, uses God's name.

Following on from the first historical use of the expression, "these are the generations" (Gen. 2:4), every other use in scripture speaks of lifetimes and genealogical fathering of children (Gen. 6:9; 10:1; 11:10,27; 25:12,19; 36:1,9; 37:2; Num. 3:1; Ruth 4:18; 1 Chron. 1:29). This is not surprising since the Hebrew lying behind 'generations' derives from the usual verb for the bearing of children (first used in Gen. 3:16, then in 4:1). Against this background, why its use in Genesis 2:4 about the heavens and the earth?

As is implicit in the fact of Genesis 1 being about God's creation, the chiastic structure makes it explicit that 'the LORD God' has a generational relationship to 'the heavens and the earth' which he created. But that it is a generational relationship, in particular, clearly pertains to this historically first use of God's name, *yhwh*, and to the detail that man is the centrepiece of God's purpose – 'the heavens and the earth' being for man and in man. In the language of later scripture, God creates man to be a people for his name, a people who, as his children, manifest the characteristics of their father. This association of fatherhood towards that which has been made is rendered explicit at a later time about another creation. Moses testified this about the making of Israel by the God of faithfulness:

> "Is not He your Father who has bought you? He has *made* you and established you" (Deut. 32:6, NASB)

There can be no shadow of doubt that this is why the closing oracles of the Hebrew scriptures and why, continuing this theme, the early apostolic writings both speak of this relationship of the Lord's fatherhood to his creative works:

> "Have we not all one *Father*? Has not one God *created* us?" (Mal. 2:10)

> "Every good gift and every perfect gift is from above, coming down from the *Father* of lights... Of his own will be brought us forth... that we should be a kind of firstfruits of his *creatures*" (Jas. 1:17-18)

It is such a relationship that is introduced at the beginning and made clear by the chiastic structure of Genesis 2:4. And since the creator God is introduced as the generational father whose children shall bear his name, scripture moves on to speak of this creative act by using "formed" and "[breathing] into [man's] nostrils" (Gen. 2:7) to depict a greater degree of personal and tactile involvement than the 'make' and 'create' of Genesis 1:26,27. In Genesis 1 the picture is of God speaking and things becoming so; but in Genesis 2 there is more than speaking, there is an intimate tactile involvement as a father to his child. Nevertheless, the generational aspect of Genesis 2:4 explains that the "image" and "likeness" of Genesis 1:26-28 is accomplished in a father's begetting of his children (cf. Rom. 8:29).

Harmonious historicity

Having seen there is no evidence of dis-harmony regarding the duration of creation, we can now turn our attention to noting the evidence portrayed in Genesis 2:4, consistent with Jesus' reading of these chapters, for the historical harmony of Genesis 1 and 2.

First, regarding them being harmonised records, there is multiple use of the language already employed in Genesis 1 to describe creation's completion in Genesis 2:4. The reference to "the heavens and the earth" and its chiastic parallel "the earth and the heavens" (Gen. 2:4) plainly draws on and repeats the opening headline of Genesis 1:1, "In the beginning God created the heavens and the earth" and its inclusio in Genesis 2:1, "Thus the heavens and the earth were finished." It should be noted that this reference to Genesis 1:1 and 2:1 in Genesis 2:4 is not an employment of some minor language, it is a use of a fundamental aspect of the literary make-up of the record in the opening oracle. This is clearly not accidental and trivial, it is evidence of strong harmonisation of Genesis 1 and 2. Likewise Genesis 2:4's re-use of the 'creation' and 'making' pair from Genesis 1:26,27; since a major focus of Genesis 2 is about the man and the woman, the reference to their creation in Genesis 1:26,27 by the use of this pair is highly significant. These features combine to illustrate that a large proportion of the language of Genesis 2:4 draws on the Genesis 1 record in order to establish that Genesis 2 deals with the same creation (not, be it noted, two creation stories), albeit from different perspectives whose purpose we are invited to discover.

More than this, that the revelation of God's purpose with man depends on these points of connection between the chapters shows that Genesis 1 and 2 are purposefully integral and harmonious scripture. Handle them as dis-harmonious records and we miss this aspect of God's revelation of his glorious will for man.

What does Genesis 2:4 tell us about the historicity of the record? The first thing to note, of course, is that the evolutionary creationist argument that dis-harmony between Genesis 1 and 2 evidences their non-historical nature is now without foundation – at least with respect to the duration of creation. Furthermore, the significance we have discovered regarding 'in the day of making' is that it speaks of a point-in-time of completion: all of God's creative acts described in Genesis 1 had a day in which they were all finished, the sixth day when Adam and Eve were created. Since Genesis 2:4 speaks of a day with point-in-time specificity in which creation was completed, it is clear this scripture has chronological interest. Genesis 2:4 is not alone in this since the statement about creation reaching completion in the expression, "Thus the heavens and the earth were finished" (Gen. 2:1) displays the same interest. Furthermore, the mention of a beginning and the marking of days in Genesis 1 reflects an identical concern. Indeed, Jesus' use of 'the beginning' to encompass what happened in Genesis 1 and 2 as taking place within the same timeframe and to highlight Genesis 2:24's historical precedence over Deuteronomy 24[14] powerfully reinforces such chronological interest.

It remains to be noted that chronological interest and historical precedence necessarily has historical focus, and this demonstrates that Genesis 1 and 2 are presented as historical.[15]

An ironic conclusion

In seeking to demonstrate that Genesis 1 and 2 are not to be read historically, some evolutionary creationists do attempt to read Genesis 2:4 in a strictly historical sense and consequently miss the rich literary

---

[14] See Chapter 2, 'Associating Genesis 1 and 2'.

[15] Denis Alexander argues, as part of his thesis to accommodate Genesis with evolution, that Genesis 1 is not normal history but rather proto-historical and that the text shows no interest in chronology whereas Genesis 2 is nearer to being historical and resonant with the history of Neolithic farmers (Denis Alexander, *Creation or Evolution*, 180, 288-289, 295-296, 300-301). Contrarily, it is clear that Jesus read Genesis 1 and 2 as sharing the same historical focus and timeframe and, furthermore, close attention to the text of Genesis 1 and 2 reveals a strong interest in chronological matters.

meaning on which the historicity of God's harmonious creative purpose in man is established.

When we read Genesis 2:4's literary structure and function intra-textually, contextually and inter-textually, we see there is no disparity or disharmony between Genesis 2:4 and the six days of creation in Genesis 1. Rather, Genesis 2:4 portrays a profound revelation of God's special and generational relationship to man, in whom God's purpose in creating the heavens and the earth finds its fulness. Genesis 1 and 2 are a wondrously harmonious and historical record of God's creation. As Jesus testified in a context which speaks of God's manifestation in his children, "Scripture cannot be broken" (John 10:35).

4: Different Depictions of the Beginning?

We turn now to examine the second of eight reasons marshalled by evolutionary creationists to argue for a dis-harmonious and non-historical reading of Genesis 1 and 2. It is claimed of these chapters, "The two stories depict two different primordial scenes".[1] On the one hand, it is said that Genesis 1 begins with pre-existent chaotic matter that is about to be 'tamed' by God during the six-day sequence, and that Genesis 1 shows how God makes habitable what was chaotically uninhabitable. On the other hand, it is asserted Genesis 2 depicts a similar transition from uninhabitable to habitable but does not describe the primordial state in the same way; rather, it is averred, Genesis 2 deals with a land that is not yet habitable because of an absence of plant life due to there not having been rain or anyone to work the land.

Suspect reading

We already have grounds for considering this to be a suspect reading. When the writer speaks of 'two stories' and 'two different primordial scenes' he immediately places himself again in conflict with Jesus' reading. Although the writer headlines this claimed difference by speaking of 'beginning' singular, his mention of 'two different primordial scenes' reveals that he believes Genesis 1 and 2 contain two distinct beginnings in two different stories. But against this, we have seen it is clear that the Lord Jesus Christ read Genesis 1 and 2 as portraying a single beginning across a single story whose narrative extends from Genesis 1:1 to at least Genesis 2:24.[2]

Such conflict of readings is a powerful reason for viewing this evolutionary creationist claim with great suspicion. Nevertheless, we will now consider the differences which are highlighted in this argument.

---

[1] Peter Enns, *Israel's Two Creation Stories*, http://biologos.org/blog/series/israels-two-creation-stories [referenced October 25, 2016]. See also Peter Enns, *The Evolution of Adam: What the Bible Does and Doesn't Say About Human Origins*, Brazos Press, 2012, 51.

[2] See Chapter 2, 'Associating Genesis 1 and 2'.

Genesis 2:5

Plainly, the claim about Genesis 2's primordial scene is based on the narrative in verse 5:

> "When no bush of the field was yet in the land and no small plant of the field had yet sprung up – for the LORD God had not caused it to rain on the land, and there was no man to work the ground . . ."

A suppressed premise for the claim that this depicts a dis-harmonious and different primordial scene from that seen in Genesis 1 is plainly that the chronology of Genesis 2 is co-extensive with the six days (as distinct from the sixth day) of creative work described in Genesis 1. But we have already seen that this is not an accurate reading of Genesis 2. Rather, Genesis 2:4 headlines that what follows in chapter 2 deals with the Lord God's completion of his creative work on the sixth day, a completion that awaited the creation of man.[3]

In fact, this conclusion about creation's completion awaiting the formation of man has direct relevance to understanding the statements about bushes, plants and rain in Genesis 2:5. This is seen from the fact it is the description about there being no bush or plant which sets the scene for scripture's revelation of the reason why the Lord God's work was incomplete: 'there was no man . . .' (Gen. 2:5, cf. v. 20). The absence of bushes and plants of the field in Genesis 2:5 is clearly associated with the impact of there being no man: for these to spring up, a man was needed "to work the ground".

These considerations illustrate that we need another perspective on Genesis 2:5 other than it being a dis-harmonised record of the same things portrayed in Genesis 1.

---

[3] See Chapter 3.

Another perspective

We see clearly that Genesis 2:5 most certainly has a different viewpoint from the creation of Genesis 1. This is marked by the introduction of language about created things that has not previously been employed. This new language is tabulated below:

Expression	Uses in Genesis 1 to 3
bush [*śyḥ*]	2:5
field [*śdh*]	2:5,19,20; 3:1,14,18
to spring up [*smḥ*]	2:5,9; 3:18
to rain [*mṭr*]	2:5

Note that the language we witness being employed beginning in Genesis 2:5 onwards is entirely absent from Genesis 1. What the Lord God is described as performing in Genesis 2:5, therefore, is something new and distinct from the events of the first six days prior to man's creation. This new and distinctive thing is purposefully flagged by the introduction of this completely new language about plant life and the conditions within which it would flourish. Overlooking of such a feature in Genesis 2 exposes a superficial reading of this scripture.

This conclusion is further substantiated by observing how Genesis 2 develops our understanding of the field, similarly introduced for the first time in verse 5, in which bushes and plants would spring up. Regarding this field, we are told that bushes and plants would spring up in it only when there was a man to "work [*'bd*, the common Hebrew expression for 'serve'] the ground". We next meet man in the position of working the ground in Genesis 2:15; this time he is appointed by the Lord God "to work [the garden]". The "field" of Genesis 2:5 has become "the garden" planted by the Lord God in the east (Gen. 2:8). As in Genesis 2:5, so also in Genesis 2:8, new language regarding a "garden" is introduced purposefully to mark the change of perspective in Genesis 2 from that in Genesis 1. Man having been formed, as described in Genesis 2:7, the Lord God planted the garden and caused fruit-bearing trees to spring up in it so that these could sustain the man (Gen. 2:8-9,16-17) and so that in this garden the man could fulfil his appointment of working it and keeping it (Gen. 2:15).

The clear viewpoint in this part of Genesis 2 therefore is of only a part of "the earth" of Genesis 1 in which, on the third day, God had caused the sprouting of all manner of vegetation (Gen. 1:11-13). In Genesis 2 on the sixth day, *a part of* this earth is now set aside as a field to be cultivated as a garden in which man would serve.

Serving up a conclusion

Thus, to claim that Genesis 1 and 2 depict separate and different transitions from the uninhabitable to habitable is to misread the text. And to claim further that this means that Genesis 1 and 2 are dis-harmonised and cannot be historical records is faulty reasoning. From 'the earth' which had been created and ordered in the first six days before man's creation, the Lord God separated out a field as 'a garden' in which he caused bushes and plants of the field to spring up specifically so that, being placed in this garden (Gen. 2:8), man might learn to serve; the Lord God did this on the sixth day.

Historicity

Genesis 2's introduction of new language regarding vegetation and a field which becomes a garden fit neatly with the concluding description in this verse of man working the ground. This is a description of an agrarian lifestyle and, as a portrayal of the first man and his environs, it has an historic ring about it.[4] Indeed, one evolutionary creationist

---

[4] Current anthropology dates the establishment of agrarian societies in the Middle East to about 10,000 years ago (Allen W Johnson and Timothy Earle, *The Evolution of Human Societies*, Stanford University Press, 2000, 91). Such a date does not conflict in any way with scripture's description of man's beginning and creation in Genesis 1 and 2.

acknowledges that Genesis 2 is resonant with secular history of Neolithic farmers.[5] The very nature of agriculture is to set apart a chosen portion of land that it might be worked, and this is what this early part of Genesis 2 clearly describes. Such a focus sets Genesis 2 apart from the description in Genesis 1, the latter plainly displaying a much more extensive perspective.

Later scriptures look back on this time and in doing so employ the language of Genesis 2:5 – clearly regarding Genesis 2 as a historical basis for the psalmist's claims about God. In particular, the psalmist drew on the specific detail of the setting apart of a field as a garden in which man could be appointed to serve. In drawing on this detail, the psalmist evidently handled it as an event that actually took place:

> "You [the Lord] <u>cause</u> the grass <u>to grow</u> [*smḥ*] for the livestock and plants for man to cultivate, that he may bring forth food from the earth" (Ps. 104:14)

> "[The Lord] covers the heavens with clouds; he prepares <u>rain</u> [*mṭr*] for the earth; he <u>makes</u> grass <u>grow</u> [*smḥ*] on the hills" (Ps. 147:8)

These psalms speak of the ongoing sustenance of creation by God and declare the continuation of that which he commenced in Genesis 2:5. This continuing creative care, which is described by picking up the language of Genesis 2, makes no sense without the latter's historicity. If God performs the things that are described in these two psalms then it follows he also performed the things described in Genesis 2:5. Furthermore, both psalms call for praise, thanksgiving and song to the one who performs these things (Ps. 104:1,24,33-35; 147:1,7,12,20); an empty call if they are not historically true regarding God's performance of such caring acts.

Furthermore, Psalm 147 employs its reference to Genesis 2 alongside other descriptions of the Lord's continuing care for his creation (based

---

[5] Denis Alexander, *Creation or Evolution: do we have to choose?* Monarch Books, 2nd Edition, 2014, 300-301.

on a variety of other aspects from Genesis 1 and 2) and alongside quite different works performed by God, including:

- The Lord's works on behalf of Jerusalem, Israel and individuals (Ps. 147:2-3,6,13-14).

- God's active sustenance of his creation (Ps. 147:8-9,15-18).

- The Lord's revelation of his word to his chosen people (Ps. 147:19-20).

If the Lord God did not perform what he is described as doing in Genesis 2 then what are we to make of the historicity of these other acts of the Lord? Contrarily, if, through faith, we are assured in our knowledge of God that he performs things for Jerusalem, Israel and individuals and that he sends his word to his chosen people, we can be equally assured, through faith, that the Lord God executes his caring sustenance of the creation and which he began in the manner described in Genesis 1 and 2.

An additional feature of Psalm 147 is that it narrates these works of the Lord in order to substantiate that the Lord is great, abundantly powerful and that he has an understanding beyond measure (Ps. 147:5). If the Lord God did not accomplish all the things described in Psalm 147 including, specifically, those drawn from Genesis 2 then this claim about the Lord's greatness is vain.

Note also that Psalm 104 uses language from Genesis 2 while speaking of agrarian work – "livestock and plants for man to cultivate, that he may bring forth food from the earth" – and this confirms our conclusion that such is the focus of Genesis 2.

A further illustration of the historicity of this part of Genesis 2 is the way that the garden introduced there is taken up as a figure of God's blessings of life in his kingdom. In this case it is testimony from the glorified Lord Jesus Christ:

"He who has an ear, let him hear what the Spirit says to the churches. To the one who conquers I will grant to eat of the tree of life, which is in the <u>paradise</u> [*paradeisos*, i.e. 'garden'[6]] of God" (Rev. 2:7)

Of course, the assurance of "the paradise of God" in Revelation 2:7 employs a figure about an eternal truth that is taken from Eden and called God's paradise because it was the Lord God who had first planted it there. But the use of the garden as a figure does not mean that the garden was not an historical place: it is a feature of figures in the Hebrew scriptures that they are real things which stand for eternally true and better things. As the writer to the Hebrews said of aspects of the historical and figurative law of Moses, they are "copies of the true things" (Heb. 9:24). But if the garden of Genesis 2 is not historical, the Lord's assurance in Revelation 2 is rendered an empty promise; if the garden was not planted in the east by the Lord God, how can we be confident he, through his son, will really grant to eat of the tree of life which is in the paradise of God?

Before concluding this section, we ought to note again how the Psalms and Revelation do not speak of God as creator in some generalised sense. Rather, at the detailed level of plants being caused to grow in a garden planted by God, the testimony of these other scriptures is that Genesis 2 is historically true. It ought also to be noted that it is such detailed and specific things that are employed to substantiate the Lord's greatness.[7]

Scripture's harmonious purpose

In explaining that 'the heavens and the earth' were incomplete without man, Genesis 2:5 sets the scene for man to learn more of the Lord God's purpose in creation. These details add a layer of meaning to our understanding of the Lord God's purpose in creating man: man was to learn service. In the context of the majestic creative acts of God in Genesis

---

[6] *Paradeisos* is 'from Old Persian word for garden' (Friberg, *Analytical Greek Lexicon*).

[7] See Chapter 2, 'Historical references'.

1, man was appointed to a position of glory: "dominion" over all that God had created (Gen. 1:26,28). The Lord God, through the scripture of Genesis 2, now determines that such dominion entails that man must first learn what it is to serve.

It is understanding that the garden in Genesis 2 was separated out from all else that was created in Genesis 1 which highlights that service must precede dominion. For this teaching to emerge we need to be sensitive to the interdependency between Genesis 1 and 2. This requires that Genesis 1 is also historical so that it corresponds and interrelates with the history of Genesis 2:5. Genesis 1 and 2 work together in a beautifully harmonised and historical manner to teach us these things.[8]

The Lord Jesus Christ taught his disciples about the power of God's word in the scriptures, that it is powerful to determine outcomes:

"the Son of Man goes as it has been *determined*" (Lk. 22:22)

It is in such a context that the Lord spoke also of the need for service:

". . . let the greatest among you become as the youngest, and the leader as one who serves" (Lk. 22:26)

It is incumbent on Christians that God's teaching in Genesis 1 and 2 should determine things in our lives. From the very beginning of creation, God teaches that service must precede dominion.

---

[8] Denis Alexander acknowledges that Genesis 2 explains the responsibilities of being made in God's image (Denis Alexander, *Creation or Evolution*, 196).

5: Different Order of Events?

A third reason served up by evolutionary creationists to sustain their claim that Genesis 1 and 2 'cannot be harmonized' and 'were never intended to be' is that these two chapters 'have distinct descriptions of what happens next, both in order and content.'[1] This claim about differences in the order of events features in source critical analysis.[2] Elsewhere, Peter Enns describes this claimed dis-harmony as 'particularly telling'.[3] To substantiate his argument, the two chapters are summarised in sequenced stages and contrasts then drawn between the sequences identified.

Genesis 1 is summarised as having two stages in the following arrangement:

- first, God creates the habitable space: light, separation of waters, dry land on days one to three; and

- second, he fills the space: plants, heavenly lights, sea and sky creatures, land animals, and humans, both male and female together at the end, on days four to six.

Genesis 2 is summarised by four stages in the following sequence:

- first, God creates man before there is any plant life;

- next, he creates a garden and puts the man to work there;

---

[1] Peter Enns, *Israel's Two Creation Stories*, http://biologos.org/blog/series/israels-two-creation-stories [referenced October 25, 2016]. See also Denis Alexander, *Creation or Evolution: do we have to choose?* Monarch Books, 2nd Edition, 2014, 188, 194-195, 226.

[2] See Pauline A Viviano, 'Source Criticism' in Eds. Steven L McKenzie and Stephen R Haynes, *To Each Its Own Meaning: An Introduction to Biblical Criticisms and their Application*, Westerville John Knox Press, 1999, 46 (available on Google Books).

[3] Peter Enns, *The Evolution of Adam: What the Bible Does and Doesn't Say About Human Origins*, Brazos Press, 2012, 51.

- after placing the man in the garden, God creates animals for the man as helpers; and then

- not finding a suitable helper among the animals, God forms the woman out of the man's side.

Based on these summaries, the evolutionary creationist reading of Genesis 1 and 2 is that the sequential order of creation laid out in Genesis 1 is completely overturned in Genesis 2. Disparities in their sequences are claimed to be:

- unlike Genesis 2, in chapter 1 the creation of plant life precedes humanity;

- in Genesis 1, man and woman are made concurrently and together on the sixth day, whereas in Genesis 2 they are formed separately; and

- while man is made at the end of God's creative acts in Genesis 1, he is made first in chapter 2.

Fundamental to the evolutionary creationist argument here is that Genesis 1 and 2 are co-extensive geographically and chronologically:

- The 'garden' of Genesis 2 is presumed to be co-extensive with the 'dry land' of Genesis 1.

- The creative work of Genesis 2 is supposed to take place across the six days of Genesis 1.

Misreading upon misreading

We have already seen, however, that this is not an accurate reading of the text. Rather, Genesis 2:4-24 deals with the Lord God's completion of his creative work on the sixth day, a completion that awaited the creation of man.[4] Furthermore, we have seen that Genesis 2 presents a

---

[4] See Chapter 3.

different perspective from the account of Genesis 1, one in which the garden of chapter 2 is *a part of* the earth of Genesis 1 now set aside for man's service.[5] As we trace through these evolutionary creationist readings of Genesis 1 and 2, we witness misreading of the text compounding earlier misreading.

Nevertheless, the third and fourth stages of the evolutionary creationist reading of Genesis 2 are new aspects that do need to be evaluated:

- What are we to make of the claim that the animals of Genesis 2:19 were created after man, whereas Genesis 1 says that animals were created before man?

- What are we to make of the assertion that the creation of male and female together in Genesis 1 is contrary to the woman being made separately, out of the man's side, in Genesis 2?

In order to facilitate exploration of the first of these points against the backcloth of evolutionary creationist claims about it, two possible explanations for the mention of the animals in Genesis 2:19 will be examined before adding a third interpretation, the one which this writer believes to be the most likely meaning.

The animals

Are the animals "formed" and named in Genesis 2:19-20 the same animals as those "created" and "made" in Genesis 1:20-25? Or, akin to the vegetation specifically created for the garden,[6] are the animals of Genesis 2 domesticated animals specifically created to pertain to the garden in which Adam was appointed to serve?

If the animals of Genesis 2 are the same as those in Genesis 1:

---

[5] See Chapter 4.

[6] See Chapter 4.

- As claimed by evolutionary creationists, does Genesis 2:19-20 record that the order of creation of man and the animals is indeed different here from what we see in Genesis 1?

- Alternatively, are these verses a parenthetic retrospection on the animals' earlier creation, to provide some background and explanation about the search for a suitable "helper fit for [the man]" (Gen. 2:18)?

When we examine Genesis 2's reference to the animals we find some correspondence with the language and terminology of Genesis 1:20-25:

Genesis 2:19-20	Genesis 1:20-25
"beast [_hyt_]"	"beast [_hyt_]"; "beasts [_hyt_]"
"bird of the heavens ['_wp_ hšmym]"	"birds… the heavens ['_wp_… hšmym]"; "bird ['_wp_]"; "birds [_h 'wp_]"
"living creature [_npš hyh_]"	"living creatures [_npš hyh_]"
"livestock [_hbhmh_]"	"livestock [_bhmh_]"

This consistency of language across Genesis 1:20-25 and 2:19-20 could suggest these two records speak of the same animals (while also being, be it noted, a harmonising feature of the two chapters). If this is the correct reading, is the order of creation represented in Genesis 2 in conflict with what we see in Genesis 1, or are we to read 2:19-20 as a flashback to the animals' earlier creation?

Evolutionary creationists pre-empt the latter reading by claiming that a 'pluperfect' rendering of Genesis 2:19, such as we find in the NIV,[7] is

---

[7] "Now the LORD God _had formed_ out of the ground . . ."

not warranted because the 'simple past' is used in the Hebrew through-out Genesis 2.[8] But this is a simplistic handling of Hebrew verbs, for which attention to contextual reference, narrative logic and syntax is also required in order to determine grammatical tense.[9]

The significance of these literary aspects for determining a right under-standing of tense can be seen from considering a later passage in Genesis where a verb with precisely the same form and syntax as that used in Genesis 2:19-20 is employed and which obviously has the plu-perfect sense. When scripture records, "Now the LORD *had said* unto Abram . . ." (Gen. 12:1, KJV) it is evident that the KJV accurately catches the pluperfect tense of the opening Hebrew verb because:

- the content of what is recorded in Genesis 12:1ff as having been said by the Lord includes the command that Abraham leave his country, Ur of the Chaldeans; yet we have the earlier record of Abraham leaving Ur and travelling to Haran en route to Canaan in Genesis 11:28,31 – evidently in obedience to the command retrospectively narrated in Genesis 12:1ff;

- Genesis 12:4 reiterates Abraham's obedience to the divine com-mand: "So Abram went, as the LORD had told him"; and again, this departure has already been narrated in Genesis 11:31; and, consequently

- the KJV rendering of Genesis 12:1 accurately captures the plu-perfect sense of the record; it refers back and testifies to the

---

[8] Peter Enns, *Israel's Two Creation Stories*. Use of the expression 'simple past' about the Hebrew verbs in Genesis 2 is actually unwarranted. In Genesis 2:19 (as also for other verbs in this chapter), the Hebrew verb is *waw-consecutive* with imperfect (also known as *wayyiqtol* verb form) and this requires more sensitive handling than just categorising it as 'simple past'. See also, Denis Alexander, *Creation or Evolution*, 194-195.

[9] C. John Collins, 'The wayyiqtol as "pluperfect": when and why' in *Tyndale Bulletin* 46.1 (1995), 117-140 (available at http://www.tyndalehouse.com/tynbul/library/Tyn-Bull_1995_46_1_08_Collins_WAYYIQTOL_Pluperfect.pdf); see 127-128 for a formal statement of these criteria. Notice also John Collins' explicit assessment of Genesis 2:19 in which he concludes the NIV's pluperfect rendering, "Now the LORD God had formed out of the ground . . .", is correct; see 135-140.

narrative in Genesis 11:28-31 and its earlier history to provide a covenant promise explanation for what had happened then.

Any residual doubt about this reading of Genesis 11 and 12 is authoritatively removed by Stephen's spirit-filled testimony that "the God of glory appeared to our father Abraham *when he was in Mesopotamia, before he lived in Haran,* and said to him, 'Go out from your land and from your kindred . . .'" (Acts 7:2,3). This testimony renders it clear that the Lord's command recorded in Genesis 12:1 had actually been uttered by the Lord prior to Abraham's departure as originally recorded in Genesis 11:31. Thus, apostolic testimony further confirms that the record in Genesis 12:1 carries a pluperfect tense despite the Hebrew verb being, as evolutionary creationists argue, 'simple past' in form.

Assuming a framework that the animals of Genesis 2:19-20 are the same as those in 1:20-25, it is only if one has pre-determined that Genesis 1 and 2 are not to be read sequentially[10] that one can claim there is no narrative logic driving a pluperfect reading of Genesis 2:19. But since:

- the Hebrew verb form and syntax of "Now the LORD God *had formed* . . ." (Gen. 2:19, NIV) is the same as "Now the LORD *had said* unto Abram . . ." (12:1, KJV), and since

- within the assumed framework, the narrative logic of Genesis 1 and 2, sequentially read, would demand it, the pluperfect sense of Genesis 2:19 as a flashback to Genesis 1 is seen to be a valid reading of this verse.

Domesticated animals

However, it is also plain that between Genesis 1:20-25 and 2:19-20 we see changes in the language used of the animals' origins and habitat.

---

[10] See Chapter 6 where sequential reading of chapters displaying distinct literary styles is demonstrated to be a common feature of scripture.

This is consistent with the change of perspective from earth to garden which we saw in Genesis 2's account of man's formation:[11]

Genesis 2:19-20	Genesis 1:20-25
"out of the ground [*mn h'dmh*]"	"Let the earth bring forth [*tws' h'rs*]"
"beast of the field [*hyt hśdh*]"	"beast of the earth [*hyt 'rs*]"; "beasts of the earth [*hyt h'rs*]"

In Genesis 2 we see that the animals are formed out of the ground whereas in Genesis 1, God made the animals on day six through the earth bringing forth. Assuming this signals that scripture speaks of different kinds of animals, this adds to the change of perspective between Genesis 1 and 2 that we have already witnessed. Within this change of viewpoint, we have seen that 'field' is employed for the first time as a part of the 'earth' of Genesis 1 in relation to Adam's formation and his appointment to serve in the garden. While "the ground [*h'dmh*]" has also featured previously in Genesis 1:25, this was to characterise the behaviour of the animals, not to describe the material from which they were made as in Genesis 2:19. On the other hand, the formation of the animals "out of the ground" (Gen. 2:19) resonates strongly with Adam's origins in Genesis 2:7.

These details suggest that the animals of Genesis 2:19 are distinct from all those in Genesis 1:20-25, and that, consistent with a major theme of Genesis 2, they are domesticated animals associated with the field and garden in which Adam was appointed to serve, and they were created specifically for this purpose. Indeed, the absence of any mention of sea creatures in Genesis 2:19 (cf. Gen. 1:20-22) reinforces the distinctiveness of the animals in Genesis 2. Such a reading would also explain the mention of the birds of Genesis 2:19 being formed out of the ground on

---

[11] See Chapter 4.

day six.[12] The need for an explanation of such a detail arises from the fact the birds of Genesis 1 are portrayed as swarming, associated with the waters, on day five (Gen. 1:20) and not as being brought forth from the earth on day six (Gen. 1:24). If Genesis 2:19 describes a special creation of domesticated animals on day six, separate from the animals of Genesis 1:20-25, then this apparent discrepancy is removed. Likewise, a common criticism of Genesis 2:19 that there is no possibility that Adam could name all the species of animals created in Genesis 1 within a single day (day six) is removed. If the reading of Genesis 2:19 is properly about domesticated animals only, the population of animals paraded before Adam is significantly reduced.

Finally, if this reading is correct, then the tense in the first verb in Genesis 2:19 ("Now the LORD God *had formed* . . .", NIV) is rendered irrelevant in the argument suggested by evolutionary creationists.

A third interpretation

Yet another possible reading, and the one which this writer believes to be the right one, combines the previous two analyses. It takes the opening of Genesis 2:19 as pluperfect *and* that these animals are domesticated. The domesticated animals of Genesis 2:19 are then explained as a sub-set of all the animals created in Genesis 1. The formation of these beasts and birds from the ground would then be a flashback description of the creation of a particular sub-set of the animals created as described in Genesis 1.

Purpose

While the third interpretation is favoured, any of the possible readings considered above show that the claim of evolutionary creationists – that Genesis 2 presents a different and conflicting order of creation of animals from that in Genesis 1 – is wrong. Furthermore, the pursuit of a historical reading of Genesis 1 and 2 by evolutionary creationists, thereby finding dis-harmony between the two chapters, overlooks the

---

[12] See Chapter 3 for an explanation of why Genesis 2 should be read as an account of day six.

spiritual meaning that God intends us to take from the formation of the animals in Genesis 2:19 – namely, that these animals share some commonality with Adam himself, being made from the same stuff as him. Other scriptures make just this point about the hopelessness of sinful and unredeemed man:

> ". . . what happens to the children of man and what happens to the beasts is the same; as one dies, so dies the other. They all have the same breath, and man has no advantage over the beasts, for all is vanity" (Eccl. 3:19)

Furthermore, we are to learn from this that it was not the stuff from which we are made that sets us apart from the animals, it is the image and likeness of God. And in seeking a "helper fit for [the man]" (Gen. 2:18)", it was only with such exalted things in purview that a helper could be found.

Historicity

Before moving on to consider evolutionary creationist claims about contrary differences in Genesis 1 and 2 regarding the creation of the woman, we should note again the consistency with Neolithic agrarian history that arises from a domesticated animal reading of Genesis 2:19-20.[13]

The woman

What are we to make of the evolutionary creationist assertion that the creation of male and female together in Genesis 1 is contrary to the woman being made separately out of the man's side in Genesis 2?

The most fundamental consideration that should lead us to reject this claim is how it conflicts with Jesus' reading of Genesis 1 and 2 and, specifically, his reading of the creation of man. We have seen that Jesus employed the language of both Genesis 1 and 2 to teach things about

---

[13] See Chapter 4.

man's creation as male and female (Gen. 1) and about God's declaration about marriage based on the manner of Eve's creation (Gen. 2). Such handling clearly indicates that Jesus believed these scriptures spoke of the same events in a harmonious and historic manner.[14]

Furthermore, if one were asked for a summary of Genesis 2, it would be reasonable to state that it is about the creation of man and woman. Consequently, it is entirely rational to employ the words of Genesis 1:27, "male and female he created them", to summarise the events of Genesis 2:7,18-22. It stretches credulity to claim that the records in Genesis 1 and 2 are in conflict. Such an argument seems very much like special pleading.

The same style of reasoning would charge the gospel writers with dis-harmony and lack of historicity because of differences in presentation.[15] For example, we have Matthew saying of Jesus' baptism that the voice from heaven spoke to the gathered crowd, "This is my beloved Son, with whom I am well pleased" (Mt. 3:17) while both Mark and Luke record that the voice spoke to Jesus and said, "You are my beloved Son; with you I am well pleased" (Mk. 1:11; Lk. 3:22). If we were to charge these three gospel writers with dis-harmony and consequent lack of historicity, where does that leave our confidence in their testimony about the resurrection of the Lord Jesus Christ? Rather, a reading that expects harmony between scriptural records will seek to learn from these differences. In this case, that the voice from heaven both testified to the crowd at Jesus' baptism *and* spoke encouragingly to his only beloved son in response to his obedience.

Harmonious historicity

In fact, the creation of man first, and then the woman, is an aspect of harmony, rather than dis-harmony, between Genesis 1 and 2 that also resonates with later scriptures which reference these chapters. It is not

---

[14] See Chapter 2.

[15] The more conservative evolutionary creationist to whom we have referred explicitly acknowledges that gospel differences do not render these scriptures unhistorical (Denis Alexander, *Creation or Evolution*, 188).

without significance that Genesis 1 records about man's creation, "male and female he created them" (Gen. 1:27). Obviously, scripture could have reversed the mention of male and female in this description but the reference to male first is harmoniously consistent with the order of their creation in Genesis 2.

Furthermore, rather than, as claimed by evolutionary creationists, the different portrayals of the woman's creation in Genesis 1 and 2 being evidence that these chapters are not 'recording history',[16] the apostle Paul made clear references to these scriptures as historical and harmonious background for typological roles to be fulfilled by men and women in the ecclesias.

In explaining why he did not permit a woman to teach or to exercise authority over a man, the apostle drew on Genesis 2:

> "For Adam was formed first, then Eve" (1 Tim. 2:13)

'Formed' here is a clear use of "formed" in Genesis 2:7, while the order of creation upon which he based his argument is established from Genesis 2 as a historical record. Moreover, while the apostle here employed some of the text of Genesis 2:7, he did so to assert a historical element of the creative works of God: according to the apostle Paul, Adam was formed first then Eve and it is evident that *he declared* that this is what actually happened. This is not just a reference to the text of Genesis without any regard for the historicity of the events described within it. Alongside the testimony of Genesis 1 and 2, the apostle Paul added his voice as another witness to testify how the Lord God created man and woman in the beginning.[17]

Paul's argument regarding men and women in 1 Corinthians can also be seen to rest on the historicity and harmony of the record of man's creation in both Genesis 1 and 2. When he explained that women ought

---

[16] Peter Enns, *Israel's Two Creation Stories*. See also Denis Alexander, *Creation or Evolution*, 180, 288-289.

[17] See Chapter 2, 'Historical references'.

to cover their heads whereas men ought not, he first established this teaching based upon the record in Genesis 1:

"he is the image and glory of God" (1 Cor. 11:7)

Plainly, the apostle here alluded to and expounded Genesis 1:27: "God created man in his own image, in the image of God he created him". Paul's 'the image... of God' is an explicit repetition of the language while 'the glory of God' expounds some of the significance of God's creative purpose. Of course, Paul proceeded to comment "but woman is the glory of man" (1 Cor. 11:7) and, against the background of Genesis 1:27 concluding "male and female he created them", it is only by reading both Genesis 1 and 2 sequentially and harmoniously that this image and glory relationship between God and man and then man and the woman can be consistently and truly understood. Furthermore, the apostle continued to substantiate his teaching by writing, "man was not made from woman, but woman from man. Neither was man created for woman, but woman for man" (1 Cor. 11:8-9). These statements are evidently founded on the record in Genesis 2 about the Lord God seeking a helper for the man. Note that Paul clearly relied on the historicity of the record in Genesis 1 *and* 2 of man and woman's creation in order to substantiate his teaching. Not only this, he referred to both Genesis 1 and 2 as part of the same argument indicating apostolic judgment, consistent with Jesus' reading, that these two records are harmonious in their descriptions of man and woman's creation. Indeed, the two chapters record a single story. Again, while the apostle sometimes employed features of the text of Genesis 1 and 2, he did so to assert the historicity of the events described in these chapters. Yet again, it is the independent testimony of the apostle Paul, sometimes stated even without employing the actual text of Genesis 1 and 2, that specific things happened at the time of the creation:[18]

- Man was made in the image and glory of God.

---

[18] See Chapter 2, 'Historical references'.

Genesis 1-2

- The woman was created for the man and from him.

- The woman was made as the glory of the man.

The apostle Paul did not just make a reference to the text of Genesis without any regard for the historicity of the events described within it but testified alongside the record of God's creation in Genesis 1 and 2.

Note again, that these apostolic scriptures do not just speak of God as creator of the heavens and the earth in some broad overview manner, leaving the specifics of how God performed this creative work for evolutionary science to discover and describe. Rather, they refer to highly specific aspects of the creative works and handle the record as harmonised and the events described as historical and true. In particular, these apostolic scriptures refer in this manner to specific events of both Genesis 1 and 2. And yet these two detailed aspects of Genesis 1 and 2 – the formation of Adam (Genesis 2:7) and man's creation in the image of God (Gen. 1:26-27) – are two of three particular details in Genesis 1 and 2 which are dismissed by evolutionary creationists as having any historical value since, otherwise, there would be irreconcilable conflict with evolutionary science.[19] We have previously seen that it is not only the apostle Paul who handled Genesis 1:26-27 as historical but that Jesus did too.[20] Thus, evolutionary creationists find themselves directly and specifically in conflict with both Jesus' and the apostle Paul's readings.

Finally, either the records in Genesis 1 and 2 and the events described in these chapters to which the apostle Paul[21] explicitly referred are historically true and substantiate his theological teaching about men and women or they are not historically true and his judgment is baseless.

---

[19] Denis Alexander, *Creation or Evolution*, 295-297; Peter Enns, *The Evolution of Adam*, xiv.

[20] See Chapter 2, 'Historical references'.

[21] In order to address the clear tensions between evolutionary science and scripture, Peter Enns dismisses the apostle Paul's historical treatment of Adam as a feature of his Jewish upbringing. See Peter Enns, *The Evolution of Adam*, Chapter 7.

Purpose again

Yet again, therefore, the pursuit of an evolutionary creationist argument misses the point of the differing details in Genesis 1 and 2 concerning the creation of man.

As we have seen previously,[22] while Genesis 1:26-28 describes the glorious purpose that God has for his creation with mankind at creation's head, Genesis 2 moves on to describe essential means to that end[23] and both chapters need to be read together to see how they harmoniously work to teach these things. The profound "mystery" (Eph. 5:32) portrayed in Genesis 2:18-25 is that God's purpose of mankind filling the earth and showing forth his image and likeness will finally be realised only through the work of the true husband in reconciling God and man. The truth of this work of reconciliation is founded on the historicity of God's formation of Adam and on the making of the woman out of his rib. As the gospel record tells us, "beginning with Moses and all the Prophets, [Jesus] interpreted to [the disciples] in all the scriptures the things concerning himself" – including that Christ must suffer (Lk. 24:27) for his bride (Eph. 5:23,25-27).

---

[22] See Chapters 3 and 4.

[23] Another aspect explicitly acknowledged by Denis Alexander (*Creation or Evolution*, 196).

6: Different Literary Styles?

The fourth of eight reasons commonly proposed by evolutionary creationists for handling Genesis 1 and 2 as 'two different creation stories' which 'are not meant to be harmonized or read sequentially', and one that is employed in source critical analysis, is that the two chapters 'are not written in the same literary style.'[1]

Roughly stated, it is claimed that Genesis 1 is more poetic, emphasising '*patterns* rather than *plot*', while Genesis 2 is 'more like the narratives that will occupy the rest of Genesis.'[2] It is not uncommon for this distinction to be heavily caveated along at least two lines:

- first, the distinction between poetry and narrative is more blurred than this simple statement would seem to indicate; and

- second, neither style should be taken as implying greater historicity over the other.

In fact, the claim is sometimes so heavily caveated that the evolutionary creationist comes close to dismantling completely this point himself.[3] But at the heart of the claim is the argument that different literary styles in adjacent chapters, ostensibly dealing with the same subject matter, imply two distinct stories that are not meant to be harmonised or read sequentially. Quite apart from the clear testimony of the Lord Jesus

---

[1] Peter Enns, *Israel's Two Creation Stories*, http://biologos.org/blog/series/israels-two-creation-stories [referenced October 25, 2016]. Pauline A Viviano, 'Source Criticism' in Eds. Steven L McKenzie and Stephen R Haynes, *To Each Its Own Meaning: An Introduction to Biblical Criticisms and their Application*, Westerville John Knox Press, 1999, 42-43 (available on Google Books).

[2] Peter Enns, *Israel's Two Creation Stories*.

[3] Writing at an earlier time, Peter Enns actually argues against literary differences between Genesis 1 and 2 being of any significance (Peter Enns, *The Evolution of Adam: What the Bible Does and Doesn't Say About Human Origins*, Brazos Press, 2012, 52-53).

Christ that Genesis 1 and 2 are a single story and not two,[4] thus dealing a heavy blow to the evolutionary claim that we are faced with two distinct stories, is this argument about scripture and different literary styles sustainable?

Literary styles

Even a cursory review of the Hebrew scriptures yields multiple instances of changes in literary styles (however we classify those styles), indicating that such things are a common feature of the word of God:

- Jacob's prophetic poem in Genesis 49 is clearly distinct from the narrative before and after it; and yet it connects harmoniously and sequentially with the narrative of Jacob's final words introduced at Genesis 48:20.

- The song of Moses and of the sons of Israel in Exodus 15[5] is a different literary style from the narrative adjacent to it, and yet it sits neatly and in sequence as a celebration of the destruction of the Egyptians narrated earlier.

- Moses' account of Israel's wilderness journey and his summary of various laws are stylistically different from his song in Deuteronomy 32 and from his blessing of the tribes in Deuteronomy 33; yet they befit the kind of final message that such a leader would wish to leave before his death and so read harmoniously and sequentially with the surrounding narrative.

- Likewise, Hannah's poetic prayer in 1 Samuel 2 is a beautiful and holy expression of her joy at the privilege of having borne

---

[4] See Chapter 2, 'Associating Genesis 1 and 2'.

[5] Peter Enns, in his *Israel's Two Creation Stories*, acknowledges by reference to Exodus 15 (and some historical psalms, Psalms 105 and 106) that poetry is sometimes used in scripture to recount history. But he fails to recognise, in referring to Exodus 15, that he has here an example of scripture moving between narrative and poetry without such a transition being evidence that we have two different stories that are not meant to be harmonised or read sequentially.

a child whom she now lent to the Lord – a perfect and serial fit with the previous and following narrative.

- The psalm which David appointed to Asaph to thank the Lord (1 Chronicles 16) is an entirely suitable record embedded within the narrative history of the ark's ascent to Zion and harmoniously and serially corresponds with that narrative.

Such a list is only a very small sample, but here are five significant shifts in literary style without any hint that we are dealing with stories that are not meant to be harmonised or read sequentially. Rather, quite the opposite is seen to be true. Clearly, many of the poetic aspects of these examples repeat, in poetic form, some of the history we find elsewhere in the surrounding narrative:

- Jacob referred to the immediately prior family history and employs this as a basis for the things he said about specific family members – Reuben's defiling of his father's couch; Simeon and Levi's murder of all the men of Shechem's city; and the persecution of Joseph by his brothers (Gen. 49:4,5-7,23-24,26).

- Moses and the sons of Israel referred explicitly to the Lord's victory over Pharaoh and his army throughout their song (Ex. 15:4-5,7-10,13,19), a historical matter featuring large in the previous chapter; they also sang of how other nations would react to news of this victory (Ex. 15:14-16), events to which Rahab bore testimony that they were historical (Josh. 2:9-11); and they connected these events with the prophetic history of the Lord's redemption of his people and his bringing of them into the promised land (Ex. 15:13,17).

- Moses' song persistently refers to Israel's faithlessness manifested during the wilderness sojourn (Deut. 32:5-6,15-21) and reminds them of the Lord's recent deliverance (Deut. 32:9-13) – both matters dealt with in detail in his prior account of Israel's wilderness journey. Likewise, Moses opened his blessing of the tribes with historical reference to the Lord's recent manifestation in deliverance of his people and for the giving of his law

(Deut. 33:2-4); and he referred to aspects of Levi's behaviour seen during the wilderness journey (Deut. 33:8-9), details of which Moses had recounted earlier in Deuteronomy as a back-cloth to their appointment as teachers and priests in Israel (Deut. 33:10).

- Hannah's celebratory poetic prayer refers to the enmity she had suffered at the provocations of her adversary which are narrated in the previous chapter (1 Sam. 1:6-7; 2:1,3).

These historical references within the poetic parts make these examples very similar to the creation record of Genesis 1 and 2, between which we have already seen multiple correspondences across the posited distinct literary styles and there are more to come

It is clear that in the foregoing examples the different and juxtaposed literary styles are intended to work together harmoniously, to be read sequentially and to be taken as a single yet multi-faceted historical record. Consequently, the evolutionary creationist's opening assertion is found to be without substance. No evidence has been provided to establish that different literary styles mean different stories. Rather, our examples argue otherwise and increase the burden of proof that the evolutionary creationist must present.

An apostolic example

We have an apostolic example that draws on Genesis *and* exhibits the same transition from a kind of poetic style to something closer to narrative, whilst remaining an internally harmonious record of Jesus Christ's ministry.

The prologue in John 1:1-5 is plainly distinct from the more narrative style that begins with the historical record of John the Baptist being sent from God to bear witness to the Lord Jesus Christ (John 1:6ff). This prologue also draws on Genesis 1:1 by alluding to its opening phrase in its own opening expression. There is further reinforcement of this reference to Genesis with statements about all things being made (John 1:3; cf. Gen. 1:31) and the contrast between light and darkness

(John 1:4,5; cf. Gen. 1:3-5). And yet, notwithstanding the distinctive style of John's prologue compared with the rest of his gospel, it is all clearly one story.[6] This is easily demonstrated by noting how key words and themes first mentioned in the prologue are taken up and expanded later in the gospel, as the following samples show:

- the word (John 1:1,14)

- life (John 1:4; 3:15; 6:68; 17:3)

- light (John 1:4,5; 3:19; 8:12; 12:46)

- darkness (John 1:5; 8:12; 12:35,46)

Furthermore, as the gospel proceeds, it becomes clear that the description of 'the word' in the prologue is a summary introduction of the one who "became flesh and dwelt among us" (John 1:14), a matter which is explained and exhibited in the remainder of the gospel. Seeing the ways in which John's gospel is modelled on Genesis confirms our earlier conclusion: stylistic differences are not evidence of different stories that are not meant to be harmonised or read sequentially.

Harmonious historicity

Another aspect of witnessing how John's gospel is modelled on Genesis 1 and 2 is what this tells us about the gospel writer's judgment of the historicity of these two chapters and the events referenced in them. Reject the historicity of Genesis 1 and 2 and we undermine John's sublime testimony about the one who was the word become flesh and who dwelt among us to show the glory of the father's grace and truth. This testimony from John is clearly established upon the Genesis record both typically and historically and if we deny the historicity of the latter we damage John's testimony.

---

[6] For literary analysis of John's gospel that reaches the same conclusion, see Frank Kermode, 'John' in Eds. Robert Alter and Frank Kermode, *The Literary Guide to the Bible*, Collins, 1987, 440ff.

We have also now seen examples from multiple and various scriptures that contain shifts in literary style which nevertheless are harmonious and sequential writings. These present substantive evidence for scripture commonly adopting such styles adjacently and this becomes evidence in support of Genesis 1 and 2 being read harmoniously and sequentially. This is entirely contrary to the evolutionary creationist claim. Furthermore, the scriptures in which we have traced these adjacent literary styles – Genesis, Exodus, Deuteronomy, 1 Samuel, 1 Chronicles and John – are all presented within the scriptures themselves as historical. This collective witness presents a serious challenge to the evolutionary claim that, regarding Genesis 1 and 2, '*recording history* is not the point'.[7]

Purposeful scripture

In fact, the evidence of at least two books of scripture – Genesis and John – following this pattern of transition from a near-poetic style to narrative demonstrates more than this. The common structure shared by Genesis and John shows that we are not dealing with an accident of redaction process when moving from one style to another but with purposeful scripture. It is evidently a feature of certain scriptures to be structured this way.[8] What is scripture's purpose in these two examples?

An answer to this question can be arrived at by considering other themes common to Genesis and John. Plainly, both Genesis 1 and John's prologue have in common that they present majestic and exalted

---

[7] Peter Enns, *Israel's Two Creation Stories*. But is should be noted that the same author does not regard Exodus, Joshua and Judges as historical; Peter Enns, *The Evolution of Adam*, 62-65.

[8] Another example is in Matthew's opening chapter. The gospel's construction of Jesus' genealogy in three sets of fourteen generations renders it susceptible to Peter Enns' description of Genesis 1 as emphasising '*patterns* rather than *plot*' (Peter Enns, *Israel's Two Creation Stories*). Yet the way the gospel later takes up the themes of Jesus as promised king and seed of Abraham shows that Matthew 1 is of one story with the rest of the gospel. Note also how despite Matthew 1 having a clear pattern, it nevertheless deals with historical people and descent – a matter which is critical to the gospel writer's purpose. Indeed, this is acknowledged by another evolutionary creationist writer (Denis Alexander, *Creation or Evolution: do we have to choose?* Monarch Books, 2nd Edition, 2014, 285-286).

portrayals of God's purpose. What does this commonality tell us? Anticipating light thrown on reading Genesis 1 by John's prologue, a particular pattern which is emphasised in Genesis 1 is that of God speaking; "and God said" (Gen. 1:3,6,9,11,14,20,24,26) is a design that frames all that is created, and it is an expression that is presented as that which performs the creative work. As the psalmist said: "By the word of the LORD the heavens were made . . . He spoke, and it came to be" (Ps. 33:6,9). When Genesis moves on to narrative, God continues to speak through commandment, promise and dream to further his purpose of creating man in his image. Indeed, this is what God does throughout the rest of scripture, showing that the pattern in Genesis 1 is preparatory not just for the remainder of Genesis but for all of scripture and for God's entire purpose with man.

There is a corollary to this pattern. When God later spoke through prophets, it was no less God's word than when he spoke 'and it was so' for the creation recorded in Genesis 1. God's word through the prophets is no less majestic and powerful to accomplish that for which it is purposed (cf. Isa. 55:11) than the word he spoke, without any prophetic mediation, to create the heavens and the earth and all their host.

John's prologue introduces the means of God's *new* creation in just the same way but with a transformative element. Now God's word *is the man*, not only the means by which he comes into being. This man was so much in God's image, full of grace and truth, that he *was* God's word, so that it could be said, "the Word was God" (John 1:1). Once John's gospel transitions to narrative, we see Jesus *speaking* as God because such authority had been given to him (John 3:34; 1:18). So much was this so that Jesus could declare that the words he spoke "are spirit and life" (John 6:63). As with God's words to man in Genesis 2 onwards, so also with God's word in Christ:

> "Of his own will he brought us forth by the word of truth, that we should be a kind of firstfruits of his creatures" (Jas. 1:18)

Just as God's word was majestically powerful to accomplish all he created in Genesis 1, so his word of truth through all the prophets is able to bring forth his new creation in Christ.

In these examples we see scripture's *purpose* in opening with near-poetry before transitioning to narrative. This purposeful feature of the text is diametrically opposed to the evolutionary creationist claim that such stylistic changes are evidence of there being two (or more) stories:

- The near-poetic opening sets the scene for us to see God in the subsequent narrative (in John's gospel, in the person of Christ), working out the purpose he declares in his opening. The scene is of God working out his purpose through speaking to man. As the writer to the Hebrews summarised this: "Long ago, at many times and in many ways, God spoke to our fathers by the prophets, but in these last days He has spoken to us by His Son" (Heb. 1:1,2).

- The deliberate use of two styles reinforces the conclusion that Genesis 1 and 2 are one story presented harmoniously across two chapters. One story which concerns God *speaking to create* heavens and earth that will be filled with his glory; a filling which is accomplished through his word, fulfilled in Christ and creating anew a people for his name.

- Again, it needs to be noted that identifying scripture's purpose in these two styles *depends* on Genesis 1 and 2 being read harmoniously and sequentially.

Conclusion

In fact, we have now witnessed that the majesty of the new creation in Christ, as portrayed in John's gospel, actually rests on the historicity of the creation record in Genesis 1, and on its emphasis on God speaking through a variety of means in the narrative that follows. From our perspective, looking back at God's dealings with man and the way God speaks to fulfil his creative purpose, it could seem redundant to make this point, since the truth of it appears to be so axiomatic. Yet the literary styles we witness in Genesis 1 and John's prologue have this very purpose.

So much is this so that one must question how such a fundamental feature of the way God deals with man, communicated so purposely from the beginning, can be squared with an evolutionary creationist reading of Genesis 1 and 2. If God speaking in Genesis 1 is not a realistic and historical portrayal of creation then how realistic are subsequent and copious scriptural descriptions of God speaking to men and women? Indeed, the psalmist to whom we have already referred taught us that we can trust the uprightness of the Lord's word and the faithfulness of his work in righteousness, justice and steadfast love by declaring it was the same word by which the heavens were made:

> "For *the word of the Lord* is upright, and all his work is done in faithfulness. He loves righteousness and justice; the earth is full of the steadfast love of the Lord. By *the word of the Lord* the heavens were made, and by the breath of his mouth all their host" (Ps. 33:4-6).

Thus, the psalmist made clear that the basis of our trust in the uprightness of the Lord's word to create us in his image that we might be his new creation is that the same word made "the heavens and the earth . . . and all the host of them" (Gen. 1:1; 2:1). Not only this, the pattern we have observed in Genesis 1 and 2, and in John's gospel, assures us that God's word, through his prophets, is as powerful to accomplish his purpose in their revelation as was his word when he spoke, without the mediation of prophets, in the creation of Genesis 1. And so, the Lord's faithfulness, righteousness, justice and steadfast love will assuredly be accomplished by God's word to, in and through us.

Before concluding, we should note yet more prophetic testimony about things that God performed when he created in the beginning. While the psalmist employed language from Genesis 1 and 2 in declaring that the heavens and their host were made by the Lord's word and breath, it is also plain that the psalmist himself independently testified that these things occurred as recorded in Genesis. The prophet through whom

Psalm 33 was revealed testified, alongside the record of Genesis 1 and 2, how it was that the Lord made the heavens and the earth.[9]

Finally, the focus on God's word in John's and the psalmist's reflection back on Genesis 1 which we have witnessed in this chapter is yet another reference to a detailed and specific aspect of Genesis 1 – not some generalised reference to God's creative works.[10] It this specific detail which forms the basis for our confidence in God's faithfulness, justice and steadfast love. Declare this detailed portrayal of the way God created as not historical and where does that leave our trust in those things from God on which we so much depend for fulfilment of his purpose and our salvation?

---

[9] See Chapter 2, 'Historical references'.

[10] See Chapter 2, 'Historical references'.

7: Figurative Language and Historicity

We momentarily step aside from our analysis of the eight reasons commonly marshalled by evolutionary creationists for their reading of Genesis 1 and 2. We do this now because the topic of this chapter relates to the way literary styles – considered in the previous chapter – are sometimes assumed by evolutionary creationists to have a bearing on scripture's historicity. More particularly, this assumption, whether implicit or explicit, is that for something to be historical it must be literal or non-figurative. We examine and challenge such an assumption in this chapter which is a more general examination of this position than the specific matters addressed in Chapter 6.

Examples

A subtle and implicit example of this evolutionary creationist practice is found in our lead text, *Israel's Two Creation Stories*. Having stated that the discovery of ancient Near Eastern (ANE) creation stories offers 'clear evidence to support a *nonliteral* reading of the Genesis texts',[1] Peter Enns proceeds to develop this argument by:

- approvingly referring to Philo's comfort with understanding Genesis 1 and 2 to be contradictory and this signalling to Philo that 'the two stories *were not meant to be understood historically*'; and

---

[1] Peter Enns, *Israel's Two Creation Stories*, http://biologos.org/blog/series/israels-two-creation-stories [referenced October 25, 2016]; my emphasis; cf. Denis O Lamoureux, *Evolutionary Creation: A Christian Approach to Evolution*, https://biologos.org/uploads/projects/Lamoureux_Scholarly_Essay.pdf [referenced October 31, 2017].

- asserting himself that 'two different perspectives on creation in Genesis suggest (as it did to Philo) that "recording history" is not the point'.[2]

It is evident from this shift of language from the use of 'nonliteral' to claiming the records are not to be read as history that, at some level, this evolutionary creationist requires of scriptural history that it be literal. This is despite the same author, a little later in his blog, accepting that figurative scriptures such as Exodus 15 and Psalms 105 and 106 recount history.[3] Such handling of scripture is at least equivocal and illustrates an evolutionary creationist handling of scripture that sees nonliteral literary styles having some bearing on the lack of historicity in such texts.

A more egregious and explicit example can be seen from the pen of our more conservative evolutionary creationist.[4] Having claimed 'how we interpret Genesis 1 will clearly be highly influenced by the kind of literature that we think we're reading', this writer undertakes an extended discussion of the figurative language and structure of Genesis 1 and concludes about this record, given its figurative nature, 'it cannot be history in any normal use of that term'.[5] Genesis 1 to 3 is then extensively referred to as 'theological manifesto', 'creation manifesto',

---

[2] Peter Enns, *Israel's Two Creation Stories*; Peter Enns' emphasis. Writing at an earlier time Peter Enns equates literal and historical by writing of a 'strictly literal/historical reading of Genesis' (Peter Enns, *The Evolution of Adam: What the Bible Does and Doesn't Say About Human Origins*, Brazos Press, xv).

[3] It should be noted, however, that this reference to history is downgraded somewhat by Peter Enns referring to it as 'Israel's historical memory', as opposed to it being God's authoritative history by revelation through a prophet. Regarding this, see Chapter 9.

[4] Denis Alexander, *Creation or Evolution: do we have to choose?* Monarch Books, 2nd Edition, 2014, 180,189,196,197,230. While this writer acknowledges figurative language is used of real events (see, 284-285,301) he repeatedly employs an assumed tension between figurative scripture and historicity. Ironically, Denis Alexander dismisses the historicity of Genesis 1 on the basis it is figurative language despite himself using figurative language to describe cells – things that he would rightly insist are scientific fact – as 'like little history books' (see, 247).

[5] Denis Alexander, *Creation or Evolution*, 180-189; Denis Alexander describes his preferred model for reconciling scripture's creation account with evolution as 'proto-historical'

'theological account', 'theological declaration', 'theological text', 'manifesto literature', 'theological truths', and 'theological essay', persistently tying such descriptions with statements about the text conveying these things by 'figurative language'.[6] Such descriptions are innocent enough on their own but when they are deployed toward a claim that Genesis 1 is not normal history it becomes clear it is part of a programmatic attempt to reclassify scriptural significance and to exclude historicity as part of this meaning.

Case studies

Does the figurative language or literary style of Genesis 1 and 2, or of any other scripture, entail that they and the events portrayed within them ought not to be read as historical? Before considering this position from scripture's perspective more generally, we will examine three instances of clear figurative language[7] in Genesis 1 and 2 and assess their historicity.

The spirit of God

When Genesis 1:2 states, "the Spirit of God was <u>hovering</u> [*rhp*] over the face of the waters", it employs a Hebrew term used elsewhere of an eagle's fluttering over her young which, in its turn, is a metaphor for the Lord's redemption of Israel from Egypt and his care for them:

> "Like an eagle that stirs up its nest, that <u>flutters</u> [*rhp*] over its young, spreading out its wings, catching them, bearing them on its pinions, the Lord alone guided him [i.e. the Lord's people, Deut. 32:9]" (Deut. 32:11-12)

(see, 289-294) and asserts that the portrayal of Adam in Genesis 1 to 4 is clearly not as historical as the later record about Abraham (see, 293).

[6] Denis Alexander, *Creation or Evolution*, 224-226,290,295-296,300,320,326,358. Peter Enns employs 'theological history' about the entire Hebrew scriptures (Peter Enns, *The Evolution of Adam*, 30).

[7] These examples show that one does not need comparison of Genesis 1 and 2 with ANE creation stories to realise there are nonliteral, figurative aspects in these scriptures.

Figurative Language and Historicity

It is incontrovertibly true that scripture portrays as historical both the exodus[8] of the people of Israel from Egypt and God's care for them as they wandered in the wilderness. It is also clear that the exodus generally, particular events within it, the law that was revealed during this time and things that were made during this period are typologically prophetic (e.g. Mt. 2:15; John 3:14; 1 Cor. 10:1-6,11; Heb. 3-5; 8-9); this is a feature whose relevance we shall consider shortly.

The use of the same figurative language about God's activity in Genesis 1:2 *and* his work during the exodus demonstrates that the figurative language describing the spirit of God hovering over the face of the waters does not render this as not historical. On the contrary, the use of the language of Genesis 1:2 in Deuteronomy 32 has historical reference and purpose: just as God's spirit hovered as part of his creative work recorded in Genesis 1, so also in another creative work, the establishment of Israel as his portion and heritage, the Lord repeated this act of care as an assurance of his creative purpose with Israel.[9] It is also essential to emphasise two further aspects of this:

- The assurance of the Lord's creative care, as described in Deuteronomy 32, depends on the historical reality of Genesis 1:2, that it was an event that actually took place.

- This historical event is portrayed by employing figurative language.

---

[8] It should be noted that Peter Enns does not regard Exodus, Joshua and Judges as historical (Peter Enns, *The Evolution of Adam*, 62-65).

[9] For evidence that God's redemptive work with Israel being brought out of Egypt is portrayed as another creation see, for example: Deuteronomy 32:6: "Is not He your Father who has bought you? He has *made* you and established you"; and Isaiah 43:1,7,15: "But now thus says the LORD, he who *created* you, O Jacob, he who formed you, O Israel: 'Fear not, for I have redeemed you; I have called you by name, you are mine... everyone who is called by my name, whom I *created* for my glory, whom I *formed* and *made*... I am the LORD, your Holy One, the *Creator* of Israel, your King'".

Sun, moon and stars

In a second example, Genesis 1:16 speaks of the greater and lesser lights 'ruling [*mmšlh*]'; this is an expression used elsewhere of royal dominion (e.g. 1 Kings 9:19) and so its use about the role of these lights in Genesis 1 is a further instance of figurative language in this chapter. Does such figurative language render this part of Genesis 1 as not historical? Of interest here is how the language of Genesis 1:16 is taken up in one of the psalms:

> "Give thanks to the LORD ... to him who made the great lights, for his steadfast love endures forever; the sun to rule [*mmšlh*] over the day, for his steadfast love endures forever; the moon and stars to rule [*mmšlh*] over the night, for his steadfast love endures forever" (Ps. 136:1,7-9)

This psalm makes explicit reference to God's creative acts of Genesis 1:16. This includes the psalmist mentioning the making of "the great lights" and the "stars" and his interpretation of Genesis 1:16's 'greater and lesser lights' as functions of the 'sun' and 'moon'. In making this reference to Genesis 1, the psalmist also repeated the figurative language of these heavenly bodies 'ruling' – further evidencing the psalmist's unmistakable reflection back on the Genesis record. The psalm's repeated association of these creative acts of God with the Lord's 'enduring steadfast love' requires that the truth of the latter has its counterpart in the historical value of Genesis 1:16 – despite Genesis' use of figurative language. The endurance of the Lord's steadfast love is placed alongside God's creative works so that the latter become the basis for confidence in the former. Deny the historicity of Genesis 1:16, and the events it describes, and we destroy this psalmist's basis of confidence.

The true significance of such figurative language being employed about the function of the sun, moon and stars is found by tracing the use of the heavens and the heavenly hosts as figures for rulers of nations (e.g. Deut. 32:1; Isa. 1:2,10; 13:10; Mt. 24:29) and, more importantly for the redeemed, of the rule of the glorified saints. For example:

"those who are wise shall shine like the brightness of the sky above; and those who turn many to righteousness, like the stars forever and ever" (Dan. 12:3; see also 1 Cor. 15:40-41)

The Christian's hope of resurrection to glory and rulership with Christ is inchoately presented to us in Genesis 1:16 and rejection of its historicity based on its employment of figurative language would damage this early foundation – a basis for our confidence in the Lord's 'enduring steadfast love' that this promise will surely be fulfilled by him.

Reinforcing the historicity of Genesis 1:16's creative acts are two other aspects arising from the psalm and Genesis. First, it is noteworthy how Psalm 136 narrates a host of the Lord's acts, associating each with his enduring steadfast love. Before and after the description in Psalm 136:7-9, the Lord is the one also who made the heavens, who spread out the earth, who struck down the firstborn of Egypt and brought Israel out from among them (Ps. 136:5,6,10,11) and so on. Of particular note is the final work of the Lord deployed to substantiate his enduring steadfast love:

"he who gives food to all flesh, for his steadfast love endures for ever" (Ps. 136:25)

Does the Lord provide food for all flesh or not? If he does not, then we can equally dismiss the other acts of his that are narrated in this psalm. If he does – and which Christian would argue he does not? – how can we with integrity dismiss the factuality of all other works described by the psalmist? We cannot with honesty play fast and loose with these descriptions of the Lord's acts; if he redeemed Israel from Egypt, then he also performed the creative work described in Genesis 1 and referenced by this psalm; if he provides food to all flesh, then he also performed the work of creation described in this psalm.[10]

---

[10] Psalm 136 is one of several scriptures surveyed by Peter Enns as evidencing 'the intersection between primordial divine time and present earthly time in Israel's theology' (Peter Enns, *The Evolution of Adam*, 62-65); this thesis is employed to justify classification of Genesis 1 as ancient Near Eastern literature which, consequently, ought not to be taken as historical. While Peter Enns likewise dismisses the historicity of the exodus and the period of the Judges

A second aspect arises from Genesis 1's summary statement of what took place on the fourth day, and which encompasses God's creative acts of Genesis 1:16. This is found in Genesis 1:14:

> "And God said, 'Let there be lights in the expanse of the heavens to separate the day from the night. And let them be for signs and for *seasons*, and for days and years'"

The relevance of this to assessing the historicity of Genesis 1 comes from the apostle Paul's reference to a feature of God's creative purpose in these seasons – they are a witness to God's care:

> "Yet [the living God, who made the heaven and the earth and the sea, and all that in them is (Acts 14:15)] did not leave himself without witness, for he did good by giving you rains from heaven and fruitful *seasons*, satisfying your hearts with food and gladness" (Acts 14:17; cf. Ps. 104:19)

The 'seasons' of which Paul spoke had their origin in the Genesis record of God's appointment of the lights in the expanse of heavens "for signs and for *seasons*, and for days and years". In order that, inter alia, the seasons could function as a witness to the living God, they must have their origin with him, and it is in Genesis 1 where we find the record of God's origination of them. If we claim that Genesis 1, and this specific event, is not historical we render the apostle's assertion about the witness that God has left meaningless and vain.

These two additional aspects powerfully reinforce that Genesis 1 is historical, notwithstanding its use of figurative language.

Before moving on to consider our third case study, we should note yet again how later scriptural reference to the events of Genesis 1 do not just speak of God as creator in some generalised sense. Rather they refer to highly specific aspects of the creation record and handle these

---

within the same analysis, the employment of these acts of the Lord to substantiate his enduring steadfast love is something that argues in completely the opposite direction as shown in the foregoing argument.

particularities as historically true, that is that they were events that actually happened. Psalm 136 refers to the detail regarding sun, moon and
stars (as well as other items from Genesis 1 which have been mentioned
in passing). It is these specific details of the creation record that are
presented as the basis for confidence in the Lord's steadfast love, not
just some generalised reference to God as creator.[11]

As a final point, note how the apostle Paul bore witness to a facet of
God's active use of the sun, moon and stars for things we experience in
our lives even today: the seasons. Our own experience is to have this
specific thing which was appointed in Genesis 1 as a basis for confidence in God's goodness. Our personal experience of these things
evidences for us the historicity of the events described in Genesis 1:14-
16.

Historical events

Again, we have seen that prophets independently testified to the events
of Genesis 1 and 2 and not just to the text of these two chapters without
any regard for the historicity of the events described within them. Each
prophet asserted specific events described also in Genesis 1 and 2 to be
historical. It is the testimony of these prophets that the following things
happened at the time of the creation:[12]

- The psalmist asserted that the Lord made the heavens, the earth
  and the great lights (Ps. 136:5-7).

- The apostle Paul testified that God gave the seasons as a witness
  of his creative acts (Acts 14:17).

Eve

Our third instance of figurative language in Genesis 1 and 2 takes us to
the second chapter and Eve's creation. Anticipating the necessity for
the narrative regarding Eve's special creation in Genesis 2 to be non-

---

[11] See Chapter 2, 'Historical references'.

[12] See Chapter 2, 'Historical references'.

historical in order to accommodate models which account for Genesis 2 that are 'consistent with the current scientific account of evolution',[13] Denis Alexander handles Genesis 2:18-25 as an 'obviously figurative and literary passage' with 'vivid metaphorical language to express some profound theological truths'.[14] Thus, this writer dismisses historicity on the basis that this scripture comprises, at least in part, figurative language. Within such a handling, this evolutionary creationist clearly rejects the historicity of Eve's creation and treats it rather as a 'theological text' which is about the foundations of marriage but empty of any historical reality. Other than mentioning there are linguistic plays on words in this narrative (which is not disputed) and twice dismissively referring to the making of Eve from Adam's rib as not to be taken as some kind of surgical procedure, Denis Alexander does not offer any evidence for Genesis 2:18-24 being 'vivid metaphorical language'. Given the matter-of-fact way in which the whole episode of Eve's creation is narrated, rather more evidence is called for to substantiate its lack of historicity on the basis of it being an 'obviously figurative and literary passage'.

As it happens, there is some plainly figurative language used about Eve's creation:

> "the rib that the LORD God had taken from the man <u>he made</u> [*bnh*] into a woman and brought her to the man" (Gen. 2:22)

---

[13] Denis Alexander, *Creation or Evolution*, 288. This writer lays out five models that he believes Christians employ in understanding Genesis 1 and 2 in the context of evolutionary science: models A-E (287-294, 316-319, 355-365). Only models A-C are deemed consistent with evolutionary science and therefore regarded as acceptable while the author reveals a clear preference for model C. In models A-C, neither Adam nor Eve are special creations but the product of evolutionary processes, with man and woman obtaining 'the image of God' by a variety of hypotheses, according to the model in view. Such models necessarily preclude the historicity of Eve's special creation as recorded in Genesis 2. Peter Enns disputes models A-C on the basis these models 'rewrite [Genesis]' (Peter Enns, *The Evolution of Adam*, xiv-xv, xvii-xviii, 123).

[14] Denis Alexander, *Creation or Evolution*, 229-232.

The Hebrew word rendered 'he made' is the very common expression for 'to build', such as is employed, for example, in, "He shall build [*bnh*] a house for my name" (2 Sam. 7:13). Where the 'creation' of male and female in Genesis 1:27 is explained by Adam's 'formation' in Genesis 2:7,[15] Eve's creation is elucidated by her 'building' in Genesis 2:22. Why does scripture use the language of 'building' about Eve's creation?

The apostle Paul explained the purpose of this for us. Having introduced the topic of the new creation (Eph. 2:10,15), he reversed the metaphor we have in Genesis 2 of a person being built:

> "you are … members of the household of God, built on the foundation of the apostles and prophets, Christ Jesus himself being the cornerstone, in whom the whole structure, being joined together, *grows* into a holy temple in the Lord" (Eph. 2:19-21)

Rather than a person being *built* we are introduced to an edifice *growing*, something we would expect of a person. This is part of a rich set of themes the apostle wove together in this letter, and it sets the scene for a more explicit use of the metaphor laid out in Genesis 2. This the apostle Paul did in Ephesians 4. Writing of Christ's gift of the ministers in Ephesians 4:11, he said that these are given:

> "for *building up* the body of Christ" (Eph. 4:12)

We now are presented with an aspect to do with a person, a body, being *built* – the metaphor we have first portrayed for us in Genesis 2. These two ideas are then brought together for us as the apostle concluded:

> "from [Christ] the whole body, joined and held together by every joint with which it is equipped, when each part is working properly, makes the body *grow* so that it *builds* itself *up* in love" (Eph. 4:16)

---

[15] Explored in Chapter 10.

Here, the body *grows*, as we might expect, and *builds* itself, again employing the figurative language of Genesis 2:22.

In summary, the teaching that is being laid out here is that the manner of Eve's creation is not just a figure of the bride of Christ – a matter we will shortly consider – but that her being *built* establishes from the beginning that the woman also represents a dwelling place for God (Eph. 2:22, "a dwelling place for God") and for his son (Eph. 3:17, "Christ may dwell in your hearts").

As we have now seen on numerous occasions, a lovely picture of God's glorious purpose with and for man is set out through an enacted parable detailed in the Genesis 1 and 2 creation record. The figurative language employed in Genesis 2:22 is not evidence at all that the record is not historical. Rather, the veracity of God's promise of making his "dwelling place … with man" (Rev. 21:3)[16] is founded upon his creation of Eve in the manner described in Genesis 2. Rejection of the historicity of Genesis 2:18-24 serves only to destroy the promise's historical and figurative foundation.

Furthermore, we have already seen that Jesus' masterful reading of Genesis 1 and 2 unequivocally handles the record of Eve's creation as historical.[17] There we saw that Jesus' handling of Genesis 1 and 2 places it on par with the historicity of the giving of the law by Moses in Deuteronomy – indeed, the force of Jesus' argument depends on their historical and chronological relativity. We also saw that Jesus' theological conclusion about marriage depended on the fact God uttered the words recorded in Genesis 2 'from the beginning' – if the father in heaven did not thus speak, the Lord's conclusion is without foundation.

---

[16] Note the nearby association of the holy city, Jerusalem, being described as a bride (Rev. 21:2). This is completely consistent with the weaving of bridal and dwelling themes in Ephesians.

[17] See Chapter 2, 'Historical references'. Denis Alexander refers to the Lord's words in Matthew 19 as part of his thesis but overlooks these fundamental points (Denis Alexander, *Creation or Evolution*, 231).

There is another, extended theological conclusion reached in the apostolic writings derived from the record in Genesis 2:18-24. Having written extensively about the *growing* and *building* of the body, the latter employing the metaphor of Genesis 2:22, the apostle Paul returned to consideration of Genesis 2 later in his letter. Paul wrote about Christ's relationship to the ecclesia as her head, her saviour and her nurturer because the brothers and sisters are members of his body (Eph. 5:23-30), and then substantiated his exposition by referencing Genesis 2:24:

> "Therefore a man shall leave his father and mother and hold fast to his wife, and the two shall become one flesh" (Eph. 5:31)

There are multiple figurative layers in this passage and each figurative layer employs an historical event as representative of some other spiritual matter. First, Christ's salvation of the ecclesia is deployed as figurative of how men ought to be towards their wives, and it is clear the presence of this figure does not render what Christ did as vivid metaphor without historical value. More explicitly, Christ gave his life in his death on the cross for the ecclesia and this historical event is deployed as a figure of how men ought to behave towards their wives. A second layer is that the events surrounding the creation of Eve in Genesis 2 are figurative of what Christ would fulfil. The apostle made clear that these things and the figurative relationship between the Genesis 2 narrative and their fulfilment in Christ are a 'profound mystery' (Eph. 5:32) but, as with the first figurative layer, this does not render the record in Genesis 2 just a vivid metaphor without historical value. Rather, the parallel of these two layers and the incontrovertible historicity of what Christ did as a figure of how men ought to be with their wives argues completely in favour of the historicity of Genesis 2 and the events it describes. Indeed, it is the very presence of the figurative language in Genesis 2:18-24 which alerts us to its typological and prophetic significance. To read these literary aspects of Genesis 2 as evidence of its lack of historicity mishandles its significance and purpose.

As was noted in our consideration of Genesis 1:16 so too here, Genesis 2 is typologically prophetic and a clear picture is emerging that these figures, portrayed in a variety of literary ways, are historically real in order to function effectively as prophetic typology of future things. To borrow some words from Hebrews which speak of historical aspects of the law and the tabernacle as "a shadow of the good things to come" (Heb. 10:1), the ancient but historically real figures are "copies [*antitupa*, "antitypes"] of the true things" (Heb. 9:24).

Finally, just as Jesus did not just speak of God as creator of the heavens and the earth in some broad outline but spoke of detailed aspects of Eve's creation, so the apostle Paul referred to a highly specific aspect of her creation and established this as true.[18] And yet this particular record is one of three specific details in Genesis 1 and 2 which is dismissed by evolutionary creationists as having any historical value since, otherwise, there would be irreconcilable conflict with evolutionary science. Denis Alexander excludes its historicity by tendentiously suggesting the record is not about God performing surgery.[19] Peter Enns counts the record of Eve's creation as one of the detailed aspects of Genesis 1 and 2 that 'one can no longer accept, in any true sense of the word "historical"' if evolution is correct.[20] Thus, we see that evolutionary creationism directly conflicts with the testimony of both Jesus and the apostle Paul.

More evidence

When we reflect on the range of historical things described with figurative language in scripture, one wonders what basis evolutionary creationists have for handling Genesis 1 and 2 as non-historical because of the presence of such language.

Here are some examples, chosen specifically because it is extremely unlikely that evolutionary creationists would question the truth and reality of the history lying behind these figurative descriptions:

---

[18] See Chapter 2, 'Historical references'.

[19] Denis Alexander, *Creation or Evolution*, 229-232.

[20] Peter Enns, *The Evolution of Adam*, xiv.

- Jesus' death as a sacrifice is described figuratively as: "a propitiation [*ilastērios*, used elsewhere of "the mercy seat" (Heb. 9:5)]" (Rom. 3:25); "Passover" (1 Cor. 5:7); and "a lamb without blemish or spot" (1 Pet. 1:19; cf. John 1:29,36).

- Jesus' resurrection from the dead is described figuratively as "the firstfruits" (1 Cor. 15:20,23).

- John 1 is replete with figurative language, yet few evolutionary creationists would suggest, as for the previous two examples, it follows from the use of such language that John's first chapter does not speak of historical truth regarding Jesus' origins and God's purpose in him.

- As a more general illustration of this, and manifesting equivocal handling of scripture, one evolutionary creationist acknowledges that literary structures employed in the gospels do not render their material non-historical but rather he asserts the gospel writers were 'historical in their material'[21].

- Highly figurative language is commonly used to describe God's manifestation in the earth for the salvation of his people (e.g. Ps. 18:7-17) but which Christian would claim that God does not thus act?

Regarding the first two of the above examples, for the original figures to have significance they must have historical reality. As has already been observed, it is a feature of scripture's typology that the original figures such as the exodus generally, specific events within it, the law which was revealed at that time and things which were made during that period, the creation of Eve and figures of Christ's sacrificial death and resurrection are necessarily historically real in order to function effectively as prophetic typology of future things.

---

[21] Denis Alexander, *Creation or Evolution*, 188.

Genesis 1-2

It might be argued, in relation to the figurative language used of Christ's death as a sacrifice and of his resurrection that the historicity of these events is testified in other places by non-figurative language and that it is only because of this that we can be certain of their historical reality. While this overlooks the point that the examples listed demonstrate unequivocally that the presence of figurative language does not necessarily entail that the things spoken of are not historically real – and it is this evolutionary creationist argument that was set out to be disproven – it is also the case that the same can be said of the events of Genesis 1 and 2. We have already seen that scriptures other than Genesis 1 and 2 speak of, or establish theological conclusions upon, the events of these chapters being historically true. We have previously observed this in many ways as follows:

- Jesus's authoritative testimony in Matthew 19 and Mark 10.

- In the following Hebrew scriptures: Psalms 33; 104; 136 and 147.

- In the following apostolic writings: John 1; Acts 14; 1 Corinthians 11; Ephesians 5 and 1 Timothy 2.

As we progress yet more will be added:

- In the Hebrew scriptures: Genesis 14; Psalms 8; 95; 121; 124; 146 and Isaiah 45.

- In the apostolic writings: 1 Corinthians 15.

Thus, there is ample testimony to the historicity of Genesis 1 and 2 throughout the Hebrew scriptures and apostolic writings.

Figures in scripture

In passing, it should be observed that it is a feature of scripture's richly textured meaning that figures and figurative language operate in multiple ways.

Figurative language is employed to describe historical incidents, that is, events that really did happen. We have witnessed that this is a literary feature which requires interpretation to understand what actually was taking place in the historical event. And we have observed that the presence of figurative language is a feature which points to an enacted parable being employed regarding God's ongoing work with his creation and for his purpose. Historical events in scripture are deployed as enacted parables that are figures of true things in Christ and the new creation accomplished through him.

Conclusion

The evolutionary creationist argument that dismisses the historicity of Genesis 1 and 2 on the basis that these chapters are full of figurative and metaphorical language has been demonstrated to be without foundation. Furthermore, and to the contrary, the extensive evidence of scripture is that figurative language is commonly used of historically true and real events.

8: Different Views of God?

We now resume our consideration of arguments brought forward by evolutionary creationists for reading Genesis 1 and 2 as neither harmonised nor historical. A fifth reason offered is that Genesis 1 presents God as 'transcendent' while Genesis 2 portrays him as more 'down to earth', not 'aloof or distant'.[1] This is another feature deployed in source-critical analysis of Genesis 1 and 2.[2]

Evolutionary creationists acknowledge that anthropomorphism[3] occurs in the first two chapters of scripture, and that this does not allow the drawing of 'a thick line between Genesis 1 and 2'. Yet they portray this difference as more important than other differences previously addressed.[4] The way God is portrayed in Genesis 3 – holding conversations with Adam, Eve and the serpent, and the manner in which he interacts with them – is then presented as support for these distinctive portrayals of God: it is claimed that the alleged difference in presentation between the first two chapters 'is clearer if we read Genesis 2 with what follows'.[5]

Special pleading

Before we get into detailed analysis of the different portrayals of God in Genesis 1 and 2, we ought not overlook further evidence of special pleading for the evolutionary creationist cause. To employ the language

---

[1] Peter Enns, *Israel's Two Creation Stories*, http://biologos.org/blog/series/israels-two-creation-stories [referenced October 25, 2016]. See also Peter Enns, *The Evolution of Adam: What the Bible Does and Doesn't Say About Human Origins*, Brazos Press, 2012, 51.

[2] See Pauline A Viviano, 'Source Criticism' in Eds. Steven L McKenzie and Stephen R Haynes, *To Each Its Own Meaning: An Introduction to Biblical Criticisms and their Application*, Westerville John Knox Press, 1999, 45-46 (available on Google Books).

[3] In religion and mythology, anthropomorphism refers to the perception of a divine being or beings in human form, or the recognition of human qualities in these beings.

[4] Peter Enns, *Israel's Two Creation Stories*.

[5] Peter Enns, *Israel's Two Creation Stories*.

of the evolutionary creationism apologist, if we were to 'draw a thick line' anywhere in the early chapters of Genesis, it would be between chapters 2 and 3, given the latter chapter's description of the entrance of sin and death into man's personal experience, where previously these things were not. Claiming a dis-harmonised reading of Genesis 1 and 2 supported by noting similarities between chapters 2 and 3 blithely sets aside such a fundamental issue. The evolutionary creationist's 'thick line' is not between the first two chapters, it is between Genesis 2 and 3 notwithstanding that the evolutionary creationist sees great similarities shared by these two chapters. Quite apart from the fact that Genesis 3 describes the entrance of sin and death into man's personal experience, the reality of the 'thick line' existing between Genesis 2 and 3 is seen clearly just by reading through these chapters and noting the massive changes that are thrust into man's life, even without apostolic commentary on this as seen in Romans 5 and 1 Corinthians 15. Adam and Eve discover nakedness; they become fearful of God's voice in the garden; they each receive words of rebuke from the Lord God, including that they will die as he had warned in Genesis 2; and they are dispatched from the garden, severing them from God's presence. This point ought to be sufficient of itself to cause more careful handling of Genesis 1 and 2, with a preparedness to place weight on the harmonising similarities between these two chapters, some of which have already been observed and with more to come.

Differences of presentation

Nevertheless, it is the case that God is presented as more transcendent in Genesis 1, while he participates more tangibly in the created world in Genesis 2. Indeed, we have noted this difference when we considered evolutionary creationist claims about different durations of creation recorded in Genesis 1 and 2.[6] In that chapter we considered the reason God is portrayed in these different ways: in Genesis 2 the Lord God is portrayed with more intimate, tactile involvement, as a father with his child. Yet again, it should be noted that we have also seen the Lord Jesus Christ's reading of Genesis 1 and 2 in relation to Adam and Eve's

---

[6] See Chapter 3.

creation and his handling of them in a fully harmonised manner. It is the same God who made male and female in the beginning as the one who, at that time, pronounced his teaching about marriage.[7] However, in this chapter we will consider whether this difference of presentation necessarily means that we are dealing with dis-harmonised records. We will do so by considering how the differences between Genesis 1 and 2 are taken up elsewhere in scripture.

Psalm 8

Both the transcendence of God and his intimate involvement with man are, together, arguably the principal theme of David's Psalm 8.[8] Indeed, the literary power of this psalm depends on these diverse aspects of the Lord featuring and working together. Without a recognition and acknowledgement of these different characteristics, the expression of wonder and amazement that begins and ends this psalm would have little meaning, and certainly less power. The integration of these distinctive aspects of the Lord God's creative works, within a single psalm, authoritatively illustrates that the presence of differing characteristics of God ought not to be interpreted as dis-harmony in the record.

In fact, the thematic support of Psalm 8 for a harmonised reading of Genesis 1 and 2 also works at a detailed level. The two aspects are interleaved in this psalm in such a way that source criticism would face a near-insurmountable task to argue that Psalm 8 reflects two different sources, as is claimed for Genesis 1 and 2.[9] This is illustrated in the following tabulation of Psalm 8:

---

[7] See Chapter 2, 'Associating Genesis 1 and 2'.

[8] Other psalms present the two aspects we are considering with a variety of literary purposes. See, for example, Psalms 121; 124; 146, in all of which it is the transcendent maker of heaven and earth who condescends to help his people.

[9] For an illustration of how source criticism attempts to isolate independent sources within a tightly formed narrative, see Pauline A Viviano, 'Source Criticism', 44-45, 47.

Psalm 8	God's portrayal
"O LORD, our Lord, how majestic is Your name in all the earth! You have set Your glory above the heavens!"	v. 1: as with the order of presentation in Genesis 1 and 2, the psalm begins with the Lord's transcendence.
"Out of the mouth of babes and infants, You have established strength because of Your foes, to still the enemy and the avenger."	v. 2: immediately, the psalm turns to God's involvement with man as with young children, corresponding to God's activities in Genesis 2.
"When I look at Your heavens, the work of Your fingers, the moon and the stars, which you have set in place . . ."	v. 3: setting the scene for another juxtaposition of the two aspects of God we are considering, the psalmist marvels at the creative work of God by clear reference to Genesis 1.
". . . what is man that You are mindful of him, and the son of man that You care for him? Yet You have made him a little lower than the heavenly beings and crowned him with glory and honour. You have given him dominion over the works of Your hands; You have put all things under his feet, all sheep and oxen, and also the beasts of the field, the birds of the heavens, and the fish of the sea, whatever passes along the paths of the seas."	v. 4-8: David gave voice to the wonder that the transcendent creator God cares for man, corresponding to God's involvement with man in Genesis 2, and spoke of the man being exalted through plain reference again to Genesis 1, where God appoints the man he has created to dominion.

Psalm 8	God's portrayal
"O LORD, our Lord, how majestic is Your name in all the earth!"	v. 9: with a refrain that clearly marks out the psalm's chiastic structure, the prophet concluded by reflecting again on the Lord's transcendence.

Thus, this short psalm is densely packed with an interleaving of both God's transcendence and his far-from-aloof involvement with and care for man. This demonstrates that the specific evolutionary creationist reading of Genesis 1 and 2 we are considering in this chapter has no scriptural support for the argument that distinct portrayals of God necessarily mean the record is dis-harmonised. More than this, Psalm 8 presents a substantive explanation for one reason Genesis 1 and 2 are structured the way they are – to evoke the same sense of wonder as that to which the psalmist gave voice. In Psalm 8 and in Genesis 1 and 2, the one who has spoken majestically in creating the heavens and the earth and all that is in them is also the one who is intimately involved with man.

The chiastic structure of the psalm strengthens the case against any suggestion that the two distinct aspects reflect two different sources *and* reinforces the harmonisation of the two dissimilar presentations of the way God is. The psalm's chiastic structure is as follows:

A   "O LORD, our Lord, how majestic is your name in all the earth!" (Ps 8:1a)

B   "You have set your glory above the heavens. Out of the mouth of babies and infants, you have established strength because of your foes, to still the enemy and the avenger" (Ps 8:1b-2)

C   "When I look at your heavens, the work of your fingers, the moon and the stars, which you have set in place, what is man that you are mindful of him, and the son of man that you care for him?" (Ps 8:3-4)

b   "Yet you have made him a little lower than the heavenly beings and crowned him with glory and honour. You have given him dominion over the works of your hands; you have put all things under his feet, all sheep and oxen, and also the beasts of the field, the birds of the heavens, and the fish of the sea, whatever passes along the paths of the seas" (Ps 8:5-8)

a   "O LORD, our Lord, how majestic is your name in all the earth!" (Ps 8:9)

The A-a pair is obvious and clearly signals the chiasm. In B-b, the psalmist spoke of what the Lord has done and included points of contrast and correlation: the Lord's glory above the heavens contrasts with man being made a little lower than "the heavenly beings (*'lhym*)" while the strength established in babies and infants corresponds to the dominion given to man; furthermore, the B-b pair clearly coheres the transcendence of God, whose glory is above the heavens, with his work towards man's glory and honour.

The centre of the chiasm is the heart of the psalm and voices the amazement and wonder of the psalmist that the creator of the heavens and earth condescends in being mindful of man. As has already been noted, this contrast is one of the principal themes of this psalm without which the opening and closing expressions of wonder at the Lord's majesty would have considerably weakened meaning and power. It is no surprise therefore that the chiasm places these two aspects together at its centre with the significance of the second part displaying a dependence on the first part. The central piece of the chiasm does this by including a specific reference to God's creative acts in Genesis 1 and by reinforcing this chapter's thematic harmonisation with Genesis 2, where the Lord God is seen portrayed forming man in tactile fashion.

Given this chiastic structure for the psalm and especially the coherence of God's transcendence with his condescension towards man at its centre – the principal focus of the psalm's meaning – how would it make any sense that the two distinct portrayals of God evidence a history of two different sources? And how is it reasonable that these distinct depictions of God are taken as evidence for dis-harmony? The chiastic centre of this psalm, with its integration of Genesis 1 and 2's distinct portrayals of God, *is* its purpose. A source-critical approach that disintegrates the psalm into two or more distinct sources destroys its meaning and purpose and renders it function-less. Likewise, reading the psalm as dis-harmonious across these two aspects renders the psalm's principal function as meaningless. These same things are plainly also true of Genesis 1 and 2.

Harmonious historicity

On the other hand, Psalm 8 provides substantive evidence that the creative acts of God in Genesis 1 and 2 have historical status in the eyes of later prophets of God. This is seen most obviously in the use of ideas which have a close counterpart in Genesis 1. This is easily illustrated in the following tabulation:

Genesis 1	Psalm 8
"God made the two great lights – the greater light to rule the day and the lesser light to rule the night – and the stars. And God set them in the expanse of the heavens" (Gen. 1:16-17)	"your heavens, the work of your fingers, the moon and the stars, which you have set in place" (Ps. 8:3)
"let them have dominion over the fish of the sea and over the birds of the heavens and over the livestock and over all the earth and over every creeping thing that creeps on the earth... have dominion over the fish of the sea and over the birds of the heavens and over every living thing that moves on the earth" (Gen. 1:26,28)	"You have given him dominion over the works of your hands; you have put all things under his feet, all sheep and oxen, and also the beasts of the field, the birds of the heavens, and the fish of the sea, whatever passes along the paths of the seas" (Ps. 8:6-7)

The correspondence between these two scriptures is not superficial, there is clearly a strong conceptual correlation which is reinforced by some shared use of the same underlying Hebrew terms. The first thing to note about this correlation, as has been noted about other prophetic references to Genesis 1 and 2, is that Psalm 8 does not make some vague and generalised recollection that God created. Rather it refers to God's acts at a detailed and particular level, detail which resonates conceptually between the psalm and Genesis 1.[10] The second matter of note is how the historical reference is fundamental for both aspects of the contrasting elements of the psalm's meaning: the first correspondence deals with God's transcendent creative acts while the second deals with his far-from-aloof condescension towards man. Without the historicity

---

[10] See Chapter 2, 'Historical references'.

of both these aspects of God's portrayal, what worth does David's song of praise carry?

It also plain that these two detailed aspects of God's creative works – the making of the greater and lesser lights and the appointment of man to dominion – form the integrated basis for the twice repeated lauding of God's name: "O LORD, our Lord, how majestic is your name in all the earth!" (Ps 8:1a,9). If God did not perform these detailed and specific works of creation, is it defensibly true that the Lord's name should be lauded as majestic in all the earth?

Once more, we witness the psalmist independently describing events that are also recorded in Genesis 1 and 2 and not just referring to the text of these two chapters without any regard for the historicity of the events within them. Alongside the testimony of Genesis 1 and 2, the prophet David asserted that the making of the greater and lesser lights and the appointment of man to dominion actually happened, and he did so without direct use of the language of the Genesis texts.[11]

We ought also to note how the substantiation of the historicity of Genesis 1:26,28 by the detailed and specific correlation with Psalm 8:6-7 sets evolutionary creationism directly and explicitly in conflict with God's prophets. This is because the record of man's creation in Genesis 1:26-31 is one of three detailed aspects of Genesis 1 and 2 that is dismissed by evolutionary creationists as being historical if evolution is correct.[12] Of course, the prophet David's substantiation of the historicity of Genesis 1:26,28 harmonises with Jesus' reading of these verses.[13] Furthermore, as is addressed in the next section, the fact that these very words of Psalm 8 comprise part of a prophecy about Christ serves to highlight even more the extent of the conflict between evolutionary creationism versus Jesus and the prophet David.

---

[11] See Chapter 2, 'Historical references'.

[12] Denis Alexander, *Creation or Evolution: do we have to choose?* Monarch Books, 2nd Edition, 2014, 295-297; Peter Enns, *The Evolution of Adam*, xiv.

[13] See Chapter 2, 'Historical references'.

Moreover, and anticipating a feature of Genesis 1 and 2, which is more extensively dealt with later,[14] there is a detail in this psalm that illustrates God's tactile creative acts of Genesis 2 are, in relevant contexts, appropriate to and harmonious with descriptions of his majestic and transcendent works in Genesis 1. When the psalmist wrote of the "heavens... the moon and the stars", aspects of God's creative works in Genesis 1, he declared that the heavens were the work of the Lord's "fingers" (Ps. 8:3). This is tactile and far-from-aloof language and yet it is used about God's works in Genesis 1. In this way, Psalm 8 further illustrates the harmony and integrity of Genesis 1 and 2.

A prophecy of Christ

We cannot conclude this chapter without reflecting on Psalm 8's prophetic purpose. The words of Psalm 8:4-6 are cited in Hebrews 2:6-8, and expounded in the following verses of Hebrews, to demonstrate Jesus' superiority over the angels. This superiority necessitated his momentary lowliness compared to the angels "because of the suffering of death, so that by the grace of God he might taste death for everyone" (Heb. 2:9). We see from this that Jesus' sacrifice for sin and his glorification because of his perfection "through suffering" (Heb. 2:10) is the true and full meaning of Psalm 8. Take away the historicity of God's creative acts, including at the detailed and specific level, which form the bedrock of this psalm's prophecy about God's son and where does that leave the truth of Christ's tasting of death for every man?

The correlation we have noticed between Psalm 8 and Genesis 1 adds another point in this context, one that the apostle Paul's expositions of Adam in Romans 5 and 1 Corinthians 15 takes up. The things that God accomplished in Christ were and are a perfection of his purpose in the original creation of Adam – the replication of God's image and likeness in man – a purpose which was marred by the entrance of sin and death into the world. In this we see that God's purpose in Christ is bound up with an understanding of God's original creative purpose and which is described in Genesis 1 and 2. Again, dismiss the historicity of Genesis

---

[14] See Chapter 10, where this aspect of the harmony of Genesis 1 and 2 is dealt with.

Genesis 1-2

1 and 2 and the events they describe, including the particular and specific events of these chapters, and where does that leave this aspect of God's purpose in Christ?

Conclusion

Psalm 8 shows that Genesis 1 and 2 are purposefully structured to evoke awe and wonder that the maker of heaven and earth is mindful of man. The distinctive portrayals of God in Genesis 1 and 2 do not communicate disparate stories. For, while an evolutionary creationist might read dis-harmony into these chapters, the prophet David did not. Psalm 8 shows that the distinct portrayals of God in Genesis 1 and 2 are actually a functional and purposeful harmonising feature.

Psalm 8 also wonderfully illustrates the historicity of Genesis 1 and 2. and the creative acts described in these chapters, and this forms the basis both for the meaning and purpose of the psalm. Additionally, the psalm employs a historic foundation as a prophecy which informs us that Christ will perfect God's original creative purpose with man in replicating his image and likeness.

These things demonstrate once more that evolutionary creationist readings of Genesis 1 and 2 are like a cancer at the heart of verbal inspiration of scripture.

9: 'God's Names'

Evidently relying on source criticism again, especially since different referents for God lie deep in the history of this methodology,[1] a sixth reason brought forward in support of an evolutionary creationist reading of Genesis 1 and 2 is that chapter 1 employs Elohim while chapter 2 uses Yahweh Elohim to refer to the creator.[2]

It is said that Elohim is 'a generic and universal word for the divine' whereas Yahweh 'is the personal name of Israel's God, like other nations have their personal gods'. The same writer also says that this name is 'the four letter name of the *Hebrew* God YHWH'.[3] This argument is explicitly connected with a proposition we have previously examined[4] – that the different views of God presented in Genesis 1 and 2 show that 'Genesis 1 is more universal in its scope and appeal, whereas Genesis 2 is more earthy'. The conclusion drawn from this observation is that 'the names of God used in these chapters further supports this distinction'.[5]

In this chapter we will follow three lines of investigation of this evolutionary creationist claim:

- first, we will evaluate the integrity of the evolutionary creationist argument;

---

[1] See Pauline A Viviano, 'Source Criticism' in Eds. Steven L McKenzie and Stephen R Haynes, *To Each Its Own Meaning: An Introduction to Biblical Criticisms and their Application*, Westerville John Knox Press, 1999, 35-57 (available on Google Books).

[2] The error of treating Elohim as a name is set aside.

[3] Peter Enns, *Israel's Two Creation Stories*, http://biologos.org/blog/series/israels-two-creation-stories [referenced October 25, 2016]; my emphasis. See also Peter Enns, *The Evolution of Adam: What the Bible Does and Doesn't Say About Human Origins*, Brazos Press, 2012, 18-19, 51.

[4] See Chapter 8.

[5] Peter Enns, *Israel's Two Creation Stories*.

- we will then consider the scriptural testimony for whether Elohim and Yahweh are source-critical evidence of different and potentially dis-harmonious records; and

- finally, we will explore the passing hint in this evolutionary creationist argument that Yahweh is to be regarded as a parochial, tribal name, in some way equivalent to other nations having their own personal gods.

Examining the argument

The way this argument is put together is prejudicially selective. First, in singling out the use of God's name in Genesis 2, it overlooks the fact that Elohim is carried over from Genesis 1 in the ubiquitous and repeated expression 'Yahweh Elohim' found in Genesis 2.[6] This carry-over is a harmonising component for Genesis 1 and 2, and to neglect its presence has no justification while tendentiously obscuring an aspect which argues in the opposite direction.

Second, another part of the argument claims that, 'in the second creation story, Eve and the serpent (Genesis 3:1-5) refer to God as Elohim only, not Yahweh Elohim,' opining that this suggests their 'disconnection from Yahweh'.[7] This claim:

- highlights the evolutionary creationist neglect of the presence of Elohim in Yahweh Elohim and which is addressed in the first comment above about the argument being prejudicially selective;

- cuts both ways since if, according to the argument, Elohim can be used in Genesis 3 as part of 'the second creation story' consistently with the use of Yahweh Elohim in the previous chapter of 'the same story', then this fundamentally undermines the claim that these expressions – the use of Elohim in Genesis 1

---

[6] More accurately, "Elohim" continues to be used alone in Genesis 2:1-3 while "Yahweh Elohim" is used solely throughout Genesis 2:4-25.

[7] Peter Enns, *Israel's Two Creation Stories.*

and of Yahweh Elohim in Genesis 2 – demonstrate that Genesis 1 and 2 are disparate stories, not in harmony and should not be regarded as historical records; and

- lastly, we should not overlook that this argument repeats the special pleading we identified in the previous chapter; there we noted that there is a more obvious harmony between Genesis 1 and 2 than between Genesis 2 and 3 since there is an absence of sin and its consequential entrance of death into the world in both the opening chapters; Genesis 3 sees the entrance of both; for the evolutionary creationist to lump Genesis 2 and 3 together as 'the second creation story'[8] overlooks this fact.

Scripture's testimony

Are the uses of Elohim in Genesis 1 and of Yahweh Elohim in Genesis 2 source-critical evidence for different and potentially dis-harmonious records?[9] To assess this, we will analyse seven psalms for which we have apostolic authority – including testimony at the mouth of "the apostle and high priest of our confession" (Heb. 3:1) – that they were written by a single writer, the psalmist and prophet David. We will note

---

[8] Peter Enns, *Israel's Two Creation Stories*.

[9] While this chapter does not attempt a comprehensive analysis of the Newer Documentary Hypothesis, nevertheless it should be noted that the Hypothesis commonly places the 'Yahwist' source c. 950 BC in the southern kingdom, the 'Elohist' source c. 850 BC in the northern kingdom, the 'Deuteronomist' source c. 700-600 BC in Jerusalem, and the 'Priestly' source c. 550 BC in Babylonian exile. But according to scriptural chronology, supported by some archaeological finds (https://en.wikipedia.org/wiki/David#Archaeology [referenced March 25, 2016]), David's psalms pre-date these sources. The manner in which David's psalms consistently and coherently employ Yahweh and Elohim, including especially within the same psalm, considerably undermines from a scriptural perspective the Newer Documentary Hypothesis. This is so because Elohim and Yahweh, as referents for God, lie deeply and fundamentally in the history of the formulation of this Hypothesis. See Joshua Wroten, *Are There Two Different, Contradicting Creation Narratives in Genesis One and Two?* September 2016, 11 n13. He refers to Gordon Wenham, 'Genesis 1-15', *Word Biblical Commentary*, Edited by David A Hubbard and Glenn W Barker, Waco: Word Books, 1987, Introduction, xxxv and to his summary that Wellhausen's reliance on distinctive expressions for God has garnered less and less support through the years because of similar usage elsewhere in the book of Genesis.

the range of different expressions employed in each psalm to refer to God. This evidence is set out in the following table:

Psalm	Apostolic authority	Expressions in the psalm referring to God
2	Acts 4:25,26 citing Psalm 2:1-2	Yahweh (vv. 2,7,11); Adonai (v. 4)
16	Acts 2:25-28 citing Psalm 16:8-11	El (v. 1); Yahweh (vv. 2,5,7,8); Adonai (v. 2)
32	Romans 4:6-8 citing Psalm 32:1,2	Yahweh (vv. 2,5,10,11)
69	Acts 1:16,20 citing Psalm 69:25 Romans 11:9,10 citing Psalm 69:22-23	Elohim (vv. 1,3,5,6,13,29,30,32,35); Adonai (v. 6); Yahweh (vv. 6,13,16,31,33)
95	Hebrews 3:7-11; 4:7 citing Psalm 95:7-11	Yahweh (vv. 1,3,6); El (v. 3); Elohim (v. 7)
109	Acts 1:16,20 citing Psalm 109:8	Elohim (vv. 1,26); Yahweh (vv. 14,15,20,21,26,27,30); Adonai (v. 21)
110	Matthew 22:43-45; Mark 12:36-37; Luke 20:42-44; Acts 2:34-35 citing Psalm 110:1	Yahweh (v, 1,2,4)

The range of expressions used to refer to God across these psalms, including both Elohim and Yahweh and all by *a single writer*, is quite contrary to any claim that these terms are evidence for dis-harmonious scriptures arising from a hypothesis that the terms for God represent disparate sources separated either in time or geography. The same prophetic writer employed both God's name, Yahweh, and titles such as Adonai, El and Elohim, harmoniously and pertinently to the theme and purpose of each psalm. Moreover, selections of each of God's name and his titles are found within some of the individual psalms. Clearly, and especially, the presence of these varied terms within a single psalm is not evidence of dis-harmony – unless we wish to charge the Lord Jesus and his apostles with error in identifying David as the psalmist in each case. Likewise, the uses of Elohim in Genesis 1 and of Yahweh Elohim in Genesis 2 are not evidence for dis-harmony between these chapters. Rather, as seen in the foregoing psalms, scripture uses various referential terms for God in order to carry differing meanings and purposes pertinent to the particular psalm's theme(s). Likewise, we have already had cause to reflect on reasons why Genesis 2 introduces God's name, Yahweh, having used Elohim throughout Genesis 1 and we will reflect further on this before closing this chapter.[10]

Finally, we ought to consider again scripture's testimony about Jesus' authoritative reading of Elohim and Yahweh Elohim in Genesis 1 and 2. It is clear from our earlier analysis that Jesus' reading is that Elohim who created "male and female" (Gen. 1:27) is the same God as Yahweh Elohim who, acting harmoniously with the description of man's creation in Genesis 1, pronounced "a man shall leave his father and his mother and hold fast to his wife, and they shall become one flesh" (Gen. 2:24).[11] Thus it is plain that Jesus saw no dis-harmony evidenced by the use of differing expressions to refer to his father in Genesis 1 and 2.

---

[10] See Chapter 3.

[11] See Chapter 2, 'Associating Genesis 1 and 2'.

Genesis 1-2

Historicity

Before moving on to consider the evolutionary creationist hint that Yahweh is to be handled as a parochial, tribal name, we ought not overlook the testimony in one of these psalms, sealed with apostolic authority, for the historicity of the creation record in Genesis 1. Psalm 95 offers evidence for its claim that "the LORD is a great God, and a great King above all gods" (Ps. 95:3) by continuing:

> "In his hand are the depths of the earth; the heights of the mountains are his also. The sea is his, for he *made* it, and his hands *formed* the dry land" (Ps. 95:4-5)

The description found in verse 4 is reminiscent of other descriptions of God's creative acts (e.g. Ps. 90:2) while that given in verse 5 clearly rests on the creative work described in Genesis 1:9-10.[12] It is plain from this that the evidence offered in the psalm that the Lord is a great God and king rests on the historicity of Genesis 1 and of other descriptions of God's creative acts. Without the historicity of these descriptions of God's work, the substantiation of his greatness and regality is baseless. Furthermore, yet again we have reference by the psalmist David to specific and detailed aspects of God's creative works described in Genesis 1, not some generalised statement that God created. This is a detailed and specific reference to Genesis 1 that is employed to build confidence in the Lord's greatness and regality; classify Genesis 1:9-10 as lacking historicity and what does that leave of the evidence for the Lord's greatness? And again, we witness the psalmist providing independent testimony that God performed specific creative works which are also recorded in Genesis 1; the psalmist did so without specifically referencing the text of Genesis 1. The prophet David asserted and testified that God made the seas and formed the dry land in harmony with the record found in Genesis 1.[13]

---

[12] "And God said, 'Let the waters under the heavens be gathered together into one place, and let the dry land appear.' And it was so. God called the dry land Earth, and the waters that were gathered together he called Seas. And God saw that it was good" (Gen. 1:9-10).

[13] See Chapter 2, 'Historical references'.

Note also that the detailed and specific historical references to creation sit alongside a reference to historical aspects of Israel's wilderness journey – the rebellion of the people so that they would not enter into the Lord's rest (Ps. 95:8-11) – further aspects that have apostolic seal of historicity (Heb. 3-4).[14] On what grounds would it be reasonable to dismiss Psalm 95:4-5 as lacking historicity while accepting the second half of the Psalm (95:8-11) as being historical?

Yahweh and the Hebrew scriptures

Is Yahweh a tribal name of Israel's God, in some way equivalent to other nations having their own personal gods? Before addressing this question, it should be noted that this evolutionary creationist handling of God's name is part of a systematic treatment of the entire Hebrew scriptures, at least by some evolutionary creationists. This is signalled by a couple of features of the *BioLogos* blog[15] taken as a foil in examining the harmony and history of Genesis 1 and 2. First, even the title of this blog, *Israel's Two Creation Stories*, positions Genesis 1 and 2 as principally belonging to Israel, just as other ANE creation stories belong to other nations. It is positioned principally in this way rather than, as it ought, Genesis 1 and 2 being revelation from God with an authority that supersedes the cultural and national interests of Israel. Second, when caveating his argument that different literary styles in Genesis 1 and 2 evidence dis-harmony by acknowledging that historical events are routinely recounted through poetry, Peter Enns writes, 'Here one need only think of various so-called "historical psalms" that recount *Israel's historical memory* (e.g., Psalms 105 and 106)'.[16] To refer to these psalms as 'Israel's historical memory' points to a downgrading of the historical truth of these scriptures – for Peter Enns, they are a nation's historical memory rather than God's account of that history.

---

[14] Note again that Peter Enns does not regard the scriptural record of this period of Israel's history as historical (Peter Enns, *The Evolution of Adam*, 62-65).

[15] Peter Enns, *Israel's Two Creation Stories*.

[16] Peter Enns, *Israel's Two Creation Stories*, my emphasis.

Substantiating this reading of the *BioLogos* blog is the fact that else-where and earlier, this evolutionary creationist more systematically lays out such a handling of scripture when he argues at length that Genesis is 'an Israelite product' and a 'self-defining document' of Israel. Indeed, he claims this is an accurate description of the entire Hebrew scriptures.[17] Thus, when we are examining whether Yahweh is a tribal name of Israel's God, in some way equivalent to other nations having their own personal gods, we are engaging one aspect of a wholesale mis-handling of scripture.

Yahweh

We have already had cause to reflect on scripture's purpose in intro-ducing Yahweh in Genesis 2. This chapter's teaching that God has a generational relationship to man clearly pertains to this first historical use of God's name, and to the fact that man is the centrepiece of God's purpose.[18] It is by reflecting on this purpose that any hint of Yahweh being a tribal name is ultimately destroyed.[19]

But first, among many instances of Yahweh being employed by God concerning himself, its use in Isaiah 66:1 exemplifies a common theme associated with his self-reference:

> "Thus says the LORD [Yahweh]: 'Heaven is My throne, and the earth is My footstool . . .'"

Here, God speaks of himself in cosmological and universal terms and yet refers to himself by his name Yahweh and not, as would be con-sistent with the evolutionary creationist handling of Genesis 1 and 2, Elohim. Furthermore, it is clear from this use of Yahweh that it is not

---

[17] Peter Enns, *The Evolution of Adam*, Part One. In similar fashion our more conservative evolutionary creationist suggests the Adam and Eve account is about 'the proto-historical roots of the monotheistic faith of the people of Israel' (Denis Alexander, *Creation or Evolution: do we have to choose?* Monarch Books, 2nd Edition, 2014, 358).

[18] See Chapter 3.

[19] This line of argument does not address another fundamental error in such reasoning: a misunderstanding of the fulfilment of God's promises through Israel such that all those in Christ, both Jew and Gentile, are "the Israel of God" (Rom. 9:6-8; Gal 6:16; Eph. 2:13,19).

merely a name for Israel's God in the way that other nations had personal names for their gods; it is the name God employs about himself when speaking of himself, even with regard to his cosmological and universal role.

This points to an aspect of God's own exposition of his name in Exodus 3 that it is easy to overlook, what we might term 'directionality'. For Exodus 3 is not an instance of Israel naming their God, as would certainly be true of other nations and their gods. Rather, this chapter shows us God calling himself Yahweh and emphatically revealing this name through Moses to his people:

> "Say this to the people of Israel ... Say this to the people of Israel ... This is my name for ever, and thus I am to be remembered throughout all generations. Go and gather the elders of Israel together and say to them ..." (Ex. 3:14-16)

Furthermore, in naming himself this way in Exodus 3, the Lord also expounds the significance of his generational relationship with man in Genesis 2. Briefly, the Lord's explanation of his name by, "I will be who I will be" (Ex. 3:14, AT)[20], shows that his name is prophetic, having promise of his work with and for those whom he chooses. Yahweh will be with man, and he will be seen in his redemptive work through man.

Fast-forward to the fulfilment of this promise in Christ and the work of his apostles, and we find James's insistence on Gentile circumcision (see Acts 15:1; Gal. 2:12) overturned by the testimony of Peter, Paul and Barnabas, and by James's own turn-around acknowledgement that their testimony agreed with "the words of the prophets" (Acts 15:15). Of particular note in this context is the way James described God's purpose in "[visiting] the Gentiles, to take from them a people for *his name*" (Acts 15:14). As God himself says of 'Yahweh' in various ways and on many occasions, "This is My name forever, and thus I am to be

---

[20] For a substantive argument for this rendering, see: Andrew Perry, 'The Translation of Exodus 3:14a', *Christadelphian eJournal of Biblical Interpretation*, vol. 3, no. 4, Q4 2009, 39 (http://www.christadelphian-ejbi.org/).

remembered throughout all generations" (Ex. 3:15). Thus 'Yahweh' is not merely the personal name of the Hebrew God, but the name by which he fulfils his redemptive purpose for peoples of all nations, not just the descendants of Abraham, Isaac and Jacob through the flesh.

Yahweh Elohim

The sixth argument of evolutionary creationists can therefore be seen to contain no scriptural substance at all. It is as empty as the vanities worshipped by the pagan nations surrounding Israel in David's day. The uses of Elohim in Genesis 1 and of Yahweh Elohim in Genesis 2 do not evidence that these chapters are dis-harmonised and neither do they provide any basis for a hypothesis about disparate sources. Consequently, the claim that this dis-harmony evidences the lack of historicity of Genesis 1 and 2 is shown to have no basis.

The function of Genesis 2's introduction of Yahweh Elohim is to portray the transcendent creator of Genesis 1 as one who bears a name *which he gives to himself.* This draws the reader closer to him: God has a name by which we can know him. More than this, his name speaks of God's generational relationship with man, so that we are promised that he will be with us and that his redemptive work will be seen through us. This is fundamental to true Christian hope.

10: Different Methods of Creating?

A seventh reason lined up in support of evolutionary creationist readings of Genesis 1 and 2 is substantially just a re-hashing of differences between the two chapters that have previously been discussed in this book, and yet it is also a reason employed in source critical analysis.[1] These are that, in Genesis 1, 'God creates as a sovereign monarch giving orders from on high', merely speaking so that things come into existence; whereas in Genesis 2 God 'creates in a more down-to-earth, hands-on fashion', rather than speaking life into existence. In Genesis 2 it is said that God forms man from a lump of earth, breathes life into him, plants a garden, and builds a woman from part of the man's side.[2] These headline differences – the portrayal of God as sovereign or transcendent in Genesis 1, versus the more down-to-earth, 'hands-on' depiction in Genesis 2 – have already been addressed in numerous previous chapters.[3]

In truth there is no substantive additional argument here. The motive for this approach seems to be to try to accumulate weight to the evolutionary creationist reading by classifying this information as a separate strand of evidence.

---

[1] See Pauline A Viviano, 'Source Criticism' in Eds. Steven L McKenzie and Stephen R Haynes, *To Each Its Own Meaning: An Introduction to Biblical Criticisms and their Application*, Westerville John Knox Press, 1999, 42-43 (available on Google Books).

[2] Peter Enns, *Israel's Two Creation Stories*, http://biologos.org/blog/series/israels-two-creation-stories [referenced October 25, 2016]. See also Peter Enns, *The Evolution of Adam: What the Bible Does and Doesn't Say About Human Origins*, Brazos Press, 2012, 51. Denis Alexander rejects the notion that *br'*, the expression for 'to create' in Genesis 1, and *ysr*, the expression for 'to form' in Genesis 2, indicate substantive differences of methodology (Denis Alexander, *Creation or Evolution: do we have to choose?* Monarch Books, 2nd Edition, 2014, 32-33).

[3] See Chapters 3, 6, 8 and 9.

Claiming too much

Before examining again scripture's purpose in these undoubted differences, we should note that too much is made of them by the
evolutionary creationist. First, the psalmist saw no tension between the
notion of God's sovereignty and his 'tactile' formation of man:

> "The LORD looks down from heaven . . . from where he sits
> enthroned he looks out on all the inhabitants of the earth, he
> who *fashions* the hearts of them all and observes all their deeds"
> (Ps. 33:13-15)

In this psalm, the Hebrew translated "fashions [*ysr*]" is the same verb
as rendered "formed" in Genesis 2:7. Since the psalmist clearly handled
harmoniously the two concepts we are considering – God's sovereignty, the one who is enthroned in heaven, and the one who is involved
in 'tactile' creative activity – why should we read dis-harmony into
Genesis 1 and 2? Second, in another psalm, the holy spirit in David
(Heb. 3:7; 4:7) uses Genesis 2's tactile language of 'forming' to speak
of God's acts in Genesis 1:

> "The sea is his, for he made it, and his hands *formed* the dry
> land" (Ps. 95:5)

The psalmist again used the Genesis 2:7 Hebrew expression for
"formed [*ysr*]" but this time about the creation of the dry land, an act
that is described in Genesis 1:9,10.[4] Indeed, we have already had cause
to note that the prophet David brought together the tactile language of
Genesis 2 with a reference to God's creative works in Genesis 1 when
he declared of "[the Lord's] heavens ... the moon and the stars" that
they were the work of his "fingers" (Ps. 8:3).[5]

---

[4] We see the same kind of point being made in Isaiah 45:18 where the creator of the
heavens is said to have "formed [*ysr*] the earth" (cf. Gen. 1:1,10).

[5] See Chapter 8.

The approach of these psalms – handling the manner of God's creative activities and methods in Genesis 1 and 2 interchangeably and harmoniously – is, of course, in tune with the Lord Jesus Christ's clear and harmonious combination of God's creation of male and female in Genesis 1 with the making of the woman from Adam's side as in Genesis 2.[6] Just as Eve's creation, summarised in Genesis 1:26-28, is explained by being 'built',[7] so Adam's creation is elucidated by Genesis 2's description of him being 'formed'.

Finally, on this point, the psalmist also took up the conceptual and tactile language of God breathing for Adam's formation in Genesis 2 and deployed it to describe the way the sovereign God creates in Genesis 1:

> "By the word of the LORD the heavens were made, and *by the breath of his mouth* all their host" (Ps. 33:6)

Plainly the making of the heavens and their host by the word of the Lord resonates with the sovereign God speaking to create these things (see Gen. 1:1,8; 2:1). In fact, the Hebrew lying behind "all their host [*kl sb'm*]" (Ps. 33:6) is an exact replica of that used in Genesis 2:1's "all the host of them". Yet, language associated with man's formation in Genesis 2:7 – "the breath of [the Lord's] mouth" – is used of these things created in Genesis 1. It is also noteworthy that here, seen in a typical Hebrew scripture parallelism, the psalmist associated God speaking things into existence ("the word of the LORD") with his breath accomplishing the same outcome. From this point of view, God breathing life into man in Genesis 2 can be seen to represent a speech-act.

Thus, from God's perspective, revealed through the holy spirit in the psalmist, not only is there no dis-harmony between God's sovereignty and his tactile involvement with man rather the more down-to-earth fashion of creation portrayed in Genesis 2 is also historically true of

---

[6] See Chapter 2, 'Associating Genesis 1 and 2'.

[7] See Chapter 7.

God's creative work in Genesis 1. Seeing these features in Psalms high-lights that the literary differences between Genesis 1 and 2 ought not to be read as dis-harmony and historical conflict but as purposeful scripture by which God teaches mankind.

Before turning to consider the significance of the differing creative methods portrayed in Genesis 1 and 2, we ought to note again that Psalm 33 (as also, as previously noted, Psalms 8 and 95[8]) asserts the Lord made the heavens and their host and does so without direct employment of the text of Genesis 1. This is not just a reference to the text of Genesis without any regard for the historicity of the events described within it. Rather, Psalm 33 independently provides testimony about what God did when he created the heavens and their host alongside the record of Genesis 1 and does so harmoniously.[9]

God speaks

Furthermore, whereas the evolutionary creationist rightly notes that Genesis 1 has God speaking things into existence, while Genesis 2 has him creating in a more hands-on fashion, he overlooks the fact that the Lord God is also seen *speaking* in Genesis 2. Noting this fact highlights the harmonious correspondence between Genesis 1 and 2 and not the dis-harmony as claimed by evolutionary creationists – harmonisation of language and concepts between these two chapters is something we have persistently seen in the course of our analysis. In Genesis 2 the Lord God *speaks*:

- to give commandments to man (Gen. 2:16,17);

- to describe the incompleteness of creation without the woman for man (Gen. 2:18); and

---

[8] See Chapters 8 and 9.

[9] See Chapter 2, 'Historical references'.

- as we learn unequivocally from the Lord Jesus, to initiate marriage between the man and the woman (Gen. 2:24; cf. Mt. 19:5,6).

Indeed, we later read that Adam and Eve "heard the <u>sound</u> [*qwl*, 'voice'] of the LORD God walking in the garden in the cool of the day" (Gen. 3:8). Since Adam and Eve recognised this voice, it is evident that they were accustomed to hearing God speaking prior to their sin. At that earlier time, they clearly heard God's voice without experiencing the fear they felt in this instance – a direct consequence of their sin (Gen. 3:10). The Lord God continuing to speak, as he had done in Genesis 1, is part of man's ongoing experience in Genesis 2 and 3.

This resonates with one of the conclusions reached earlier. The two literary styles of Genesis 1 and 2 reinforce the teaching that they are one story about God speaking to create the heavens and the earth which will be filled with his glory, and that God continues to speak throughout history to fulfil this purpose in man.[10] We will examine later how this theme is developed, by considering why Genesis 2 has the Lord God speaking to instruct man in his ways, as against Genesis 1 having God speaking to bring him into existence.

Harmonious historicity

In thinking about the portrayals in Genesis 1 and 2 of different aspects of the way God created man, we have already had cause to reflect on the way the apostle Paul, in 1 Corinthians 11, brought together the language of man's creation in Genesis 1:26-28 with the manner of the woman's being built from man and for man as portrayed in Genesis 2:21-22. We noted the apostle thereby established the historicity *and* the harmony of Genesis 1 and 2. Likewise, we have observed that the use of the language of 'formation' in 1 Timothy 2:13, picking up the act of Adam's 'formation' in Genesis 2:7, confirms the historicity of

---

[10] See Chapter 6.

this creative act of God.[11] Together, these apostolic scriptures add further challenge to the evolutionary creationist claim about different methods of creation evidencing dis-harmony between Genesis 1 and 2 and their claim for the consequent non-historical standing of both chapters.

There is yet another apostolic scripture that takes up the language of Genesis 2 and which unequivocally demonstrates its historicity. 1 Corinthians 15 must be one of scripture's clearest systematic uses of historical evidence through eye-witness testimony – alongside systematic use of logical reasoning – to establish the truth of a central tenet of the gospel: that Christ was raised from the dead and that this assures us of the hope of the resurrection for all in Christ. The apostle brought forward a host of eyewitnesses (1 Cor. 15:5-8) while relying on his own and others' integrity (1 Cor. 15:14-15) to establish the historicity of Christ's resurrection. Then, having established the historical truth of Christ's resurrection from the dead, the apostle Paul employed this fact as assurance for the believers' hope.

While employing the historical fact of Christ's resurrection this way, the apostle wove two distinct yet related threads together. The two threads of Paul's argument are introduced in 1 Corinthians 15:21-22:

> "For as by a man came death, by a man has come also the resurrection of the dead. For as in Adam all die, so also in Christ shall all be made alive"

Much could be made of this apostolic statement to point out the reliance of the apostle's teaching on the historicity of Adam and of death's entry into the world, thus establishing apostolic authority for the historicity of Genesis 3 and the events described in that chapter. It is also clear that within Genesis there are fundamental points of relationship between Genesis 3 and 2 which lie behind the apostle's statements in 1 Corinthians 15:21-22:

---

[11] See Chapter 5.

- the disobedience of Genesis 3 presupposes the commandment prohibiting Adam from taking of the tree of the knowledge of good and evil which is revealed in Genesis 2; and

- Genesis 3's exclusion of Adam and Eve from the garden of Eden lest they take of the tree of life assumes Genesis 2's explicit permission that they could eat of that tree.

Given these clear inter-dependencies, the apostolic sanction in 1 Corinthians 15:21-22 of the historicity of Genesis 3 extends also to Genesis 2's historical value as well.

But now, since our focus in this chapter is on the methods God used for the creation of man, we note that this is the apostle's introduction of two threads that he employed again, later in this chapter. The first thread is Adam, his experience and the consequences for all in him; the second thread is Christ, his resurrection and the consequences for all in him. Paul continued with these two threads later in 1 Corinthians 15, this time in a context where we witness the apostle's use of the language related to the method of Adam's creation in Genesis 2:

> "It is sown a natural body; it is raised a spiritual body. If there is a natural body, there is also a spiritual body. Thus it is written, 'The first man Adam became a living being'; the last Adam became a life-giving spirit … The first man was from the earth, a man of dust; the second man is from heaven" (1 Cor. 15:44-47)

There are two clear references to Genesis 2 in the first of the apostle's two threads. "Thus it is written" introduces a direct citation of Genesis 2:7, the place where we read of Adam's 'formation' preparatory to having the breath of life breathed into him that he might become "a living creature". The second reference is the statement about the first man being "from the earth, a man of dust" – a plain allusion to what is said in Genesis 2:7 about Adam being formed "of dust from the ground". The second thread features again as the spiritual body, which is raised because the last Adam, the man from heaven, became a life-giving spirit.

Genesis 1-2

As we saw earlier in the apostle's clear reference to Genesis 3, so also here. Paul's two plain references to Genesis 2 establish unequivocally that the apostle handled Genesis 2 as comprising and portraying historical truth.

But the highly significant aspect to observe is how, in both 1 Corinthians 15:21-22 and 44-47, the apostle wove together his two threads – the first, of Genesis' record about Adam and the second, of Christ's work of redemption and his resurrection. In order to appreciate the strength of this point, it will be helpful to consider an analogy which draws on a scriptural parable – the weaving of cloth from these two threads.

Paul's cloth is woven in such a manner that should one of the threads be suspect the whole cloth would be destroyed – including the teaching about Christ's resurrection along with it. If Genesis 2 and, specifically, the manner of Adam's 'formation' is not historical, as claimed by evolutionary creationists, then we must question the historicity of Christ's redemptive work and his resurrection. Contrariwise, the historical truth of Christ's work and his resurrection is evidence for the historical truth of Adam and the manner of his 'formation'. Christ is clearly, and multiple times, placed as a counterpoint with Adam and as the second of two threads in the apostle's cloth. Given the strong focus on the historicity of Christ's resurrection in 1 Corinthians 15, the counterpoints are not merely something of theological significance – though they are certainly that, as Romans 5 explains in more detail – they also carry historical relevance. The statements made about death coming into the world through Adam, the fact that in Adam all die and the manner of Adam's creation in being made a living creature, are all as historically true as Christ's resurrection.

Furthermore, while the apostle's appeal to the manner of Adam's creation is a reference to the text of Genesis 2:7, his assertion that the first man was "from the earth, a man of dust" is not such a use of any language found there. Rather, the apostle himself asserted what we also find testified in Genesis 2, that the Lord God formed man "of dust from the ground" (Gen. 2:7). Thus, the apostle Paul again independently testified to the historicity of this creative act of God. He did not just make a reference to the text of Genesis without any regard for the historicity of the events described within it but testified to the truth and historicity of this creative act alongside the witness of Genesis 2.[12]

Mark yet again how 1 Corinthians 15 refers to detailed and specific events of the creation record in Genesis 1 and 2 and not to some generalised concept that God created. Note also that the apostle Paul's reference to Genesis 2:7, and its historicity, places evolutionary creationism directly in conflict with him. This is because the record in Genesis 2:7 is one of three specific details in Genesis 1 and 2 that is claimed to be not historical since, otherwise, there would be irreconcilable conflict with evolutionary science.[13]

Authoritative scriptures

Before returning to a consideration of the distinct language employed in Genesis 2 for Adam and Eve's creation in order to explore scripture's purpose, there is another aspect of 1 Corinthians 15 that we ought to ponder. This is that, alongside the apostle's systematic use of historical evidence, through eyewitness testimony, to establish the truth of a central tenet of the gospel, he deployed another authority: scripture itself. We see this at the beginning of his argument and even before he introduced his historical evidence (and his systematic logical reasoning). In doing so, he placed the authority of the Hebrew scriptures ahead of these things. In fact, the apostle employed this authority twice at the beginning of 1 Corinthians 15:

> "Christ died for our sins *in accordance with the Scriptures*" (1 Cor. 15:3)

> "[Christ] was raised on the third day *in accordance with the Scriptures*" (1 Cor. 15:4)

---

[12] See Chapter 2, 'Historical references'.

[13] Peter Enns, *The Evolution of Adam*, xiv. See also Chapter 2 of this book, 'Historical references'.

These two declarations demonstrate that, for the apostle Paul, the Hebrew scriptures have both predictive force and an instillation of God's authority that assures their fulfilment.[14] As God states elsewhere in a context where he claims there is none like him: "I have spoken, and I will bring it to pass; I have purposed, and I will do it" (Isa. 46:11).

This is similar to the authority the apostle Paul employed later, when he referred to Genesis 2 to prove what he said about there being a natural body: "Thus it is written" (1 Cor. 15:45) introduces authoritative scripture, in this case from Genesis 2, by which we can know for certainty the truth of the apostle's claim. This again underlines the sense of historical truth we witness in the record of God's creation of Adam and Eve in that chapter. It is clear from the apostle's "thus it is written", that Genesis 2 is scripture with true authoritative instruction for the future, at least in terms of the relationships between godly men and women. But we have also already seen that it has predictive force with an instillation of God's authority that assures its fulfilment. We witnessed this when we noted the typological significance of Genesis 2 for Christ's work of redemption of his bride, the ecclesia.[15]

This authoritative and powerful function of scripture, including of Genesis 2, argues strongly against evolutionary creationist handling of Genesis 1 and 2 and it is a theme to which we shall return before concluding this chapter.

Tactile involvement

The tactile 'forming' and 'breathing', employed of Adam's creation in Genesis 2, set the scene for how the Lord God will continue to work with man so that his image and likeness will be seen in him; likewise the language of planting and building. This is seen from the way these acts of the Lord God are taken up in other scriptures.

---

[14] See Chapters 4 and 6.

[15] See Chapter 5.

The language of Adam's formation is employed in other places to describe the Lord's work with man at both national and individual levels. For example:

> "the people whom I <u>formed</u> [*ysr*] for myself that they might declare my praise" (Isa. 43:21; see also 44:2,21)

> "the LORD says, he who <u>formed</u> [*ysr*] me from the womb to be his servant, to bring Jacob back to Him; and that Israel might be gathered to him" (Isa. 49:5; see also Jer. 1:5)

In the first of these examples, we witness the Lord's testimony that he had 'formed' his people at the national level, notably that they might declare his praise – declaring the Lord's praise being an aspect of God's image and likeness being manifest in this people. In the second example, the Lord speaks of the 'formation' of his servant, historically the servant in Hezekiah's day, prophetically the Lord Jesus Christ, and subsequently (because of his apostleship to the gentiles) Paul. Through each of these individuals, the Lord redeems his people. Isaiah's description of this man being honoured by the Lord, and the statement that God is his strength (Isa. 49:5) such that the Lord would be glorified in him (Isa. 49:3), further resonates with the concept of God's image and likeness being seen in each of them.

Adopting a similar approach to other of the 'tactile' language for God's acts of creation in Genesis 2 yields similar conclusions:

- The act of planting can be seen to be figurative of the way in which the Lord God works with man to tend for our needs, especially our spiritual nurturing; indeed, many times his people metaphorically become the garden itself.[16]

- Building, as a metaphor for the establishment of God's people as his dwelling place, is so commonplace in scripture that it

---

[16] See: Ex. 15:17; 2 Sam. 7:10; 1 Chron. 17:9; Ps. 44:2; 80:8,15; Isa. 5:2; 51:16; Jer. 1:10; 2:21; 11:17; 18:9; 24:6; 31:28; 32:41; 42:10; 45:4; Ezek. 36:36; Amos 9:15; Mt. 15:13; 21:33; Mk. 12:1; Lk. 13:6; 20:9; Rom. 6:5; 1 Cor. 3:6-8; 9:7. Jas. 1:21.

hardly needs stating.[17] The metaphorical use of 'to build' for the creation of Eve out of Adam's rib (Gen. 2:22, where "he made" is the Hebrew *bnh* 'to build'), is part of scripture's richly textured meaning in which the woman as a metaphor for the Lord's bride (Eph. 5:31,32) is simultaneously presented as a house for God's glory (Eph. 2:19-22).[18]

God-breathed

We now turn our attention to the final piece of 'tactile' language, the description of God enlivening a body formed of dust from the ground by breathing into it. This language is likewise taken up in other scriptures to describe God's active involvement in his creation, to develop his image and likeness in man. A key apostolic scripture conveys this while also furthering our understanding of the ongoing role of God 'speaking' to instruct man in his ways – something we have already noted as a feature of Genesis 2.

The apostle Paul wrote:

> "All Scripture is breathed out by God and profitable for teaching, for reproof, for correction, and for training in righteousness, that the man of God may be complete, equipped for every good work" (2 Tim. 3:16,17).

The allusion to Genesis 2:7 in "breathed out by God" is unmistakable, and it is reinforced by its association with a new Adam, "the man of God". Just as the formation of Adam was accomplished by God speaking (Gen. 2:7; 1:26), so also the new man in Christ, the man of God, is made competent for every good work by God's 'breathed' scripture – recall the conceptual association of God's word and his breathing laid out for us in Psalm 33.

---

[17] See: 2 Sam. 7:13; 1 Chron. 17:10; Ps. 78:69; 102:16; 127:1; 147:2; Jer. 24:6; 31:4,28; 33:7; Amos 9:11; Mt. 16:18; Acts 20:32; Eph. 4:12; 1 Pet. 2:5.

[18] See Chapter 7.

This function of scripture, God's word, to transform the natural man into a man of God, manifesting his image and likeness, is made clear as early as Genesis 2 when God continues to speak to instruct man in his ways. It is yet another illustration that scripture has both predictive force and an instillation of God's authority that assures its fulfilment. The different portrayals of God in Genesis 1 and 2 we have been considering make this teaching evident.

The book of truth

For scripture to be able to accomplish the completion of the man of God, as asserted by the apostle Paul, necessarily it must be intrinsically complete since "a diseased tree" cannot "bear good fruit" (Mt. 7:18), "Neither can a salt pond yield fresh water" (Jas. 3:12).

Indeed, in another place where the equipping of the saints and the achievement of "a mature person" is described in terms of the metaphor of Eve being built, the apostle Paul said of our "work of ministry" that we are to 'practise the truth' (Eph. 4:12-16, NET). For God-breathed scripture to be able to accomplish such a thing in the saints in their 'work of ministry', scripture likewise must be intrinsically true – as scripture claims about itself (Ps. 19:7-9; Prov. 30:5).

Clearly, many Hebrew and apostolic scriptures refer to Genesis 1 and 2, and the events referenced in those chapters, as historically true and employ its truth in spiritual instruction. We cannot play fast and loose with this historical value, in order to accommodate other matters external to scripture, without losing the truth of its spiritual instruction. Yet reading dis-harmony into Genesis 1 and 2 and claiming that we ought not to handle these chapters as harmonious or historical, perpetrates exactly that.

11: Different Views of Humanity?

While evolutionary creationists acknowledge that Genesis 1 and 2 share a 'high view of humanity', in an eighth argument borrowed from source critical analysis for their thesis, they also claim that 'the difference in how humanity is depicted is one of the more significant differences between the two stories' and, consequently, among the stronger reasons for Genesis 1 and 2 not being read as historical descriptions.[1] These alleged differences fall into two distinct categories: scope and portrayal.

Regarding scope, evolutionary creationists state that Genesis 1 speaks of 'the mass creation of humans (male and female) at one time'. On the other hand, Genesis 2 is said to begin 'with one man, then one woman from the man in a separate act'.[2] Regarding portrayal, evolutionary creationists point out that Genesis 1 'presents humans as royal figures . . . created in God's image' and, as such, 'the pinnacle of God's creation'. By contrast, it is noted that Genesis 2 'presents humans . . . as servants in the garden', a garden which 'is God's sanctuary, his temple, where the man-priest is placed to care for it'.[3]

We need to consider both of these distinct categories to test whether they evidence the evolutionary creationist claim that Genesis 1 and 2

---

[1] Peter Enns, *Israel's Two Creation Stories*, http://biologos.org/blog/series/israels-two-creation-stories [referenced October 25, 2016]. See also: Peter Enns, *The Evolution of Adam: What the Bible Does and Doesn't Say About Human Origins*, Brazos Press, 2012, 51. Pauline A Viviano, 'Source Criticism' in Eds. Steven L McKenzie and Stephen R Haynes, *To Each Its Own Meaning: An Introduction to Biblical Criticisms and their Application*, Westerville John Knox Press, 1999, 46 (available on Google Books).

[2] Peter Enns, *Israel's Two Creation Stories*. See also Peter Enns, *The Evolution of Adam*, 10; Denis Alexander, *Creation or Evolution: Do We Have to Choose?* 224-226,301. It is noteworthy that Denis Alexander refers to Psalm 8 to help establish his claim that Genesis 1 is about 'humankind' – the mass of humanity – but completely overlooks apostolic interpretation of Psalm 8 in Hebrews 2 as referring to one man, Jesus Christ.

[3] Peter Enns, *Israel's Two Creation Stories*. Note we have previously seen that, in common with Genesis 1, chapter 2 reinforces that man is the pinnacle (or centrepiece, as it was stated) of God's creation: see Chapter 3.

are dis-harmonious and therefore ought not to be read as historical descriptions. Addressing scope, we will assess the accuracy of the assertion that Genesis 1 presents 'the mass creation of humans'. Turning to portrayal, we will explore scripture's purpose in the undoubted differences noted and consider whether scripture sees the 'royalty' of Genesis 1 as dis-harmonious with the 'priestly' service of Genesis 2.

Scope

In the Genesis 1 record of the creation of man, there are a couple of notable features missing that one would have expected if these verses spoke unequivocally of 'the mass creation of humans'. There is a complete absence of any numbering of those created, compounded by the lack of any adjective such as 'many'. Of course, the pronoun "them" (Gen. 1:26,27) is plural, but two human beings satisfy this description just as much as thousands would.

Further aspects of Genesis 1, and their relationship to other scriptures, challenge the evolutionary creationist claim that it speaks of man's mass creation. Male and female having been created by God, the record states:

> "God blessed them. And God said to them, '*Be fruitful* and *multiply* and *fill* the earth and subdue it'" (Gen. 1:28).

The commandment to multiply and fill the earth suggests humanity's small beginnings, not mass creation. However, before noting how this blessing and commandment is taken up in a manner that reinforces this reading, we should consider an earlier part of Genesis 1 which might be interpreted as arguing against it.

On the fifth day, we witness God likewise blessing the sea creatures and birds with a commandment to multiply:

> "God blessed them, saying, '*Be fruitful* and *multiply* and *fill* the waters in the seas, and let birds multiply on the earth'" (Gen. 1:22)

This is clearly the same language as that used of man. The aspect of God's creative work on this fifth day that might be interpreted to argue against reading the commandment to be fruitful and multiply as an indication of small beginnings, is the earlier record of God's creation speech on the same day:

> "God said, 'Let the waters swarm [*šrṣ*] with swarms of living creatures, and let birds fly above the earth across the expanse of the heavens.' So God created the great sea creatures and every living creature that moves, with which the waters swarm [*šrṣ*], according to their kinds" (Gen. 1:20-21)

It might be suggested that the description of sea creatures 'swarming' – an expression whose usage elsewhere certainly indicates abundance – shows that God created very many sea creatures on the fifth day and yet still commands them to multiply. If such is the case, then this would certainly argue against reading the commandment that man should multiply as a certain indication of small beginnings.

However, when we examine the way the language of 'swarming' interacts with associated descriptions of fruitfulness and multiplication, we find the situation confirms the reading of Genesis 1:28 as speaking of small beginnings. For example, when God commanded Noah to leave the ark, he instructed him about what should be done with the animals which had been rescued from the flood:

> "Bring out with you every living thing that is with you of all flesh – birds and animals and every creeping thing that creeps on the earth – that they may swarm [*šrṣ*] on the earth, and *be fruitful* and *multiply* on the earth" (Gen. 8:17)

This commandment indicates that the 'swarming' of the pairs of animals that left the ark – clearly in small numbers of each kind – was actually an outcome that was associated with them being fruitful and multiplying.[4] Seen in this light, the commandment in Genesis 1:20 that

---

[4] We see the same association described in Genesis 9:7 about the small number of eight people who left the ark ("And you, *be fruitful* and *multiply*, teem [*šrṣ*] on the earth and *multiply*

the waters should 'swarm' with sea creatures is a statement that reaches beyond the creation of the first of their kind in Genesis 1:21a ("God created the great sea creatures and every living creature that moves") to the time when, fulfilling God's commandment that they should multiply, they 'swarmed' the waters.

Further support for this reading is the fact that, after Genesis 1:22 and 28, the threefold expression "be fruitful... multiply... fill" is used only in contexts of small beginnings out of which fruitfulness and multiplication follows as part of God's blessings:

- "God blessed Noah and his sons and said to them, '*Be fruitful* and *multiply* and *fill* the earth'" (Gen. 9:1): we know for sure that this speaks of small beginnings since it is about the eight persons who were saved in the ark and who then multiplied and spread across the earth as summarised in Genesis 10.

- "The people of Israel were *fruitful* and increased greatly [*šrṣ*]; they *multiplied* and grew exceedingly strong, so that the land was *filled* with them" (Ex. 1:7): likewise, we know this speaks of small beginnings – the seventy persons, descendants of Jacob, who entered Egypt (Ex. 1:4) – whose multiplication resulted in the new king of Egypt feeling threatened (Ex. 1:9).

In the absence of contrary factors in Genesis 1:22,28, these later uses of the threefold expression argue that Genesis 1 likewise speaks of small beginnings.

We resume now by considering the way in which the blessing and commandment of Genesis 1:28 are used in God's later dealings with man, and which reinforce the reading that this verse speaks of humanity's small beginnings. Picking up both the blessing and the commandment of Genesis 1, the Lord declared to Abraham: "I will surely *bless* you,

---

in it") and in Exodus 1:7 about the multiplication of Israel from the seventy persons who entered Egypt to the vast population by which the Egyptians felt threatened ("the people of Israel were *fruitful* and increased greatly [*šrṣ*]; they *multiplied* and grew exceedingly strong, so that the land was *filled* with them").

and I will surely *multiply* your offspring as the stars of heaven and as the sand that is on the seashore" (Gen. 22:17). Several things flow from noting these points of contact. The shared language shows that we are to see in the Lord's covenant promise to Abraham a new creative act by him, one that resonates with his act of creation as recorded in Genesis 1 and 2.[5] With this foundation, it then becomes clear that there is at least one other correspondence: just as Genesis 1 speaks of God's original act of creation from one man – Adam – so his covenant of promise speaks of this new creation from one man – Abraham. This repeated pattern strengthens the reading of Genesis 1 that sees it as humanity's small beginning in the first couple.

Finally, we have already noted that Genesis 2 is evidently a more detailed explication of Genesis 1:26-27, and especially that Jesus read it this way.[6] Both Genesis 1 and 2 speak of God creating one man and one woman, and the evolutionary creationist's claim about 'mass creation' in Genesis 1 is found to have no substance.

Covenant choice

Before moving on to consider the portrayal of humanity in Genesis 1 and 2, it is probably helpful to pre-empt a typical evolutionary creationist argument – namely, that we should read Adam as a 'covenant choice', from among the large population of evolutionary developed humans who were in existence at that time.[7]

A posited pattern to support such an argument is that, just as Abraham was called out of a large population of humans that were around in his

---

[5] Note the creation language of Genesis 1 and 2 ("created" and "formed") used of Israel in, for example, Isaiah 43:1; see also Chapter 10, where such language is examined. The point is that Israel is the "offspring" of Genesis 22:17 which is multiplied by God's promise, and that this is an act of creation.

[6] See Chapters 2 and 5.

[7] See, for example, Denis Alexander, *Genetics, Theology, and Adam as a Historical Person, Part 4,* http://biologos.org/blogs/archive/genetics-theology-and-adam-as-a-historical-person-part-4 [referenced 5 Oct. 2016] and Denis Alexander, *Creation or Evolution,* 293,304. Another evolutionary creationist (Peter Enns, *The Evolution of Adam,* 123, 138) rejects such a model, considering it not to be faithful to the apostle Paul's understanding of Adam.

time, so too was Adam. The failure of this argument is that, unlike the shared language of blessing and multiplication as part of a creation theme, there is in Genesis 1 and 2 no language of 'calling out' from country or kindred, as is employed for Abraham (Gen. 12:1). Thus, the posited pattern does not support a claim that Adam was a 'covenant choice' from a large population of evolutionary developed humans.

Furthermore, the absence of calling or choosing terms in Genesis 1 and 2 not only prevents an analogy with Abraham's calling out, the fact that such language could so easily have been employed about Adam, but was not, shows that those who want to claim this as an explanatory model in order to accommodate evolutionary science are playing fast and loose with scripture.[8]

Likewise, to model a calling out of Eve from thousands of other humans around as a result of evolutionary processes completely overturns the clear revelation of Genesis 2:

> "the LORD God caused a deep sleep to fall upon the man, and while he slept took one of his ribs and closed up its place with flesh. And the rib that the LORD God had taken from the man he made into a woman and brought her to the man. Then the man said, 'This at last is bone of my bones and flesh of my flesh; she shall be called Woman, because she was taken out of Man'" (Gen. 2:21-23)

As we have previously seen, this scripture has unequivocal sanction of truth and historicity – at the level of specific and detailed events – from the Lord Jesus Christ and from the apostle Paul.[9] If calling out from a multitude of other humans is how Adam and Eve came into a relationship with God, then why does not God say so? If that is really what

---

[8] For further comment on this evolutionary creationist argument see Robert Roberts, 'The First Man', *The Christadelphian*, vol. 25 (1888), The Christadelphian Magazine & Publishing Association, Birmingham, UK, 618-619, 679–681.

[9] See Chapters 2, 5, 7 and 10.

happened, why does God deceptively portray Adam's and Eve's origins the way that is recorded (borrowing some words of the apostle Paul, "I speak in a human way" (Rom. 3:5))?

Portrayal

We turn our attention now to the portrayal of humanity in Genesis 1 and 2 and consider whether scripture sees the 'royalty' of chapter 1 as dis-harmonious with the 'priestly' service of chapter 2. The mind that is scripturally alert will have raced ahead as soon as the portrayal issue was defined in these terms. But we will hold off from the obvious conclusion until we have explored the seed of its significance in the narrative of God's creation of man in Genesis 1. We do this by noticing how, even within the context of God's blessing in Genesis 1:28, the seed is sown for understanding that work of some sort lay ahead for man before he could realise his royal destiny which was set out in God's creation. One of the functions of Genesis 2 is to supply a fuller explanation of what this work was to be.

Having spoken of man's royal "dominion" (Gen. 1:26), God made clear that the accomplishment of this dominion required work of some kind from man. This is seen in his commandment that man should "subdue" the earth (Gen. 1:28). It is evident from this that without man performing this work of subduing the earth, his dominion would be unfulfilled. Indeed, we can further reflect on the other part of God's commandment, that man must "Be fruitful and multiply and fill the earth" (Gen. 1:28), and conclude that this too was part of the work that lay ahead of him for his royal dominion to be fulfilled.

We should note that later scriptural teaching concerning the spiritual qualities expected of mankind uses the language of fruitfulness (for example, Ps. 128:3; Isa. 11:1; Mt. 7:20; Gal. 5:22), of multiplication (2 Cor. 9:10; 1 Pet. 1:2), and of filling the earth (Num. 14:21; Isa. 11:9; Hab. 2:14). These features demonstrate that when we read Genesis 1:28 in the light of the whole counsel of God, we are meant to be thinking beyond the merely physical significance of man's dominion. In fact, this is what Genesis 2 explains about man's work of subjugation. His work was to begin with the subjection of his own will to God in obedience to the Lord God's commandment concerning the fruit of the garden:

> "the LORD God commanded the man, saying, 'You may surely eat of every tree of the garden, but of the tree of the knowledge of good and evil you shall not eat, for in the day that you eat of it you shall surely die'" (Gen. 2:16,17).

This need for the man to begin with the subjection of his own will to God's is confirmed when we later witness the introduction of unruliness – a lack of subjection to man's will – into God's creation, as part of God's response to man's failure in this first and principal matter (Gen. 3:17-19; cf. Gen. 1:29). Man's dominion over God's creation was rendered more difficult as a direct consequence of man's failure to place the Lord God's will in dominion over himself. In doing so, the Lord God struck a correspondence between unruliness in the created order and the unruliness of man's will – made evident by Adam's disobedience.

A priest on his throne

This brings us to the point to which the scripturally alert mind immediately wanted to go when we first raised the question whether the royalty of Genesis 1 is dis-harmonious with the priestly service of Genesis 2. This is such a major theme running through scripture that it is difficult to see how any sensible handling of scripture could reasonably depict the portrayals in Genesis 1 and 2 as dis-harmonious; the prevalence of the theme points in totally the opposite direction.

It was only after Jesus fulfilled his priestly function of sacrificing himself for sins (Heb. 10:11,12), which involved the subjection of his own will to his father (Mt. 26:39-44; Heb. 10:7), that he was given the dominion purposed at man's creation, when he sat at the right hand of God (Heb. 10:12; 1:13; Ps. 110:1; 1 Pet. 3:22). This is commemorated by Jesus having been made a priest for ever after the order of Melchizedek (Heb. 5:6; 6:20; 7:17,21; Ps. 110:4). The scripturally alert mind will recognise that this speaks of one who is a priest occupying a royal throne (Zech. 6:12,13), a perfect fulfilment of the pattern set out in Genesis 1 and 2. Jesus' perfect fulfilment of this pattern is proven by the testimony of Hebrews 2, which elucidates for us that Jesus is the one who truly fulfilled the prophecy of Psalm 8 about the son of man, regarding whom God put "everything in subjection under his feet" (Heb. 2:8; Ps. 8:6). One of the functions of Psalm 8, of course, is to identify the one who would successfully accomplish the dominion that God appointed to Adam (Gen. 1:26,28) but in which Adam had failed.[10]

While this purpose of God is perfectly and fully accomplished only by his son, it is a theme easily recognised in God's work with Israel (Ex. 19:6; "a kingdom of priests") and with the elect of Christ (1 Pet. 2:9; "a royal priesthood"; Rev. 5:10; "a kingdom and priests to our God, and they shall reign on the earth"). We have previously seen that Genesis 2 speaks of the work of preparation for man's glory introduced in Genesis 1.[11] Likewise this difference in portrayal. If we desire dominion as royal priests, then unlike Adam, who failed, and rather like Christ, who succeeded, we must learn to subject our own will to God's sovereign will.

A harmonious conclusion

Thus, far from the distinct portrayals of humanity seen in Genesis 1 and 2 being among the stronger reasons for them not being read as historical descriptions, their theme of priests becoming kings is taken up copiously in the rest of scripture:

- we see it in the life of Melchizedek (Gen. 14);

- it is central to the establishment of Israel as God's people (Ex. 19);

- David reflected on its prophetic significance against the background of foreshadowing events in his own life (Ps. 110);

---

[10] For the relationship of Genesis 1:26,28 to Psalm 8, see Chapter 8.
[11] See Chapter 4.

- the prophets dwelled on the matter as an aspect of Israel's future hope (Zech. 6);

- it is supremely fulfilled in Christ (Heb. 5-7); and

- it is central to the promise of life in God's kingdom for the redeemed (Rev. 5).

The prevalence of this theme throughout scripture demonstrates that the distinctive portrayals of humanity in Genesis 1 and 2 point in entirely the opposite direction from these being evidence for dis-harmony between these chapters. Rather Genesis 1 and 2 is written in the way it is, in order to communicate God's creative purpose and promise of man being his royal priesthood. This communicated purpose and promise is actually evidence for the harmony of Genesis 1 and 2. Not only do we see that Genesis 1 and 2 are a harmonious and purposeful record, but we see it as strongly in harmony with God's purpose in Christ and with mankind, as testified in the rest of scripture. More significantly than this, the veracity of God's promise that the redeemed shall be priests reigning on earth with Christ is rooted in the historical truth and harmony of Genesis 1 and 2. Write off these things with the claim that they should not be read as historical records because they are dis-harmonious, and where does God's promise stand?

Historicity

Before closing this chapter, we should note the references to God's creative activity as relevant historical foundation for the promise of royal priesthood – as first introduced in scripture's early historical record. One of the reasons for this, as we have seen, is the way that Genesis 1 and 2 reveal God's work establishes an expectation from the beginning of creation that a royal priesthood would develop the image and likeness of God. These things are seen in the first two subsequent mentions of the royal priesthood.

The historical record of the encounter between Melchizedek and Abraham – which is later seen to have been figuratively prophetic of God's work in Christ (Ps. 110; Heb. 5-7) – testifies that both parties speak about "God Most High" being also "Possessor of heaven and earth" (Gen. 14:19,22). The mention of "heaven and earth" by both Melchizedek and Abraham has a clear resonance with the record of creation between the inclusio of "the heavens and the earth" at Genesis 1:1 and 2:1. The most high God's possession of heaven and earth clearly follows from the fact of his creation of them; the heavens and the earth comprising the entirety of his creative outcomes encompassed inside the inclusio scripture. It is evident that this creative work of God forms a basis for the truth of God's new creation through the Melchizedek priesthood. In this context, God as creator is clearly, and seamlessly, part of the understanding of who God is and why he can be trusted on the part of faithful men and women.

The second mention of a royal priesthood continues this theme. When promising the people of Israel that they would be his "treasured possession" and "a kingdom of priests", the Lord explained he can do this because "all the earth is [his]" (Ex. 19:5-6). Following on from the confessions of Melchizedek and Abraham, it is again clear that all the earth being the Lord's rests on the fact he created it, as recorded in Genesis 1. Lest this interpretation be doubted, the psalmist David testified that this is a true reading. Picking up the Lord's declaration in Exodus 19:5, he opened Psalm 24 by declaring, "The earth is the Lord's" (Ps. 24:1). He then moved on to explain this is because "[the Lord] has founded it upon the seas" (Ps. 24:2) – a clear reference to and development of Genesis 1:9-10 but also a statement which itself asserts things about God's creative activity, independently testifying what Genesis 1 also records.[12] Yet again, therefore, this creative work of God forms a basis for the veracity of God's creation of a people who will be royal priests. In Exodus 19, God as creator is in a context where he is portrayed as speaking about himself – it is a fundamental aspect of how he reveals himself as one who redeems his people.

Finally, let us note that this set of promises about a royal priesthood, and their relationship to God's initiation of this purpose from the beginning – communicated in the way Genesis 1 and 2 distinctively

---

[12] See Chapter 2, 'Historical references'.

portray man's creation – are matters dealt with in a context where an apostolic writer testified, regarding the unchangeability of God's promise to Abraham, "it is impossible for God to lie" (Heb. 6:18). More generally, the apostle Paul testified about the eternal life promised by God before the ages began – eternal life which is essential to the royal priesthood after the order of Melchizedek (Heb. 7:24) – that God "never lies" (Tit. 1:2). The creator of the heavens and the earth and all the host of them no more lies about this work of creation, and his record of it in Genesis 1 and 2, than he does about his promise of a royal priesthood after the order of Melchizedek.

12: Evolutionary Science and Scripture

The purpose of this book has been to refute the handling of scripture practised by evolutionary creationists. Over the course of the book, the posited dis-harmonies between Genesis 1 and 2, claimed by evolutionary creationists as evidence for lack of historicity, have been, for the most part, dismissed reasonably easily. This being the case, then the question inevitably arises as to why the evolutionary creationist who spots the differences between Genesis 1 and 2 then draws conclusions about dis-harmony between the two chapters, rather than seeing them function harmoniously and purposefully in the way that has been a constant theme in this book. This calls for some critique of the approaches to scripture adopted by evolutionary creationists.

It was noted in the Preliminary Remarks that evolutionary creationists point to liberal biblical criticism, evolution and biblical archaeology as three 19th century forces that demand Genesis is read differently from that which would be typical among conservative biblical critics. The two forces that particularly lead to evolutionary creationist mis-handling of Genesis 1 and 2, and of scripture's commentary on these chapters, are liberal biblical criticism and evolution.[1] How evolution is handled by evolutionary creationists will be examined first, before turning our attention to their deployment of liberal biblical criticism. As will be seen, this ordering reflects the fact that evolutionary science is the catalyst that leads to evolutionary creationist adoption of liberal biblical criticism as a reading strategy.

There are three aspects of evolutionary creationist deployment of evolution in relation to scripture's interpretation which will be addressed in this chapter:

---

[1] Evolutionary creationists' employment of liberal biblical archaeology leading to mis-handling of scriptures is outside the scope of this book.

- First, the way prior acceptance of evolution as scientific fact is positioned as the rationale for reading scripture differently.

- Second, inconsistency regarding evolutionary creationist claims about anachronistic reading of Genesis 1 and 2.

- Finally, evolutionary creationist assertions about what Genesis 1 and 2, as ancient literature, could have said about evolution.

Evolutionary science as a catalyst

One evolutionary creationist avers that overwhelming 'evidence for evolution' makes it clear that 'models [for interpreting Genesis 1 and 2] are needed that do not force these data into existing models that are ill-suited to handle them'.[2] Different models are needed, according to this writer, Peter Enns, because, as he says elsewhere, 'Evolution … is a game changer. The general science-and-faith rapprochement is not adequate because evolution uniquely strikes at central issues of the Christian faith' and because, 'If evolution is correct, one can no longer accept, in any true sense of the word "historical", the instantaneous and special creation of humanity described in Genesis, specifically 1:26-31 and 2:7,22'.[3]

This line of reasoning highlights where evolutionary science stands in the thinking of evolutionary creationists. It is their prior acceptance of the conclusions of evolutionary science that leads them to identify different models for reading and handling Genesis 1 and 2. This explains why the same evolutionary creationist places 19th century liberal biblical criticism alongside evolution as the basis for easing evolution and Christianity toward meaningful dialogue.[4] The different interpretive

---

[2] Peter Enns, *How the Incarnation Helps Us Understand the Bible*, http://biologos.org/blogs/archive/an-incarnational-model [referenced October 31, 2016]. The writer uses 'model' to refer to an intellectual construct deployed to explain why scripture is like it is.

[3] Peter Enns, *The Evolution of Adam: What the Bible Does and Doesn't Say About Human Origins*, Brazos Press, 2012, xiv. See also, xiii, xvi, 7-8, 138.

[4] Peter Enns, *The Evolution of Adam*, Chapter 1.

'models' evolutionary creationists have adopted, in order to accommo-date their prior acceptance of evolutionary science, fall within the disciplines of liberal biblical criticism. It is clear that evolutionary cre-ationists start with their acceptance of evolutionary science and that it is this that has led them to adopt liberal biblical criticism as a reading strategy – for evangelical evolutionary creationists, this is something entirely contrary to their heritage.[5]

It is important to keep this in mind when, in the following chapter, we turn to critique evolutionary creationist adoption of liberal biblical crit-ical methodologies. Such methodologies are not self-evidently true approaches that demand their employment, they are methodologies that have been chosen in order to accommodate evolutionary creationists' prior acceptance of evolution.

Crucially, for the immediate analysis, evolutionary creationists have taken evolutionary science as their reason for reading and handling scripture in the manner that is practised by them. This approach is adopted rather than, and against, taking scripture's qualities as God's word as the ultimate authority and guide. From a Christian perspective, this clearly conflicts with faith and the gospel.

Anachronistic reading

In their handling of scripture, evolutionary creationists emphasise that it is anachronistic to read Genesis 1 and 2 through the lens of modern science, or to treat them as a scientific commentary on what happened at creation.[6]

Of course, Genesis 1 and 2 certainly do not purport to be a modern scientific text. Furthermore, they are chapters that are purposed to be understood by all men and women, ancient or modern, scientist or not.

---

[5] Norman L. Geisler and Douglas E. Potter, *A Seismic Shift in the Inerrancy Debate*, 2018, available from www.academia.edu [referenced April 9, 2018].

[6] See, for example, Denis Alexander, *Creation Or Evolution, do we have to choose?* Monarch Books, Oxford, UK and Grand Rapids, Michigan, USA, 2nd edition, 48-57, 196-197, 284; Peter Enns, *The Evolution of Adam*, 33, 36.

It follows that a modern scientific lens is assuredly not required in reading them. However, such observations do not require that Genesis 1 and 2 are divorced from any connection with the physical things described in them. It necessarily follows from the historicity of Genesis 1 and 2 – a fact that has been amply demonstrated in the previous chapters – that the descriptions in the text relate to the physical world, at least phenomenologically[7].

In another context where Peter Enns again employs the 'fact' of evolutionary science as a reason for reading scripture differently, we witness him also employing evolutionary science as determinative of the genre and meaning of Genesis 1 and 2. Confronted with the dilemma that 'evolution uniquely strikes at central issues of the Christian faith' and wishing to preserve 'Christian faith'[8], Peter Enns settles on the need to 'Rethink Genesis and Paul'.[9] 'Rethinking' here amounts to the challenge of evolution affecting 'how Christians read Genesis and Paul' and indeed more than that, 'how *the Bible* is to be read'.[10] We could add that such rethinking demands that we change how we read Jesus.[11] As part of this 'rethinking', Peter Enns expresses the view that evolution (together with, as will be seen, biblical scholarship placing Genesis in its ancient Near Eastern (ANE) cultural context) has 'calibrated for us the genre of Genesis' and that, 'A literal reading of the Genesis creation stories does not fit with what we know of the past. The scientific data do not allow it …'.[12]

---

[7] See P Wyns and A Perry, *Evaluating Other Texts about Creation*, in *Christadelphian eJournal of Biblical Interpretation*, vol. 10, no. 4, Q4, 2016, 5 (http://www.christadelphian-ejbi.org/).

[8] Peter Enns, *The Evolution of Adam*, xiv.

[9] Peter Enns, *The Evolution of Adam*, xvi-xviii. In 'rethinking' Paul, he specifically has in mind the apostle's teaching regarding Adam.

[10] Peter Enns, *The Evolution of Adam*, xix-xx. My emphasis.

[11] See Chapter 2.

[12] Peter Enns, *The Evolution of Adam*, 79. Note Peter Enns' misuse of 'literal' in a context where he is seeking to dismiss the 'historicity' of Genesis 1 and 2.

In other words, for Peter Enns, the conclusions of modern evolutionary theory are important or crucial determinants for the genre and meaning of Genesis 1 and 2, and they affect how we ought to read these chapters.

Yet the more our reading of Genesis 1 and 2 is constrained or shaped by the conclusions of evolutionary science, the closer one gets to the very trap such interpreters claim we must avoid – of not reading Genesis 1 and 2 through the lens of modern science. To determine that these chapters cannot have a particular meaning, if that meaning is contrary to evolutionary science, is anachronistic and places scientific theory as determinative of the meaning of God's word. This is not to say there is no conflict between the scriptures and evolutionary science that requires resolution in some way. Rather, it is to assert that it is unequivocally anachronistic to deploy evolutionary science as interpretive of scripture's genre and meaning since to do so is to read Genesis 1 and 2 with at least one eye through the lens of modern science.

While he does not state the point in quite this way, the thrust of the argument presented here is something with which another evolutionary creationist agrees. Denis Alexander comments, 'modern science may shed light on a biblical passage, but I do not think it should be used as a tool for interpreting the passage'.[13] Nevertheless, and despite positioning himself in such a way, even this evolutionary creationist obviously feels sufficiently constrained by his prior acceptance of the conclusions of evolutionary science that he interprets the meaning of the record of man's creation through a series of models[14] that Peter Enns considers 'rewrites' Genesis 1 and 2[15]. Denis Alexander evidently falls into the very approach against which he argues.

Thus, across the spectrum of opinion among evolutionary creationists, we find them deploying the conclusions of evolutionary science as determinative of the genre and meaning of Genesis 1 and 2. This is as

---

[13] Denis Alexander, *Creation or Evolution*, 178.

[14] Denis Alexander, *Creation or Evolution*, 288-294, 297-304, 316-318.

[15] Peter Enns, *The Evolution of Adam*, xiv-xv. This is an assessment the author persistently reiterates, see, xvii-xviii, 123.

anachronistic as evolutionary creationists claim is the case when handling these chapters as modern scientific commentary and evidences their inconsistency on this matter. A truly non-anachronistic reading of Genesis 1 and 2 needs to determine whether their meaning is seen to be, within themselves and through other scriptural commentary as, inter alia[16], a historical description of creation and of the origins of the existing human inhabitants of the world. If such a reading does so, and this has been demonstrated clearly in this book, then the conclusions of evolutionary science *do not* call for a re-writing, re-reading or re-calibration of Genesis. Rather, for those who believe Genesis is God's "prophecy of Scripture" (2 Pet. 1:20), the task before us is to come to terms with the conflict between God's record of his creative works and evolutionary science while placing unshakeable trust in God's authoritative record.

Genesis 1 and 2 and evolutionary processes

Evolutionary creationists assert that the evolutionary origins of man and the fact of common descent could only have been described in scripture by a 'scientific … account' that 'no one would have understood'.[17]

This is demonstrably false because it is clear that Epicurean philosophers in the period 300 BCE to 200 CE taught a form of evolution without modern scientific language. Such a teaching is seen in the Epicurean view that uncreated matter organised itself according to strict causal laws.[18] With this in mind, it is evident that God could likewise have described, in a non-scientific manner, the creation of Genesis 1

---

[16] The point in the use of 'inter alia' is that Genesis 1 and 2 should not be solely categorised as a historic record since, as scripture, it carries many other purposes communicated via a variety of literary methods.

[17] Denis Alexander, *Creation or Evolution*, 173-174.

[18] Anthony Long, *Evolution vs. Intelligent Design in Classical Antiquity* in *Townsend Center for the Humanities UC Berkeley*, November/December 2006, 3-5 (available here: http://townsendcenter.berkeley.edu/publications/evolution-vs-intelligent-design-classical-antiquity) – the work of Stephen Palmer is acknowledged in drawing attention to this resource; Alasdair Richmond, *Epicurean Evolution and the Anthropic Principle* in *American Philosophical Quarterly*, Vol. 37, No. 2 (Apr., 2000), 149-161.

and 2 and man's origins as having taken place through evolutionary processes, *if* these processes were factually what had happened. These chapters *do not need* to have been a scientific commentary to have communicated evolution as God's creative process, *if* that is what occurred. Yet, if evolution and the common descent of man is the reality of God's creation and our origins, why does God cut across this by revealing a special creation, as in Genesis 1 and 2, and by introducing Adam as our sole progenitor (cf. Acts 17:26; 1 Cor. 15:22)?

Arguing that such ideas would make God into a deceiver, evolutionary creationists reject some young earth creationist suggestions that planet earth only has the appearance of being old[19] or that God, having specially created man, implanted into him genomic material from the apes to give the appearance of common descent.[20] But in declaring evolutionary creationism to be how God created, the shoe is on the other foot. Evolutionary creationist reasoning that the appearance of age or of common descent would make God into a deceiver would be, in such circumstances, equally applicable to the creation record we have in Genesis 1 and 2. *If* it is the case that common descent through evolutionary processes is the real picture concerning man's origins then God has perpetrated a great deception in his record of what happened, as laid out in Genesis 1 and 2. Once again, borrowing some words of the apostle Paul, "I speak in a human way" (Rom. 3:5).

Conclusion

Thus, evolutionary creationist use of evolutionary science has led to a doubling-up of scripture's mishandling. Of itself, deployment of evolutionary science in interpreting scripture has yielded illegitimate and anachronistic determination of scripture's meaning. Moreover, evolutionary creationist prior acceptance of evolutionary science as fact has become the cause for further mishandling of scripture through their

---

[19] Denis Alexander, *Creation or Evolution*, 164-167.

[20] Denis Alexander, *Creation or Evolution*, 250-251.

choice of liberal biblical criticism as a reading strategy in their response to the claims of evolutionary science.

Contrariwise, and as argued briefly in Preliminary Remarks[21], Christians ought to start with the authority of God's word in scripture rather than with evolutionary science.

It is to evolutionary creationist use of liberal biblical criticism that we now turn our attention in the following chapter.

---

[21] Chapter 1, 'Scripture's authority'.

13: Liberal Biblical Criticism

There are at least three readily observable aspects of evolutionary creationist handling of scripture that fall within the general category of 'liberal biblical criticism':

- First, espousal of the conclusions of liberal source criticism.[1]

- Second, classification of what is perceived to be scripture's various genres through adoption of the conclusions of liberal comparative studies.[2]

- Third, evolutionary creationist views of what scripture is. In some respects, this is a more generalised view that encompasses the first two aspects.

In this chapter, each of these areas will be critiqued briefly.

Liberal source criticism

Throughout, we have witnessed that the majority of the differences identified by evolutionary creationists, and which are claimed as evidence for dis-harmony between Genesis 1 and 2, are features of the text also employed by liberal source critics in their work. In fact, of the eight

---

[1] Source criticism, as the term is used in biblical criticism, refers to the attempt to establish the sources used by the author and/or redactor of the final text. For an introduction to source criticism, see Pauline A Viviano, 'Source Criticism' in Eds. Steven L McKenzie and Stephen R Haynes, *To Each Its Own Meaning: An Introduction to Biblical Criticisms and their Application*, Westerville John Knox Press, 1999, 35-57 (available on Google Books).

[2] Comparative studies are a method of drawing data from different segments of cultures into juxtaposition with one another in order to assess what might be learned from one to enhance understanding of the other through a common cognitive environment. For an introduction to comparative studies, see John H Walton, *Ancient Near Eastern Thought and the Old Testament: Introducing the Conceptual World of the Hebrew Bible*, Baker Academic, Grand Rapids, Michigan, 2006, Part 1.

differences identified by evolutionary creationists, seven of them have been flagged as standard inclusions in analysis presented by liberal source criticism. Consequently, it is clear that liberal source criticism and, more particularly, the Newer Documentary Hypothesis for the Pentateuch's composition, features heavily in Peter Enns' analysis presented in his *BioLogos* blog.[3]

Noticing the differences, and positing different original sources, is not the problem, per se. Rather, it is the neglect of the overriding claims of scripture about itself that it is "sure" and "true" (Ps. 19:7,9) that presents the difficulties. If these qualities of scripture are accurate, then it necessarily follows there can be no dis-harmony between one part of scripture and another, notwithstanding different sources: truth cannot be dis-harmonious with truth. It is this inerrant quality of scripture, plainly, that is set aside by liberal source critics from having any bearing on their analysis and conclusions. Despite claiming a belief that scripture is God's word, evolutionary creationists clearly espouse this liberal source critical position and set aside, in some fashion, scripture's claim about itself that it is sure and true.

This book has not set out specifically to examine the methodologies and arguments of liberal source criticism and, specifically, of the Newer Documentary Hypothesis. But it is plain from the analyses presented that no evidence, whatsoever, has been found for the claims of liberal source critics and evolutionary creationists about Genesis 1 and 2 being dis-harmonious. Rather, the exegesis offered has found these early chapters of Genesis to cohere with scripture's own claims about its qualities so that, notwithstanding multiple posited original sources, the text we now have is entirely harmonious and purposeful.

---

[3] Thus, Peter Enns does not just make a passing and general reference to liberal biblical criticism as a background force of the 19th century that bears upon the conclusions of evolutionary creationism; he explicitly employs such criteria. Apart from his use of 'dis-harmonies' between Genesis 1 and 2 previously identified by liberal source criticism, he writes of Genesis 1 being penned by 'authors' and he refers approvingly to the work of Julius Wellhausen, credited with being the principal architect of the Newer Documentary Hypothesis (see Peter Enns, *The Evolution of Adam: What the Bible Does and Doesn't Say About Human Origins*, Brazos Press, 2012, 52, 5, 20-22, 37).

Furthermore, one specific piece of analysis presented in the book is devastating to the liberal source critical approach. Elohim and Yahweh, as distinct referents for God, are fundamental to the beginning and formulation of the Newer Documentary Hypothesis – the Hypothesis even employs such referents for God as category names for what they claim to be distinct sources.[4] Thus, since Chapter 9 of this book shows that Elohim and Yahweh are harmoniously deployed by a *single* prophetic author, rather than being evidence for multiple and distinct writers, it has been demonstrated that the Hypothesis is faulty even at this most fundamental and seminal level. Indeed, assurance of such a conclusion has been seen to be provided by apostolic testimony, including that of the Lord Jesus Christ himself, so that the original basis for the Newer Documentary Hypothesis is completely undermined and dismantled.

Liberal comparative studies

Having written in detail about ancient Near Eastern (ANE) stories of origins[5], and about Israel's focus on self-definition through reflecting on ANE views of primordial time[6], Peter Enns summarises his conclusions about his handling of scripture that flows from this as follows: 'A literal reading of the Genesis creation stories does not fit with what we know of the past ... modern biblical scholarship places Genesis in its ancient Near Eastern cultural context ... These factors have calibrated for us the genre of Genesis'[7]. Likewise, regarding such comparative interpretations of Genesis 1 and 2, the same author writes: 'When faced as we are with the strong, even overwhelming, evidence for . . . the presence of Mesopotamian creation . . . stories that look like what we see in Genesis, it is clear that models are needed that do not force these data into existing models that are ill-suited to handle them.'[8]

---

[4] Pauline A Viviano, 'Source Criticism', 37-41.

[5] Peter Enns, *The Evolution of Adam*, Chapter 3.

[6] Peter Enns, *The Evolution of Adam*, Chapter 4.

[7] Peter Enns, *The Evolution of Adam*, 79; see also 6-8, 140.

[8] Peter Enns, *How the Incarnation Helps Us Understand the Bible*, http://biologos.org/blogs/archive/an-incarnational-model [referenced October 31, 2016].

Although less systematic in his employment of ANE texts this way, a more conservative evolutionary creationist – Denis Alexander – rests some of his handling of Genesis 1 and 2 on such things. In seeking to understand these early and later chapters of Genesis, for example, he refers to the context of 'ancient Near East culture' and to the Gilgamesh Epic.[9] He also refers approvingly to the work of John Walton – in many respects a principal modern architect of classifying Genesis 1 as ANE literature.[10]

The evolutionary creationist approaches illustrated above are the bread and butter of liberal comparative studies.[11] Such approaches amount to a claim that the discovery of Mesopotamian creation stories has shown that a 'literal reading'[12] or, as Peter Enns expresses it elsewhere, a 'literalist/historicistic model'[13] for interpreting Genesis 1 and 2, fails adequately to explain these chapters. In other words, the discovery of ANE creation stories demands that we read Genesis 1 and 2 in a non-literal and non-historic manner, because their meaning is delimited by ANE genre – Genesis 1 and 2 are interpreted within the evolutionary creationist approach as ANE literature.[14]

---

[9] Denis Alexander, *Creation Or Evolution, do we have to choose?* Monarch Books, Oxford, UK and Grand Rapids, Michigan, USA, 2nd edition, 178 (referring to 'the ancient Near East culture'), 190, 192, 225, 323 (referring to contemporary legal literature and the Gilgamesh Epic).

[10] Denis Alexander, *Creation or Evolution*, 184. Denis Alexander refers to John H Walton, *The Lost World of Genesis One: Ancient Cosmology and the Origins Debate*, Downers Grove, IL: IVP Academic, 2009.

[11] John H Walton, *Ancient Near Eastern Thought and the Old Testament*.

[12] Peter Enns, *The Evolution of Adam*, 79.

[13] Peter Enns, *How the Incarnation Helps Us Understand the Bible*.

[14] For an illustration of comparative study methodologies employed in exploring the meaning of Genesis 1 in the context of an ANE text, see Peter Enns, *Genesis 1 and a Babylonian Creation Story*, http://biologos.org/blogs/archive/genesis-1-and-a-babylonian-creation-story [referenced October 31, 2016]. It is salutary to note that such comparative study methodologies have been employed to demonstrate that other scriptures are not authentically historical. For example, based on comparison of the gospel records with Greco-Roman biographies, Michael Licona (notably, an evangelical academic) has asserted that the resurrection testimonies of the gospel writers contain legends at the point where history ends (*The Resurrection of Jesus: A New Historiographical Approach*, IVP Academic, 2010). In another example,

Genesis 1-2

Such a classification is required, according to such an evolutionary creationist reading, no matter how Genesis 1 and 2 present themselves intra-textually and contextually or how they are handled inter-textually by the rest of scripture. Yet the ample evidence laid out in this book shows that these chapters are historical, both within themselves as well as being testified to be such by the rest of the scriptures and by the Lord Jesus Christ. It follows from these things that Genesis 1 and 2 are literal in their historicity – contrary to evolutionary creationist claims.

It is also the case that the evolutionary creationist options posed for reading Genesis 1 and 2 – ANE literature versus 'literalist/historicistic'[15] – sets up a false dichotomy. This is because the evidence from the analysis of Genesis 1 and 2 presented in this book has yielded far richer and multi-layered meaning in these chapters than a simple categorisation such as 'literal' or 'history'. While the demonstrated historicity of these chapters of Genesis has indicated the presence of literal elements, in the course of the exposition we have witnessed a far broader range of features in them:

- The use of metaphorical language in both chapters.

- The use of a variety of literary structures in them as a means of communicating meaning.

- Purposeful stylistic differences between the two chapters.

- Both chapters functioning as prophetic typology.

- Teaching from God in Genesis 2 regarding marriage.

---

equivalent conclusions are reached based on, inter alia, comparison with contemporary historiography, about the speeches recorded in Acts, particularly Peter's speech at Cornelius' house, Paul's speech on the Areopagus, his farewell speech at Miletus and his speech of defence to the Jews' who accused him of defiling the temple by taking Trophimus into it (Martin Dibelius, 'The Book of Acts', Edited by K C Hanson, Fortress Press, Minneapolis, 2004, Chapter 5. See also, James M Robinson, *Acts* in Eds. Robert Alter and Frank Kermode, *The Literary Guide to the Bible*, Collins, 1987, 468).

[15] Peter Enns, *How the Incarnation Helps Us Understand the Bible.*

It is only scripture that is capable of both accurately recording historical events while also performing these multiple other functions. This is a hallmark of scripture's qualities and its God-breathed origin.

Indeed, this range of features, plus more, are true of all scripture, not just Genesis 1 and 2. Volumes of scriptures in the Pentateuch, in the records of David's, Solomon's and other kings' lives, and in many other parts of scripture, are presented in literal terms as historical accounts of things that actually took place. And yet the same accounts abound with metaphorical descriptions, parables, literary structures, poetry and song, wisdom, law and prophetic typology pointing forward to Christ's sufferings and the glory that should follow.

Thus, in arguing that Genesis 1 and 2 cannot be 'literal' or 'history', when the chapters are set in their ANE context, establishes a false dichotomy. Given the richly textured function of scripture, it is clear that the fullest answer to a query regarding the genre of any particular scripture is that it is 'God's word'. From this perspective, liberal comparative analysis that classifies the genre of Genesis 1 and 2 as ANE literature is most certainly wrong.

Scripture is first and foremost God's word since this is what scripture authoritatively says about itself. Other categories such as history, prophecy, poetry, song, wisdom, law and so on are literary and semantic vehicles for scripture's message. These vehicles are discernible in the necessary mix, as determined by its author, God himself, through proper interpretation of the text but plainly they are not the primary genre.

What is scripture?

There is a significant difference between two alternative views of what scripture is, which can be summarised as follows:

- Scripture is a product *of its time and place* which also functions as God's word; versus

- Scripture is revelation *from God* within the time and place it was communicated through his prophets.

It is evident that evolutionary creationists adopt the first of these competing views of scripture.

We have already considered evolutionary creationist handling of Genesis 1 and 2 through comparative analysis with ANE culture and texts and noted this has led them to classify the genre of these scriptures as within the milieu of the pagan texts. This is a clear instance of treating scripture as a product *of its time and place*. But it is important to note that evolutionary creationists do not limit themselves to handling the early chapters of Genesis as such a product. To varying degrees, this is a practice adopted for all of the rest of scripture – especially where it is needed to further their evolutionary creationist claims.

Peter Enns summarises such a position clearly: 'The most faithful, Christian reading of sacred Scripture is one that recognizes Scripture as *a product of the times* in which it was written... unalterably so... the Bible [is] of ultimately divine origin yet also thoroughly *a product of its time*'.[16] This position yields his conclusion that the entire Hebrew scriptures are a product of Israel's self-definition which found completion of expression, editing and compilation in the post-exile period as a product of and response to the Babylonian exile – a conclusion he shares with liberal source criticism.[17]

Likewise, regarding the writings of the apostle Paul. About these, Peter Enns writes: 'in the same way that we must calibrate the genre of Genesis by looking at the surrounding culture, we must also understand Paul's interpretation of the Old Testament within his ancient world'.[18] Specifically regarding Genesis 1 and 2 and Adam's role therein, and as part of this calibration, Peter Enns concludes, 'Paul's understanding of Adam as the cause [of the reign of death sin in the world] reflects *his*

---

[16] Peter Enns, *The Evolution of Adam*, xi; my emphasis.

[17] Peter Enns, *The Evolution of Adam*, Chapter 4.

[18] Peter Enns, *The Evolution of Adam*, 95; see also, 80-81, 98.

time and place.[19] Illustrative of such handling is that he positions Paul's interpretation of Adam on a similar footing with a variety of other contemporary or earlier Jewish interpretations of Adam.[20]

In a comparable fashion, Denis Alexander justifies his handling of the early chapters of Genesis, and what he calls the apostle Paul's interpretation of Adam as the federal head of sinful humanity, using such claims. He writes about scripture bearing 'the indelible stamp of [the inspired authors'] own particular interests, context and culture' and he emphasises that scripture is accommodated to the limitations of the common people.[21]

There are two principal features underlying this notion that scripture is a product of its time and place:

- The first is that it is clear evolutionary creationists' believe – belying Peter Enns' caveat that they are 'of ultimately divine origin' – scripture's origination lies principally or significantly with the human writers rather than with God.[22] While evolutionary creationists declare unequivocally that scripture is God's word, they plainly see that this latter aspect arises from God cooperating with the human writers in their own endeavours – as opposed to God being the originator of the revelation of his word, with the prophets acting cooperatively as his penmen.

- A second feature of this evolutionary creationist belief that scripture is a product of its time and place is their conviction that the human writers were ancient (and therefore naive) men – naive readers of scripture and necessarily naive about man's

---

[19] Peter Enns, *The Evolution of Adam*, 124; my emphasis. See also, 127

[20] Peter Enns, *The Evolution of Adam*, 98-103.

[21] Denis Alexander, *Creation or Evolution*, 25, 55-57, 358-361.

[22] This is the fundamental thesis of Part One of Peter Enns, *The Evolution of Adam* and which the author summarises as follows in Part Two: 'It was during this time of political and religious turmoil [i.e. 'the postexilic transformation of Israel's preexilic faith'] that Israel's Scripture was formed as a marker of their national identity' (see, 96).

origins, and about any other matters on which modern science has pronounced conclusions.

What does scripture say about itself?

The apostle Peter expressly opposed the idea that scripture originates with man:

> "Knowing this first of all, that no prophecy of Scripture comes from someone's own interpretation. For no prophecy was ever produced by the will of man, but men spoke from God as they were carried along by the Holy Spirit" (2 Pet. 1:20-21)

There are two telling aspects of what the apostle wrote here. First, it is clear that he specifically opposed the notion that scripture originates with man – "no prophecy was ever produced by the will of man" – and he asserted, in its place and contrarily, that scripture is "from God": God is the originator through the work of the holy spirit carrying men along as the spirit of the Lord spoke by them, God's word being on their tongue (cf. 2 Sam. 23:2).

The second aspect is what the apostle Peter said about no prophecy of scripture being "from someone's own interpretation". The key word here is "own [*idios*]", an apostolic expression which is employed about matters peculiar to the individual regarding whom it is used.[23] Since the things the apostle averred in the following verse about prophecy being *from God* are an explanation of why no prophecy of scripture is "*from someone's own* interpretation"[24], it is evident Peter was asserting in this latter statement that scripture is not from anything peculiar to the prophets themselves but that it is from God. This directly contradicts any idea that scripture bears the indelible stamp of a prophet's 'own particular interests'.[25]

---

[23] See any of the following standard lexicons: Friberg, *Analytical Greek Lexicon*; Liddell-Scott, *Greek-English Lexicon*; Gingrich, *Greek NT Lexicon*.

[24] This is the significance of the opening "for [*gar*]" (2 Pet. 1:21).

[25] Denis Alexander, *Creation or Evolution*, 25, 55-57, 358-361.

Broadening the scope, this also argues against the idea that any aspect of a prophet's make-up that 'reflects his time and place'[26] shapes the significance of scripture. It would be perverse to argue that, on the one hand, 2 Peter 1:20-21 denies a prophet's individual and peculiar traits are involved in revelation of God's word but that, on the other hand, "cleverly devised myths" (2 Pet. 1:16), which were abroad in the pervasive culture of ignorance and darkness, and which were part of the prophet's upbringing and make-up, had a part to play. Again, this directly opposes any idea that scripture bears the indelible stamp of a prophet's 'own particular... context and culture'.[27]

On the contrary, since the scriptures are "from God", he is the one that shapes scripture's significance. In doing so, God employs whomsoever he will as his prophet and as part of his revelation – as evidenced by the multiple instances on record of individual prophets being called and commissioned.

This second aspect also addresses the claim that God's prophets were ancient and naive men and, therefore, naive in both their reading of scripture and in their explanations of God's creative works and man's origins. Even assuming they were naive, the fact they were men who "spoke from God as they were carried along by the Holy Spirit" (2 Pet. 1:21) prevented any naivety that was their own from imposing itself on scripture. Furthermore, even if God's prophets and their readers were naive, this does not require that Genesis 1 and 2 and subsequent prophetic commentary could not have been articulated in a manner to describe evolutionary processes as God's creative methodology – if that is what happened – as has already been shown.[28]

---

[26] Peter Enns, *The Evolution of Adam*, 124. See also, 127.

[27] It is telling that the apostle Peter's teaching about how prophecy is produced through the holy spirit was specifically against the misuse of myths practiced by false teachers in the apostolic age, and that such practices correspond to the use of liberal comparative studies in modern times. See Peter Heavyside, *Rightly Handling God's Word: Misusing Myths* (https://tinyurl.com/yb7c2n36).

[28] See Chapter 12.

Genesis 1-2

Some evolutionary creationists claim that Jesus was naive and a man of his time and place.[29] Was this so? Were his sayings, consequently, ignorant of the reality of God's creative works and man's origins? Were the things he taught shaped by Judaism and his upbringing in that cultural context? The apostolic writings explicitly oppose such ideas.

Against any posited suggestion that Jesus, having been raised within Judaism, adopted Judaism's exegetical methods and ideas, the gospel writer stated clearly that he was different from his contemporary teachers:

> "[Jesus] was teaching [the crowds] as one who had authority, and *not as their scribes*" (Mt. 7:28)

Not only did Matthew assert this difference from the scribes, he exemplified it in his record of the Lord's distinctive teaching on the mountain. Matthew's repeated testimony that Jesus introduced his instruction by declaring, "But I say to you ..." (Mt. 5:22,28,32,34,39,44) – without the customary appeal to the sages and his contemporary teachers[30] – demonstrates that Jesus was a man who was certainly not of his time or place in his teaching.

Moreover, the record of Jesus' own testimony about the things he spoke are expressly contrary to any suggestion that in the revelation of God's words he spoke from himself. Consequently, it is doubly clear that what Jesus said was in no way shaped by any naive, cultural context and upbringing.

> "Jesus said to [the Jews], 'When you have lifted up the Son of Man, then you will know that I am he, and that *I do nothing on*

---

[29] Kenton Sparks, *After Inerrancy: Evangelicals and the Bible in a Postmodern Age*, available here:

https://biologos.org/files/modules/sparks_scholarly_essay.pdf [referenced January 4, 2018].

[30] Theodore H Robinson, *The Gospel of Matthew*, London: Hodder and Stoughton Ltd, 1960, 67-69.

my own authority, but speak just as the Father taught me'" (John 8:28)

"I have not spoken on my own authority, but the Father who sent me has himself given me a commandment – *what to say and what to speak"* (John 12:49)[31]

The testimony of the Lord Jesus Christ represented here is entirely consistent with what the apostle Peter wrote about prophecy of scripture. The only way one could claim Jesus was a naive man of his time and place and whose naivety prevailed in some measure when he spoke about God's creative works and man's origins, would be to dismiss this testimony as that of a delusional or deceptive man.

The apostle Paul's testimony about Adam is also categorised by evolutionary creationists as the interpretation of 'an ancient man'[32] and, consequently, that of a naive man. But if Paul was such, then so also must Jesus have been. This is the case because we have seen the apostle Paul's writings about Genesis 1 and 2 are completely in harmony with Jesus' reading of these chapters. Since we have seen that scripture's testimony is clear that Jesus certainly did not speak as a naive man of his time and place then, consequently and undoubtedly, we cannot dismiss what the apostle Paul taught about Adam as the erroneous understanding of an ancient man.

It is plain that the clear testimony of scripture is directly and expressly contrary to any claim that scripture is a product *of its time and place.* Indeed, if God's truth revealed in prophecy of scripture will, as Jesus testifies, "set [us] free" (John 8:32) then it is impossible that scripture is bound in any way by those things from which we are to be set free. Likewise, if we are to be Jesus' disciples and, like him, "not of the world" (John 17:14,16) then God's word of truth, which is what will "sanctify" us (John 17:17), *must* qualitatively not be '*of* the world'. Given these things, it becomes clear that reading scripture as a product

---

[31] Cf. John 5:19,30; 6:38.

[32] Peter Enns, *The Evolution of Adam*, Part Two and, in particular, Chapter 6.

of its time and place yields a wholesale mishandling of scripture and a neutering of its power to liberate and sanctify.

A pervasive challenge in the Hebrew scriptures is that Israel must not think like the other nations. How could this be affected if God permitted the culture and ideologies of these other nations to be infused in his word?

Scripture's record

In the interests of avoiding misunderstanding, none of the foregoing analysis and rejection of evolutionary creationist adoption of liberal biblical criticism denies or ignores that God, at times, inspires a sure and true record of things that are not his original word.

The extensive and blasphemous speech of Rabshakeh against Hezekiah and his God (2 Kgs. 18; Isa. 36) certainly does not comprise God's original word. However, the things that are recorded, since they are part of scripture, are assuredly a sure and true record of what he said – placed on record as part of God's revelation of his polemical defeat of Assyria and their gods.

Likewise, for example, the expressions of doubt and complaint by the prophets in their experience of God's revelatory work through them (e.g. Jer. 20:7) are not God's original word. Rather, they are the out-pouring of the prophet's innermost thoughts – sometimes, perhaps, the prophets' innermost doubts complaints being revealed to them by God himself – as they wrestled with their prophetic task. Yet they are also certainly a sure and true record of the prophet's words – in this case, placed on record as part of God's revelation of his work of fellowship with the prophets.

But these features of scripture are readily discernible and plainly form part of God's revelatory purpose in his word. They are not impositions of the socio-cultural time and place that have found their way into scrip-ture due to the frailties of the prophets through whom God revealed the scripture of truth. Nor are they an accommodation by God to falsehoods which he is prepared to overlook in the interests of condescending to men and women in their ignorance. Rather, these features are present because God has chosen that they must be there as part of his revelation, while he has also rendered them distinguishable from the truth that he reveals.

14: Competing Inspiration Frameworks

The rejection in Chapters 12 and 13 of the deployment of evolutionary science and liberal biblical criticism in evolutionary creationists' handling and interpretation of scripture calls, finally, for a brief critique of the inspiration framework adopted by them – a framework that is clearly adopted in order to sustain their handling of scripture with these methodologies. This is what we shall proceed to do in this penultimate chapter.

Inspiration and the incarnation

In order to accommodate their adoption of liberal biblical criticism and their interpretive deployment of evolutionary science, evolutionary creationists have characterised their view of inspiration as an incarnational model.[1] This model draws upon the analogy of the incarnation, suggesting that just as Jesus was of divine origin, as well as a thoroughly human figure of first-century Palestine, so also is scripture. Evolutionary creationists argue that the frailties and socio-cultural experiences of the prophet involved in revelation impose a counterpart frailty and culturally-bound element into their prophetic oracles, including in scripture.

We can see how this finds expression in their espousal of liberal biblical criticism. For evolutionary creationists, dis-harmony is an expected feature of human redaction of multiple sources and of socio-cultural

---

[1] See: Peter Enns, *Inspiration and Incarnation: Evangelicals and the Problem of the Old Testament*, Grand Rapids: Baker Academic, 2005 and his *BioLogos* blog, *How the Incarnation Helps Us Understand the Bible*, http://biologos.org/blogs/archive/an-incarnational-model [referenced October 31, 2016]; Kenton Sparks, *After Inerrancy: Evangelicals and the Bible in a Postmodern Age*, available here:

https://biologos.org/files/modules/sparks_scholarly_essay.pdf [referenced January 4, 2018]; Denis O Lamoureux, *Evolutionary Creation: A Christian Approach to Evolution*, https://biologos.org/uploads/projects/Lamoureux_Scholarly_Essay.pdf [referenced October 31, 2017].

influences on the text. Also, for them, such posited dis-harmony together with ANE genre classification are evidence for the non-historical nature of Genesis 1 and 2. The one who reads scripture in this way, readily conceives that it has limitations arising from its contemporary sociological, religious and political cultural context. For such a reader, cultural background is a weighty or overriding determinant of the meaning of scripture – both at the level of genre and of individual words – rather than God's word being able, independently and creatively, to reveal and teach new things, however challenging to the understanding of contemporary humans that might be. In such a reading, dis-harmony is not a problem but a natural consequence of differing cultural human elements and, sometimes, the frailties of the redaction process.

Yet every element of dis-harmony between Genesis 1 and 2, claimed to be so by evolutionary creationists, has contrarily been seen to be harmonious. Not only have the chapters been seen to be harmonious, but it is also evident that God's purpose within creation and for man has been communicated by the way the chapters symphonically work together. Furthermore, and contrary to liberal biblical critical interpretation of Genesis 1 and 2, what has been abundantly evident in this book is that, intra-textually, contextually and inter-textually, these chapters are presented as, inter alia, historical regarding creation and the origins of man, and that God presents things the way he does in order to reveal his purpose with and for man.

This is not, as Peter Enns characterises what he calls a wrongheaded position, 'insisting that because the biblical creation accounts are God's Word they *must* be historical'[2]. Rather, it is a conclusion based on extensive observation, laid out in this book, of how Genesis 1 and 2 are presented intra-textually and contextually and how these chapters are handled inter-textually by the rest of scripture – by the prophets and apostles, and especially by both the Lord Jesus and the apostle Paul. Scripture presents the events recorded in Genesis 1 and 2, including at

---

[2] Peter Enns, *The Evolution of Adam: What the Bible Does and Doesn't Say About Human Origins*, Brazos Press, 2012, 56.

the detailed and particular level, as historical – the detailed events narrated in Genesis 1 and 2 are presented and handled as actually having happened. We have also witnessed multiple prophets, including the Lord Jesus Christ, independently testifying to the historicity of many of God's creative acts as are also recorded in Genesis 1 and 2.[3]

The fact of the biblical creation accounts being God's word comes into play at the next stage of consideration. The question Christians must answer is this: Do I trust interpretations of scripture's meaning through exploring what scripture, as God's word, says within and about itself, or do I trust interpretations based on liberal biblical criticism or evolutionary science to determine scripture's significance – especially when such interpretations are contrary to what scripture says about itself?[4] The abundantly demonstrated harmonious and historical nature of Genesis 1 and 2, as laid out in this book, evidences that choosing liberal biblical critical approaches to scripture, and that relying on evolutionary science to interpret the meaning of scripture's creation record, are fundamental to evolutionary creationist mishandling of scripture.

The involvement of the prophets

Many Christians, not just evolutionary creationists, speak of the prophets' characters and special interests being evident in the scriptures. It is argued that the scriptures must bear evidence of such things on the basis that a prophet's consciousness and understanding is involved in the process of revelation of the scriptures. It is reasoned that this must mean there are elements of the prophet's character or special interests in the scripture we have on record. Nevertheless, not all would follow the path taken by evolutionary creationists in claiming that the scriptures are unalterably a product *of their time and place*, thereby carrying within them the socio-political and cultural ignorance weaknesses and errors

---

[3] See Chapter 2, 'Historical references'.

[4] Elsewhere, it has been shown that the deployment of ANE creation stories in the interpretation of Genesis 1 and 2 is the kind of thing that the apostles Paul and Peter had in mind in their condemnation of "myths" (1 Tim. 1:4; 4:7; 2 Tim. 4:4; Tit. 1:14; 2 Pet. 1:16); see Peter Heavyside, *Rightly Handling God's Word: Misusing Myths* (https://tinyurl.com/yb7c2n36).

of that time. But, given this element of shared thinking, it is appropriate to comment briefly on this.

For sure, the veracity of the involvement of the prophet's consciousness and understanding is evidenced by the many interactions between God and his prophet which we witness in the scriptures. The competing view of scripture that it is revelation *from God* within the time and place it was communicated through his prophets does not exclude participation of a prophet's consciousness or understanding in the process of inspiration, in the revelation act. On the contrary, the fact that God has chosen to reveal his word through prophets is evidence, per se, that the man or woman is involved in some way. But does this mean, as evolutionary creationists argue, that the prophet's ignorance, weaknesses, naivety or cultural make-up results in scripture bearing within itself such features? More generally, and as thought to be so by many Christians, does it mean that scripture necessarily bears within itself the prophet's character and special interests – irrespective of whether God wants his word to bear such an imprint?

The analysis offered throughout this book argues strongly and cumulatively against such a conclusion. In the course of this analysis, we have seen scripture is characterised by the following features:

- Scripture's origination is from God and not by the will of man.[5]

- Since scripture is from the faithful and true God, scripture itself is sure and true.[6]

- Scripture is powerful to accomplish determined outcomes given its authoritative and predictive capability.[7]

---

[5] Chapter 1; Chapter 13, 'What is scripture?'

[6] Chapter 1.

[7] Chapters 4 and 10.

- God's word, through his prophets, is as powerful to accomplish his purpose as when he spoke without the mediation of prophets.[8]

- Scripture is inherently perfect and true so that it can equip the man of God for all good works and for his liberation and sanctification.[9]

The first of these features expressly opposes the notion that scripture necessarily bears within itself the prophet's character and special interests – unless God wills that his word should bear such an imprint. The other features present a collective picture of veracity and power which is entirely contrary to scripture bearing any frailties or erroneous ideas of its prophetic writers.

Further evidence

Apart from this multiple and cumulative testimony, there are a couple of additional scriptural illustrations to demonstrate – against evolutionary creationist arguments – that the prophet's ignorance, weaknesses, naivety or cultural make-up *do not* result in scripture bearing within itself such things. These illustrations also demonstrate, more generally, that without God's will that it should be so, scripture does not bear the imprint of the prophet's character or special interests.

The first is that, while it is clear that most prophets worked cooperatively and in fellowship with God during the process of revelation, there are plain examples of prophets of God where this is not part of what happened. Balaam's prophecies, for example, are not what he wished to enunciate nor what he was paid to do. Rather, as Balaam himself confessed, he could only speak what God put in his mouth (Num. 22:18,38; 23:16,26; 24:13). While Balaam's consciousness and understanding were clearly involved in the prophetic utterances recorded in Numbers – as evidenced by the wrestling that took place in his mind,

---

[8] Chapters 6 and 10.

[9] Chapters 1 and 10; Chapter 13, 'What is scripture?'

as recorded in that scripture – this is a lucid illustration of how his own will and preferences had no part in what was said. More than this, it is plain that he was not able to impose any of his own will or preferences – especially his wilfulness or avarice – on what was uttered, despite him wishing otherwise.

A second illustration relates to those prophets who, unlike Balaam, worked cooperatively and in fellowship with God during the process of revelation. It is evident that, even with such faithful participation by the prophets, they did not understand everything that was revealed through them – indeed it was sometimes the prophets' lack of understanding that yielded interaction between God and his prophets as they struggled to achieve understanding. That the prophets did not understand everything that was revealed through them is evident from what the apostle Peter said about the prophets enquiring into those things that had been revealed through them:

> "Concerning this salvation, the prophets who prophesied about the grace that was to be yours *searched and enquired carefully, enquiring* what person or time the Spirit of Christ in them was indicating when he predicted the sufferings of Christ and the subsequent glories" (1 Pet. 1:10-11)

Such research and enquiry would be completely unnecessary if the prophets understood everything at the point it was revealed. It is evident that, at least with respect to those aspects of revelation through them that they did not understand, the prophets' understanding and consciousness could not possibly introduce any aspect of their character or special interests, let alone socio-cultural elements or personal frailties, into the oracle. This aspect also strengthens the conclusion that God is the prime mover – and therefore author – of the scriptures, since only he understood perfectly all that was being revealed at any point in time.

It might be responded that the prophet's own interests, frailties, culture or dark ignorance could unconsciously have imprinted itself into scripture. But this ignores the clear teaching of 2 Peter 1:20-21 which has been addressed in the previous chapter.

It is clear therefore, that the involvement of God's prophets in the revelation of scripture is not a reason for thinking there is any validity in the evolutionary creationist incarnational model of inspiration.

True inspiration

Having argued against evolutionary creationists' incarnational model for scripture's inspiration, and the associated idea that scripture is a product *of its time and place*, it seems necessary to complete the picture by describing the inspiration framework underlying the exegesis presented in this book. Albeit briefly, that is what is laid out in the remainder of this chapter. The previous chapter introduced a competing view of what scripture is: this is that scripture is revelation *from God* within the time and place it was communicated through his prophets. What is the significance of this and how does it bear on understanding inspiration? It is fitting that, in answering this question, we begin at the beginning.

In the beginning

It has already been observed that Adam, having learned things from his creator, reasoned together with God following the creation of Eve. From the outset of mankind's creation, there was a work of cooperative fellowship between man and his God. This work is ongoing and is part of God's creative work with all men and women both to exhibit and to develop further his "image" and "likeness" in them (Gen. 1:26,27). In Adam's case, this creative work was bound up with his prophetic role – the first instance in mankind's history of God's word being revealed through one of his prophets.[10]

There is no aspect of Adam's prophetic pronouncement which suggests his words were anything other than God's words communicated cooperatively with and through Adam – the analysis by Jesus of Genesis 1 and 2 confirms this unequivocally.[11] Indeed, given that this utterance

---

[10] See Chapter 2.
[11] See Chapter 2.

preceded the entrance of sin into the world *and* the inchoate state of mankind's history, it is not possible that this prophetic word could include any frailties or socio-cultural experiences of the prophet. Furthermore, given the manner of Adam's ignorance of anything other than what God revealed to him about the Eve's creation, it is not possible that Adam could impose anything of his own character or special interests in the things he prophetically spoke.

Thus, Adam's prophetic experience was a work of both cooperative fellowship and of the development of God's image and likeness in him, and it sets the scene for understanding inspiration. This includes that the revelation of God's word through his prophets is part of his ongoing purpose in creating his image and likeness in men and women. It is also clear that Adam's prophetic experience, involving his consciousness and understanding as he reasoned in response to God's instruction, included exhibition of the image and likeness of God in him. Adam's prophetic experience and his reasoning with God were part of his manifestation of his God.

God manifestation

This beginning of God's prophetic ministry points to an inspiration framework which is in quite the opposite direction to that of an incarnational model, in which scripture ends up thoroughly human and a product of its time and place. Rather than God's word being brought down to man's way of thinking, rather than God accommodating himself to man's weaknesses in his revelation, God's purpose is to elevate man's understanding to be like God's. This speaks of God's work of inspiration in man being a God-manifestational model – the purpose of revelation is to create his likeness in men and women and the prophetic experience itself exemplifies this as the prophet works cooperatively with his God.

Especially after the entrance of sin into the world and in order to ensure this God-manifestational purpose might continue[12], it is essential that God's will and not man's should prevail in the revelation of his word – as we have seen was testified by the apostle Peter (cf. 2 Pet. 1:20-21)[13]. Thus, when inspiring prophets with his holy spirit, God does not empty his words of his divinity – or reduce or erode their divinity – so that the socio-cultural concepts of the surrounding time and place can find a place. Rather, his word essentially communicates his divinity, so that his image and likeness might be manifest in men and women of God by taking his word into their hearts and minds. Prophets who cooperate in fellowship with God in this work set aside their frailties in order that God's word and virtues might be seen in them. Yet, it is also plain from the example of Balaam[14] that, when God's prophet is uncooperative, due to the wilfulness of sin, God's will still prevails so that his divine word is that which is spoken. In such circumstances, God is made manifest solely by the word which is spoken and not also from any fulfilment of God's will by the prophet. In this respect, God is always the author of scripture though he used prophetic writers in this work.

This is not to oppose the notion of God's condescension toward mankind – the cause of such amazement in the psalmist David in Psalm 8[15] – it is to identify God's purpose to be fulfilled in such condescension. God does not condescend in order that he or his word become less than his divinity – as in the incarnational model – he does so in order to elevate man's thinking to be like his, so that men and women might manifest the likeness of God.

Following on from God's first historic prophetic utterance through Adam, and with the entrance of sin into the world, the necessity arose for God's word becoming transformative as part of its creative power.

---

[12] For more detailed discussion of Genesis 1 and 2's explanation of how God would continue to speak, as he had at the beginning, for the creation of his image and likeness in mankind, see Chapters 6 and 10.

[13] See Chapter 13.

[14] See Chapter 13.

[15] See Chapter 8.

No longer was his word only to develop his image and likeness in mankind, it was necessary also that it would effect change from the ignorance and darkness of sin to the enlightening knowledge of God. This additional purpose in God's word accomplishing his manifestation in the earth reinforces that this word must be distinctive from the surrounding socio-cultural dark ignorance and errors. In order to accomplish this necessary change, it cannot be that God's word is characterised by that from which we are to be changed. Rather, scripture's qualities must have the character of that which we are to become, in manifesting God's virtues – including that mankind is liberated and sanctified by the word of truth (cf. John 8:31-32; 17:17).[16]

Scripture's distinctiveness

Many bible students, including evolutionary creationists, highlight the challenge that exists for a modern reader in understanding scripture in its original and ancient cultural context. Rightly so. But, without underestimating this challenge, there is a far greater trial facing any reader of scripture – whatever their time or place, be they ancient or modern, eastern or western. This much weightier challenge arises from scripture's distinctiveness; a consequence of its origin – "breathed out by God" (2 Tim. 3:16) – and of its qualities that necessarily flow from that, especially in this context that God's word is "sure" and "true" (Ps. 19:7,9). The immensity of this trial is rendered plain by the Lord himself, in an oracle in which he speaks of his word going forth out his mouth (Isa. 55:11):

> "my thoughts are not your thoughts, neither are your ways my ways, declares the LORD. For as the heavens are higher than the earth, so are my ways higher than your ways and my thoughts than your thoughts" (Isa. 55:8-9)

Scripture portrays unredeemed mankind as futile in our darkened understanding (cf. Eph. 4:17-18), and herein lies our greatest challenge – wherever and whenever a person reads scripture. It is the cultural chasm

---

[16] See Chapters 1 and 13.

between our darkened minds and the light of God's word, and between our ignorance and God's understanding "beyond measure" (Ps. 147:5). This is a cultural chasm as expansive as the heavens are higher than the earth and one which far exceeds the challenge anybody faces in understanding scripture in its original and ancient cultural context.

It follows from these things that while scripture is revealed within the time and place it was communicated through God's prophets, the relevance of which we shall consider in a moment, scripture actually has its own time and place from which it speaks throughout history. This is a time and place which is set apart from the futile darkness of contemporary societies and cultures. This 'time and place' is where God dwells; somewhere the Lord himself tells us is "eternity":

> "thus says the One who is high and lifted up, *who inhabits eternity*, whose name is Holy" (Isa. 57:15)

It is for this reason that God's word is described as living and abiding "forever" (1 Pet. 1:23,25); God's word shares the same time and place as God himself.

Of additional significance in this declaration by the apostle Peter, in which he drew on the words of the prophet Isaiah, is the explicit contrast he set up between God's eternally living and abiding word and the frailties of mankind:

> "All flesh is like grass and all its glory like the flower of grass. The grass withers, and the flower falls, but the word of the Lord remains forever" (1 Pet. 1:24-25; cf. Isa. 40:6-8)

Such a contrast speaks directly to the cultural chasm between unredeemed man, likened to withering grass, and God's prophecy of scripture, which remains forever. It is clear then, that scripture has its own culture, its own time and place, a culture which confronts every secular and religious culture and society that encounters it at any time and place of mankind's history and experience.

This utter distinctiveness of God's word in scripture fills out our understanding of a God-manifestational inspiration model. It is scripture's utter distinctiveness, clearly, that equips it for accomplishing God's manifestation in men and women. This characterisation of inspiration is what underpins scripture as revelation *from God* within the time and place it was communicated through his prophets. It is a model of inspiration that necessarily calls for methodological choices that differ from those adopted by evolutionary creationists so that, in the words of the apostle Paul, we might engage in "rightly handling the word of truth" (2 Tim. 2:15). These choices and priorities are in direct response to what scripture says about itself and its distinctive purpose.

Rightly handling the word of truth

Right handling of scripture calls, first and foremost, for incorporation of this distinctiveness in our choice and prioritisation of methodologies for its exposition. Scripture's origin and qualities demand that intra-textual, contextual and intertextual analysis of scripture are placed above all else if it is to be handled aright. This is because such an approach is about determining scripture's meaning by discovering what it says within and about itself. What scripture, within its own time and place, says about itself is necessarily of much more importance than insights gained from understanding the societal and cultural time and place within which it was first communicated by the prophet. The uniqueness of scripture's genre as the word of God necessarily means it bears an intra-textual, contextual and intertextual relationship to itself and all other parts of scripture that is massively stronger than to contemporary extra-biblical culture and its beliefs and literature. Given the identity of scripture's author, and that he is God "from everlasting to everlasting" (Ps. 90:2) with "understanding beyond measure" (Ps. 147:5), there is more in common between Genesis and Revelation across a span of more than 1,500 years, than between scripture and contemporary literature or, more particularly, between Genesis 1 and 2 and ANE texts.

Indeed, such an approach has apostolic sanction because Paul wrote that his teaching by the spirit was performed in exactly such a manner: "comparing spiritual things with spiritual" (1 Cor. 2:13, ESVm). Such an approach includes comparing scripture with scripture to determine its meaning.[17] This approach is also evidenced from the way that scripture 're-uses' itself through citation, allusion and echo. In this practice, inspired prophets have laid down a foundation for proper handling of scripture which is to be found through discovering what scripture says about itself. In this scripturally authoritative approach, scripture interprets the meaning of scripture. Since scripture is "breathed out by God" (2 Tim. 3:16), scripture's interpretation of the meaning of scripture is about discovering God's meaning, and there is no room for excluding this meaning on the basis of modern scientific claims or of liberal biblical criticism.

First and foremost, therefore, we are obliged to compare scripture with scripture to determine its meaning rather than employ the methodologies adopted by evolutionary creationists. It is this approach that has formed the bedrock of the exposition of Genesis 1 and 2 presented in this book.

Of course, scripture also interacts with, and reveals things about, its contemporary cultures; but its purpose in doing so is to call out from those cultures a people for God's name and to create a new likeness in them – God's manifestation. Since scripture interacts with, and takes place within, specific cultures, a knowledge of those cultures will sometimes help sharpen our understanding of the thrust and focus of the relevant oracles in their appeal to people to turn to God, and in their polemics against their cultural frameworks. From this perspective, the application of comparative studies to the understanding of scripture can be helpful. In fact, sound comparative analysis has been deployed by

---

[17] See Peter Heavyside, '*Comparing spiritual things with spiritual': the whole counsel of God as the basis of sound doctrine*, in *Testimony*, vol. 55, no. 652, April 1985, 131 (http://testimonymagazine.com).

scholars both to raise serious challenges against liberal source criticism, such as that championed by Julius Wellhausen in his Newer Documentary Hypothesis, and to authenticate the biblical text.[18]

But there is a world of difference between a right handling of scripture in the context of its cultural background and one which proceeds on the basis that the cultural background determines scripture's literary genre and meaning. Comparative studies necessarily must have a distant second place to comparing scripture with scripture. Comparative analysis can inform our discovery of scripture's meaning but ought not to be used to determine its meaning; God does that in his revelation.

It is evident that the same can be said, and more so, about the deployment of evolutionary science towards scripture's interpretation.

Likewise, with regard to source criticism. Recognition of multiple sources lying behind the scriptural text we now have can be helpful, for example, in appreciating the way God has persistently and consistently revealed himself to men throughout history, since he created mankind. From this point of view, the methodologies of source criticism can be of interest, it is only its misapplication and erroneous conclusions which are objectionable. Liberal source criticism displays a complete lack of sensitivity to scripture's own claims about its revelatory truth. However, even soundly applied source criticism ought to enjoy only a distant second place to comparing scripture with scripture.[19]

Thus, the remedy to the key methodologies underlying evolutionary creationists' mishandling of scripture is proper intra-textual, contextual and intertextual analysis, allowing scripture to define its own meaning.

---

[18] Ironically, this point is made by John H Walton in *Ancient Near Eastern Thought and the Old Testament: Introducing the Conceptual World of the Hebrew Bible*, Baker Academic, Grand Rapids, Michigan, 2006, 30-32, 34-36.

[19] For an illustration of sound employment of such a methodology, sensitive to scripture's own claims about its revelatory truth, see Edward Whittaker, *For the Study and Defence of the Holy Scripture*, The Testimony, Norwich, 1987, 11-35 and Bernard Burt, *Gems from early Genesis: 1. Authorship* in *Testimony*, vol. 85, no. 1001, January 2015, 3 (http://testimonymaga-zine.com).

Genesis 1-2

Only such an approach will exclude anachronistic or inappropriate socio-cultural interpretations. Such a practice accepts all of scripture as inerrant, coherent and harmonious within its own spiritual cultural unit – not only at a particular time and in a particular place but, given that its author is from everlasting to everlasting and his understanding beyond measure, across mankind's history.

15: Concluding Remarks

In Chapter 14, it has been argued that different ways of handling scripture relate to one's understanding of the qualities of scripture which emerge from competing inspiration frameworks. There is certainly a wrong way of handling scripture since the apostle Paul wrote about those who "tamper with God's word" (2 Cor. 4:2). On the other hand, there is clearly a right way of handling scripture because the apostle instructed Timothy that he must present himself approved to God by "rightly handling the word of truth" (2 Tim. 2:15). Nevertheless, and as was mentioned in the Preliminary Remarks, even if there is disagreement with the model of scripture's inspiration presented in the previous chapter, and with the proper handling of the word of truth that flows from that, we are still left with the exegesis of Genesis 1 and 2 that has been presented in the main body of this book. Any claim that these early chapters of Genesis are dis-harmonious and not historical must address this exegesis at a detailed level and show where it is wrong.

In many instances, differences between Genesis 1 and 2 have been acknowledged; and yet handling these within the framework of believing that God's word is 'sure' and 'true' in all of its facets has yielded very different conclusions from those reached by the evolutionary creationist. We have seen that the differences are not an indication of contrariness or contradiction between one scripture and another, but that they are intentionally part of scripture's own harmonious portrayal of God's purpose with and for mankind, and of how God works out that purpose with us. The harmony that has been demonstrated shows that the differences are intentionally placed there by scripture's author to highlight aspects of his purpose. In fact, to be able to discern the purposefulness of scripture, we have witnessed that Genesis 1 and 2 need to be read together and to be handled as covering the same historical events, albeit with Genesis 2 being narrower in scope with a focus on just part of the sixth day of creation. There is a strong and harmonious interdependency between the chapters which assists our understanding of both; each of Genesis 1 and 2 assists in our understanding of the other.

We have also seen how the rest of scripture handles Genesis 1 and 2 as historical, as describing events that actually took place. This is true of the things recorded in Genesis 1 and 2 at a detailed and specific level not just some generalised reference to God as creator. Thus, these mentions by other scriptures are not general statements about the creation of the heavens and the earth leaving evolutionary science to fill in the details of how God created. The detailed and specific works of God laid out in Genesis 1 and 2 have become part of the fabric of scripture and of God's self-revelation. We have extensive reference to God as the creator of the heavens and the earth, including at a detailed and specific level, presented in the rest of scripture as the basis for believers' confidence in God's covenant promises, in his faithfulness and steadfast love and in his greatness and power.

Often, these extensive references independently assert that God performed the creative works recorded in Genesis 1 and 2, without direct reference to the text of these chapters and certainly not using these texts without any regard to the historicity of the events they describe. Thus, there is multiple testimony in scripture to the detailed creative acts of God laid out in Genesis 1 and 2.[1] In this respect, there are many more than two or three witnesses establishing the truth of the detailed creative acts which are first testified in Genesis (cf. Deut. 19:15; Mt. 18:16; John 8:17; 2 Cor. 13:1).

More specifically, we have witnessed that evolutionary creationist rejection of the historicity of three specific details in Genesis 1 and 2, since they cannot be reconciled with evolution – man's creation in the image of God (Gen. 1:26-31), Adam's formation as a living creature (Gen. 2:7) and the manner of Eve's creation from Adam's rib (Gen. 2:22)[2] – positions evolutionary creationism directly and specifically in

---

[1] See Chapter 2, 'Historical references'.

[2] Denis Alexander, *Creation Or Evolution, do we have to choose?* Monarch Books, Oxford, UK and Grand Rapids, Michigan, USA, 2nd edition, 229-232, 295-297; Peter Enns, *The*

conflict with God's prophets and especially against the Lord Jesus Christ and the apostle Paul.[3]

One of the evolutionary creationists whose claims we have considered, when arguing against young earth creationists' misrepresentation of the earth's age argument on the basis that God is not a deceiver, raises the question: 'if God were such a deceiver, how could we be sure about his great covenant promises?'[4] This is a question which old earth creationists can ignore. But there are two questions which cannot be ignored by evolutionary creationists:

- If Genesis 1 and 2, and the events described within these chapters, are not historical, when so much of scripture reads them as thus and rests upon these historical acts believers' confidence in God's ability to perform that which he has promised, and when God's prophets, including the Lord Jesus Christ, independently asserted creative events happened exactly as recorded in Genesis, how can we be sure about God's great covenant promises and about his ability to accomplish them?

- And if evolutionary creationists are right about God's creative processes which, as has been seen, could have been portrayed in Genesis 1 and 2 without recourse to modern scientific language, then if God were such a deceiver, how can we be sure about his great covenant promises?

In the absence of proving the exegesis laid out in this book to be faulty, a believer in scripture's claims about itself – that it is God's word – is compelled to take Genesis 1 and 2 as authoritative about God's creation as these chapters describe it. This is the case whatever liberal comparative studies, evolutionary science or liberal source criticism might claim. But the evolutionary creationist's principal authority evidently

---

Evolution of Adam: What the Bible Does and Doesn't Say About Human Origins, Brazos Press, 2012, xiv.

[3] See Chapters 2, 5, 7, 8 and 10.

[4] Denis Alexander, *Creation or Evolution*, 251.

and necessarily lies elsewhere, despite claiming to take Genesis 1 and 2 as God's word. Their authority is found in the conclusions of evolutionary science, in interpretations of Genesis 1 and 2 based on liberal comparative analysis with other ANE creation stories, and in liberal source criticism. For the evolutionary creationist, scripture's record of creation is always subject to these other 'authorities' because they have made this methodological choice, a choice driven by prior acceptance of the conclusions of evolutionary science.

Taking scripture as authoritative above all else, Genesis 1 and 2 are presented as two portrayals of the same events, with subsequent scriptural commentary on them handling them as historical. If other scripture handles Genesis 1 and 2 and the events described in these chapters as historical and harmonious, then they must be historical and harmonious. More than this, if Jesus read Genesis 1 and 2 as harmonious and historical, including independently asserting events described in these chapters actually occurred, then this is what the chapters must be because his perfect obedience to his father, in which he spoke only those things that God commanded him, demands that we accept his reading as authoritative from his father.

Taking our lead from the Lord Jesus Christ's reading of Genesis 1 and 2, the approach adopted has witnessed that the rest of scripture agrees with Jesus' reading of these chapters.

Genesis 1 and 2 are harmonious and historical.

But it is hoped that we have witnessed even greater things than this. The approach adopted in the exegesis has yielded insights into the deeper things of God (cf. 1 Cor. 2:10). However, as the apostle Paul taught, in a context where he advertised his approach to teaching through the holy spirit – "comparing spiritual things with spiritual" (1 Cor. 2:13, ESVm) – those who bring the natural mind to the things of God's spirit do not, sadly, accept these things because they cannot discern them.

Addendum: Responding to Criticism

A1: Introduction

Christadelphians Origins Discussion (COD)[1] is a blog[2] which describes itself as dealing with 'Creation and Evolution for Christadelphians'. During the period August 2019 to January 2020, COD published a series of critiques of *Genesis 1-2: A Harmonised and Historical Reading. Replies* to the critiques were posted to the COD site and can be viewed there.

In this Addendum, the *Replies* are gathered as a supplement to the original edition of the book. The material is, for the most part, organised around the relevant chapter of *Genesis 1-2*, and then on major themes within these chapters as critiqued over time by COD. The one exception is the charge of 'literalism' which pervades many of COD's critiques; this criticism is dealt with outside the original chapter structure at the conclusion of this Addendum.

A standout feature of the discussion with COD that emerges when organised this way is how much of the debate was focused on the exposition of Jesus' reading of Genesis 1 and 2.[3] This seems to confirm, if the exposition presented in the book is true, how devastating to the evolutionary creationist case is Jesus' reading of the first two chapters of Genesis. It is submitted that COD's criticism has not demonstrated that the exposition of Jesus' reading is erroneous. Rather, it is proposed that the discussion with COD has served to confirm and underline the accuracy of the original exposition.

---

[1] COD also has a Facebook page with a slightly different name: *Christadelphian – Origins Discussion.*

[2] The blog can be accessed here:
https://christadelphiansoriginsdiscussion.wordpress.com/.

[3] Chapter 2, 'Jesus' Reading'.

Genesis 1-2

The original *Replies* have been slightly edited to correct mistakes and to clarify the arguments presented.

For completeness, it should be mentioned that COD posted further responses to the *Replies*, but since it is judged that these did not present any further argument, no further response was offered. COD's further responses can be viewed on the COD blog.

A2: Jesus' Reading (Chapter 2)

Original Post

The original post published by COD criticised the exposition of Jesus' reading of Genesis 1 and 2 as laid out in Chapter 2 of *Genesis 1-2*.[1] There are three major aspects of the criticism: what Jesus said about marriage; interpretation of scripture; and Adam's prophetic role. The *Replies* to COD are laid out under these headings.

What Jesus said about marriage

Critique 1

COD claim that the analysis of Jesus' statement in Matthew 19:5, as laid out in *Genesis 1-2* reads words and meaning into Matthew's record of what Jesus said which are not there. This claim is made on the basis that Jesus did not say anything which explicitly ties together, (a) the timing of the making of male and female (Gen. 1:27) and (b) the pronouncement about a man leaving his parents and holding fast to his wife (Gen. 2:24). COD point out that Jesus did not say things along the lines of 'also in the beginning', or 'at the same time'.

Reply 1

Matthew's record of what Jesus declared is as follows:

> "he who created them from the beginning made them male and female, and said, 'Therefore a man shall leave his father and his mother and hold fast to his wife'" (Mt. 19:5)

---

[1] The *Original Post* can be accessed here:

https://christadelphiansoriginsdiscussion.wordpress.com/2019/08/20/peter-heavysides-genesis-1-2-a-harmonised-and-historical-reading/.

Genesis 1-2

The phrase, 'he who created them from the beginning' is a nominal expression which is the subject of both the verbs 'he made' and 'he said'.[2] Consequently, the subject of Jesus' statement, "[he] said, 'Therefore a man shall leave his father and his mother and hold fast to his wife'" is 'he who created them from the beginning'. Thus, the nominal expression – which includes within it the time register 'the beginning' – extends across both clauses about making and saying. This ties the timing of both 'making' and 'saying' together and obviates the need for a statement along the lines of 'also in the beginning', or 'at the same time'.

Furthermore, as is demonstrated in detail in *Genesis 1-2*, the force of Jesus' teaching about divorce derives from the chronological precedence of what God did *and said* over the revelation of the law of Deuteronomy 24. The expressions that register this chronological precedence are, "from the beginning" (Mt. 19:4) and "from the beginning of creation" (Mk. 10:6). This feature of the dialectical discourse substantiates the conclusion that Genesis 1:27 and 2:24 coincide chronologically, at 'the beginning'.

Critique 2

COD also state the analysis in Chapter 2 is incorrect because it fails to take account of how composite quotes in the scriptures work. They point to multiple citations found in Mark 1:2 and Acts 13:22 to demonstrate that such quotations work on thematic linkages and not through contemporaneous events being described.

Reply 2

It is essential that we distinguish the manner of Jesus' use of expressions from Genesis 1 and 2 from the way that Mark 1:2 and Acts 13:22 employ the Hebrew scriptures.

---

[2] This is plainly evident in the Greek of Matthew and reasonably easily seen in most English language versions.

The gospel writer used a common 'proof text' introduction of the Hebrew scriptures with the words, "As it is written" (Mk. 1:2). Acts records that the apostle Paul introduced the Hebrew scriptures he employed about David by, "[God] testified and said" (Acts 13:22). No such introductory, 'proof text' expressions are found in either Matthew 19 or Mark 10. In Matthew 19, "Have you not read?" (Mt. 19:4) is not such an expression. Rather, *Genesis 1-2*, Chapter 1, shows that expressions such as these are not introducing a citation, or 'proof text', but challenging the way the Pharisees, chief priests, scribes, elders of the people and the Sadducees mis-read the meaning of scripture. In Matthew 19 it is also evident that "Have you not read?" does not introduce a 'proof text' citation because the expression that immediately follows on from this – "he who created them from the beginning" – cannot be read in Genesis 1 and 2, though this phrase obviously refers to those chapters.

The absence of typical 'proof text' language from Matthew 19 and Mark 10 shows that it is wrong to equate what happens in these chapters with the manner of scripture citation in Mark 1 and Acts 13. See also *Reply 3* below.

Furthermore, in both Matthew 19 and Mark 10, we have a clear chronological marker about the Hebrew scriptures employed by Jesus, but no such language is found in either of Mark 1 or Acts 13. This underlines the case that it is a mistake to equate what happens in these chapters with the manner of scripture citation in Mark 1 and Acts 13.

Critique 3

COD oppose *Genesis 1-2*'s argument that Christ revealed the reason why a man will leave his father and mother and hold fast to his wife is that God made man male and female. COD also object to the conclusion that Jesus added this explanation as a reason additional to that given in Genesis 2 – that God made Eve from Adam. COD explain that this reads into Matthew 19:5 more than is there in its context because Jesus 'simply segues from one proof text to another' to decry divorce, not to add to what Genesis says.

Genesis 1-2

Reply 3

See *Reply 2* in relation to COD's claim about Jesus' use of 'proof texts'. A further point to be added is that *Genesis 1-2*, Chapter 2, shows that Jesus did not rest his argument solely on saying something along the lines of, 'this is what Genesis 1 and 2 tell us.' Rather the gospel writers represented Jesus as independently testifying what we learn in Genesis 1 and 2 – he employed the language of Genesis to do so but the words were his, as the son of God. This is seen particularly clearly in Mark's record:

> "Jesus said... from the beginning of creation he made them male and female..." (Mk. 10:6, NET)

Thus, to speak of Jesus using 'proof texts' misses the significance of our Lord's testimony to the Pharisees. As is shown in *Genesis 1-2*, the gospels present Jesus as another prophetic witness to the historical veracity of what the Genesis writer recorded. And in this role, Jesus revealed that, in addition to the explanation in Genesis 2 that a man should leave his father and mother because Eve was made from Adam, God instituted marriage because he made male and female.

Interpretation of scripture

Critique 4

COD seem to object to a position adopted in *Genesis 1-2* which they characterise as 'science of any kind is not sufficient evidence for any conclusions.' Labelling this a 'typical literalist approach', COD claim that it is an inconsistency since, it is asserted, literalists accept modern biological science regarding the function of the heart and kidneys against the bible's emphatic and incorrect statements about their function.

Reply 4

This criticism misses the point of an argument that runs as a seam throughout *Genesis 1-2*. This argument has several key points:

- Scripture, and its teaching, is an authoritative source which is shared by both creationists and evolutionary creationists – at least nominally (see especially Chapter 1).

- Scripture, as a unique 'semantic milieu', demands that it be interpreted by reference to its own meaning – discovered through intratextual, contextual and intertextual analysis (see especially Chapters 13, 14).

- For a variety of reasons that are explored in *Genesis 1-2*, external domains, such as science and culture, cannot be determinative of scripture's meaning, especially when the external domains generate conclusions which are contrary to scriptural analysis (see especially Chapters 12, 13).

- Since the common ground shared by creationists and evolutionary creationists is the authority of scripture, the only sensible and mutually agreed basis for reaching sound conclusions about God's creative activity is the scriptures themselves (see especially Chapters 1, 15).

- This is the reason *Genesis 1-2* insists that criticism from any who disagree with its exposition of Genesis 1 and 2 must do so solely on the basis of what is presented in the book (see especially Chapters 1, 15).

This is not a position which can accurately be characterised as 'science of any kind is not sufficient evidence for any conclusions.' Rather, this is an argument that the deployment of science for proper interpretation of scripture is not legitimate. It also argues that scripture is a mutually agreed basis for determining what is true, one which is shared by creationists and evolutionary creationists, and it is to scripture alone to which we should therefore turn. It also follows from the foregoing that any evolutionary creationist theory developed which is contrary to the meaning of scripture necessarily must be rejected as false by people who accept the scriptures as authoritative.

Genesis 1-2

Regarding the comments about scripture's portrayal of the function of the heart and kidneys, and the charge of literalism, see *Reply 5*.

<u>Critique 5</u>

COD speak of the bible making 'emphatic and incorrect statements about the function of the heart and kidneys' and of Jesus, echoing the 'Old Testament' pattern, making 'biologically incorrect remarks.'

COD ally these comments to another in which it is averred that 'Jesus freely spoke of demons and is never recorded as correcting this medical and theological misunderstanding for the benefit of his first audience.' COD suggest this is a reason for questioning *Genesis 1-2*'s conclusions about Jesus speaking at a detailed level of the historicity of events recorded in Genesis 1 and 2. Regarding this, COD state, 'Bro Heavyside omits to present a unified framework in which Jesus can make biologically incorrect remarks and yet be historically accurate about another aspect of God's creation.'

<u>Reply 5</u>

These are strange assertions in a context of the use of 'literalist' about *Genesis 1-2* in a pejorative manner (see Chapter A6). The only way COD's assertions could be accurate is by insisting that scripture's and Jesus' remarks about the heart and kidneys are read literally, rather than figuratively. It is evident, contrarily, that scripture employs such terminology figuratively. This is seen no more clearly than when God speaks of his own heart. Here is one example (notably in the verse immediately following the first ever mention of man's heart in which there is a statement about its wickedness of the kind which COD invoke in their critique):[3]

> "And the LORD was sorry that he had made man on the earth, and it grieved him to *his heart*" (Gen. 6:6)

---

[3] "The LORD saw that the wickedness of man was great in the earth, and that every intention of the thoughts of *his heart* was only evil continually" (Gen. 6:5).

Given this plain figurative use, why would anybody insist that when, for example, Jesus spoke of man's heart being the origin of evil, this *necessarily* should be read literally and draw the conclusion that Jesus made 'biologically incorrect remarks'? Jesus was not teaching physiology.

There have been, for many years, interpretations of demons in the apostolic writings which compete with the 'accommodationist' approach adopted by COD. These interpretations demonstrate that the figurative language of demons was being used for apologetic purposes by Jesus, and his apostles and prophets.[4] Such interpretations render this aspect of COD's critique redundant. In any event, in whatever way demons are interpreted, it is unlikely anybody – apart from some of those who would want to deny that Jesus was a healing miracle worker – would question the historical reality of the physical and mental illnesses referred to by the language of demons. Consequently, Jesus speaking about demons is not at all a reason for questioning the historicity of things to which he referred. And so, COD's comments about the absence of a 'unified framework' are irrelevant.

Adam's prophetic role

Critique 6

Mentioning an invitation to test the validity of the book's historical and harmonious reading by demonstrating the interpretation of scripture presented within it to be mistaken (this invitation is in *Genesis 1-2*, Chapter 1), COD object to the claim that Adam was speaking prophetically when the words of Genesis 2:24 – "Therefore a man shall leave his father and his mother and hold fast to his wife, and they shall become one flesh" – were spoken by him. COD counter that the Hebrew for 'Therefore' is 'standard language used in Genesis to explain history, names and customs' and that it introduces the words of the narrator.

---

[4] More recently, for example: Andrew Perry, *Demons, Magic and Medicine*, Willow Publications, Third Edition, 2017; Peter Heavyside, *Demons and Unclean Spirits* (https://tinyurl.com/yb7c2n36).

Genesis 1-2

Apart from listing several scriptural examples which COD offer as evidence for this (Gen. 10:9; 11:9; 16:14; 19:22; 21:31; 25:30; 26:33; 29:34; 30:6; 32:32; 47:22)[5], COD also reference a couple of scholarly works in support.[6]

Reply 6

The first point to note is that the invitation to rebut the conclusions reached in *Genesis 1-2* is focused on the exposition presented for the historical and harmonious reading of Genesis 1 and 2. The interpretation opposed in this COD criticism pertains to introductory comments about Adam's prophetic role, which set the scene for a later examination of competing inspiration frameworks. This is presented in *Genesis 1-2*, Chapter 14, where the case is made for a God-manifestational model of revelation (as opposed to an incarnational model, one which is commonly adopted by evolutionary creationists). Consequently, even if the criticism offered by COD stands, it does not render faulty *Genesis 1-2*'s exposition which sets out to demonstrate the historical and harmonious nature of the first two chapters of Genesis. Nevertheless, COD's critique calls for assessment.

It is certainly the case that the Hebrew expression underlying "Therefore [*'l kn*]" (Gen. 2:24) is employed throughout the Hebrew scriptures, as Brown-Driver-Briggs states, 'where the origin of a name, or custom, or proverb is assigned.' But there are a couple of queries we need to raise to assess COD's assertion that this is its function in Genesis 2:24. First, is 'Therefore' a sufficient criterion *on its own* to determine the presence of what COD says is a comment of the narrator? We will witness some instances of 'Therefore' within Genesis itself where this is not so. Second, are there other features present alongside the use of

---

[5] There is a mistake in COD's list of verses, and, in one instance, the verse number of the MT is used. The list shown here corrects the mistake and employs the verse numbering of English language versions.

[6] Clines, D. J. A. (Ed.). (1993–2011), *The Dictionary of Classical Hebrew* (Vol. 6, p. 330), Sheffield, England: Sheffield Academic Press; Sheffield Phoenix Press, and Brown, F., Driver, S. R., & Briggs, C. A. (1977), *Enhanced Brown-Driver-Briggs Hebrew and English Lexicon* (p. 487) Oxford: Clarendon Press.

'Therefore' in the case of clear instances of a prophetic narrator's comment which contribute to the identification of this function, features which are absent from Genesis 2:24? We will see that there are.

Here are two examples from Genesis in which 'Therefore' does not function to assign 'the origin of a name, or custom, or proverb':

> "Then God said to [Abimelech] in the dream, 'Yes, I know that you have done this in the integrity of your heart, and it was I who kept you from sinning against me. Therefore [*'l kn*] I did not let you touch her'" (Gen. 20:6)

> "Then [Joseph's brothers] said to one another, 'In truth we are guilty concerning our brother, in that we saw the distress of his soul, when he begged us and we did not listen. That is why [*'l kn*] this distress has come upon us'" (Gen. 42:21)

These are clear instances of 'Therefore' on its own in which its function is certainly not a narrative comment; rather, the uses of 'Therefore' are fundamental to the speeches being made by God in the first instance and by Joseph's brothers in the second. Furthermore, the structural similarity of these two cases to the record of Adam's speech in Genesis 2:23-24 is obvious, and this not only negates COD's assertion, rather it argues in the opposite direction.

What about the presence of other features alongside uses of 'Therefore' where its use is clearly about assignment of 'the origin of a name, or custom, or proverb?' We will examine each of the examples listed by COD.

Genesis 10:9 has a fuller expression than "Therefore" alone. It reads, "Therefore *it is said* ...". It is this longer phrase which explains the origin of the saying about Nimrod, *not* 'Therefore' on its own.

Likewise, Genesis 11:9 has the fuller phrase, "Therefore *its name was called* ...". Again, it is this longer expression which provides an explanation for the naming of 'Babel'. Similar analysis applies to the following Genesis examples listed by COD: Genesis 19:22; 21:31; 25:30; 29:34; 30:6.

Both Genesis 16:14 and 26:33 can be analysed in a similar fashion, but they also include further features. Genesis 16:14 has the addition of a geographic comment about Beer-lahai-roi's location, while Genesis 26:33 adds the comment "to this day." In both cases, it is this longer expression which provides an explanation for 'the origin of a name, or custom, or proverb'.

Genesis 32:32 introduces an Israelitish custom, and the presence of "to this day" is employed alongside "Therefore" to make this clear.

In Genesis 47:22, "Therefore" features within a narrative statement about the experience of the Egyptian priests as an explanation of why they did not need to sell their land. It is not obvious why this should read as 'the origin of a name, or custom, or proverb' – it speaks of a unique circumstance.

None of the additional expressions which feature alongside 'Therefore' in the foregoing examples occur in Genesis 2:23-24. Consequently, none of the evidence offered by COD demonstrates that Genesis 2:24 is a narrator's comment. On the other hand, the evidence of Genesis 20:6 and 42:21 favours reading Genesis 2:24 as a continuation of Adam's speech which begins in the preceding verse.

Strengthening the case for this reading are the following points:

- *Genesis 1-2*, and the additional evidence presented above, show that God spoke the words of Genesis 2:24 'in the beginning' and this argues against them being read as a narrator's comment when Genesis was later penned. This is further reinforced by noting that Jesus made it clear that 'Therefore' was part of what God said at that time, it does not introduce a later comment by the narrator.

- *Genesis 1-2*, Chapter 2, in the context of discussing Adam's prophetic role, briefly mentions that Adam's words recorded in

Genesis 2:23 are evidently prophetic (as also confirmed by their use in Ephesians 5:28-30) and this shows that we are to view Adam in a prophetic role in this part of Genesis 2.

Summary

- COD claim that *Genesis 1-2* 'fails to account for the nature of composite quotations.' But it has been shown that COD conflate 'proof texts' with use of language from an earlier source which function as later testimony and confirmation of what has been originally revealed.

- COD say that *Genesis 1-2* 'reads in temporal markers to Jesus words which are not there.' However, the evidence presented in *Genesis 1-2*, and the additional details above about the nominal expression of Matthew 19:5 extending the chronological marker 'the beginning' across both the making of male and female *and* the statement about man leaving his father and mother, demonstrate otherwise.

- There is multiple evidence against the COD assertion that *Genesis 1-2* wrongly 'attributes prophetic ability to Adam' because a 'clear transition to a narrator,' evident from the use of 'Therefore', has been missed. This evidence argues for Genesis 2 introducing Adam in a prophetic role and this includes: the use of Genesis 2:23 in Ephesians 5:28-30; Jesus' testimony; and the distinctive functions of 'Therefore' in Genesis.

- COD classify as speculative the argument in *Genesis 1-2* that Jesus added yet another reason for marital unity to that given in Genesis 2. Contrarily, this criticism misses the evidence presented in *Genesis 1-2*, and above, that Matthew and Mark portray Jesus as an independent witness to what took place in Genesis 1 and 2 – while employing the language of these chapters to do so.

- COD criticise *Genesis 1-2*'s acceptance of Jesus' words as the ultimate standard of historical truth because it neglects 'obvious

189

examples of Jesus using incorrect language.' However, as shown above, this ignores the use of figurative language and Jesus' apologetics against demonology. Not only Jesus' words but the words of all of scripture are the only shared authoritative basis which are determinative of what God did in 'the beginning.'

To repeat a conclusion reached in *Genesis 1-2*, Chapter 2 and to which COD object based on reasoning which has been countered in this section, it is evident from Jesus' use of Genesis 1 and 2 that 'evolutionary creationists find themselves directly and specifically in conflict with Jesus' reading.'

COD answered these *Replies* to their original post with four further posts, and these are dealt with in the remainder of this chapter.

First Follow-up Post

The arguments in the first of the further posts can be summarised under the following topics:[7] the grammar of Matthew 19:4-5; the issue of chronological precedence and priority; the thrust of Jesus' argument in Matthew 19:4-5; and differences between the records in Matthew and Mark.

The further *Replies* to COD are laid out under these headings. But before doing so, it is important to revisit, in summary form, the full argument laid out in *Genesis 1-2*, and which is briefly summarised at the conclusion of *Reply 1*. This is because it is crucial to note that the grammatical issue addressed in this dialogue with COD is not the sole nor even the main argument underlying the claim in *Genesis 1-2* that Genesis 1:26-27 and 2:7,18-24 speak of the same event which took place at 'the beginning'. The grammatical argument has been added as

---

[7] COD's *Post* can be accessed here:

https://christadelphiansoriginsdiscussion.wordpress.com/2020/01/03/does-the-grammar-of-matt-193-5-link-genesis-1-2-responding-to-bro-peter-heavyside/.

a narrowly focused reply to COD's demand for an 'at the same time' statement within Matthew 19:4-5.

Restating the argument

Chapter 2 of *Genesis 1-2* lays out two principal arguments in support of the claim that Genesis 1 and 2 both record events that took place at 'the beginning'.

- First, it is the case that in both Matthew and Mark, Jesus employed the time register 'the beginning' to demonstrate that God's revelation about the creation of male and female *and* about marriage pre-dated the Deuteronomy law and so takes precedence. It is worth teasing out an aspect of this which is embedded within the argument. Jesus reached a conclusion in his dialogue with the Pharisees as follows: "So they are no longer two but one flesh. What therefore God has joined together, let not man separate" (Mt. 19:6; Mk. 10:8-9). It is evident that the crucial feature from Genesis 1 and 2 which Jesus employed to sustain his conclusion is his use of Genesis 2:24 – this is the scripture which describes the two becoming one flesh. For Jesus' conclusion to have cogency, it is necessary that the time register which he employed, 'the beginning', is as applicable to his use of Genesis 2 as it is to Genesis 1. It unequivocally follows from this that the words of Genesis 2:24 were spoken in 'the beginning'.

- Second, there is detailed analysis of the reason given in Genesis 2 and of the reason provided by Jesus, as recorded in Mark, for man leaving his father and mother and holding fast to his wife. This analysis shows that God's making mankind 'male and female' coincides with Adam's statement about Eve being called woman because 'she was taken out of Man'. It follows from this that Genesis 1:26-27 and 2:7,18-24 describe the same creative event.

These are cogent arguments and, if they are to be gainsaid, strong evidence is needed from COD or others to demonstrate that they are faulty.

Genesis 1-2

This is the case even if the grammar of Matthew 19:4-5 does not perform in the way that has been argued – not that this is the case, as is restated and reinforced in detail below.

The grammar of Matthew 19:4-5

<u>Critique 7</u>

COD suggest that *Reply 1* rests dubiously on grammar, claiming that the grammatical analysis is unsubstantiated *and* that the evidence in the Greek is contrary such that there is not a tight nominal tie in the Greek grammar. COD argues this through reference to three Greek scholarly resources while pointing out that *Reply 1* does not provide any references to support the claims about Greek grammar.

<u>Reply 7</u>

COD's argument from the Greek scholarly resources is dealt with below. But it is important to note that grammatical analysis of what Jesus said in Matthew is not complex such that academic references are needed. Analysis of the Greek grammar is a task that could be performed by anybody who has ably studied just an introductory book on the Greek of the apostolic writings, such as J W Wenham's *The Elements of New Testament Greek*. Yet, even English language versions evidence the point, as mentioned in *Reply 1*.

Let us revisit the Greek of Matthew 19:4-5. The Greek text[8] is laid out below, together with the author's translation.[9] This is presented in detail to facilitate further comments about the gospel writer's syntax:

o de apokritheis eipen	ouk anegōte oti	o ktisas ap' archēs
and he answering said	have you not read	the one who created from (the) beginning

arsen kai thēlu	epoiēsen autous	kai eipen	eneka toutou
male and female	he made them	and he said	for this cause

kataleipsei anthrōpos ton patera kai tēn mētera	kai kollēthēsetai tē gunaiki autou
a man shall leave the father and the mother	and he shall be joined to his wife

---

[8] There are textual variants that have *o poiēsas* ('the one who made') in place of *o ktisas* ('the one who created') but the reading adopted here is that which is chosen by *H KAINH DIAΘHKH*, The British and Foreign Bible Society, 2nd Edition, 1958, *The Greek New Testament*, Edited by Kurt Aland, Matthew Black, Carlo M Martini, Bruce M Metzger and Allen Wikgren, United Bible Societies, 2nd Edition, 1968 and by the ESV, NASB and NET. But the difference in these variant readings is immaterial to the argument presented here (or, for that matter, the argument laid out in *Genesis 1-2*). This is because the pericope of Genesis 1 that Jesus had in mind uses terminology for both "to make ['*śh*]" (Gen. 1:26) and "to create [*br'*]" (Gen. 1:27).

For completeness, though the number of manuscripts reading this way are so paltry it is hardly worth mentioning, it should be noted that there are a small number of manuscripts that omit *ap' archēs* ('from (the) beginning') and *autous* ('them'). Of course, *H KAINH DIAΘHKH*, *The Greek New Testament* and the ASV, ESV, KJV, NASB and NET do not adopt this poorly attested reading.

[9] For those that want to check, it can be readily observed that the translation corresponds to major English language versions.

| *kai esontai oi duo eis sarka mian* |
| and the two shall be unto one flesh |

Let us raise some questions about this record:

1. Who is 'he' in the opening clause, 'and *he* answering said'?

2. Who is 'he' in the clause, 'and *he* shall be joined to his wife'?

3. Who are 'the two' in the clause, 'and *the two* shall be unto one flesh'?

It is difficult to imagine any reasonably competent bible reader who could not readily answer as follows:

1. This is the "him" of Matthew 19:3 and it is evident that this is Jesus, named earlier in the record in Matthew 19:1.

2. This is the "man [*anthrōpos*]" referred to earlier in Matthew 19:5.

3. These are the man referred to in point 2 and his "wife [*gunē*]" to whom he is said to be joined in the same verse.

Discerning such references can often be a more complex task than this, such that linguists have developed the discipline of discourse analysis and, in specific relation to this discussion, participant reference analysis. It is with such disciplines in mind that *Reply 1* speaks of 'dialectical discourse'.

Turning now to the pronouns implicit in the verbal forms *epoiēsen* ('he made') and *eipen* ('he said'), to who do these pronouns refer? Again, who could not easily discern that this is the one referred to as, 'the one who created from (the) beginning'? Stating this another way, participant reference analysis informs us that:

- the one about whom Jesus said, "male and female *he made them*" (Mt. 19:4) is 'the one who created from (the) beginning'

- and, as pointed out in *Reply 1*, the one about whom Jesus stated that '*he said*' the things about man leaving his parents and joining his wife is, again, 'the one who created from (the) beginning'

Thus, it is unequivocal that the pronouns of both 'he made' and 'he said' refer to the same one as identified in the nominal expression, 'the one who created from (the) beginning'.[10] And so, as originally stated in *Reply 1*, 'the nominal expression – which includes within it the time register "the beginning" – extends across both clauses about making and saying. This explicitly ties the timing of both "making" and "saying" together and obviates the need for a statement along the lines of "also in the beginning", or "at the same time".'

In fact, now that we are revisiting Matthew 19:4-5, we will take the opportunity for further reinforcement of this grammatical conclusion.

The first thing to mention is the presence of 'the one who created' within the full nominal expression that Jesus used. This reference to God as the creator – tied to the events of Genesis 1 by the statement, 'male and female he made them' – sits alongside the time register and reinforces that the person who said the things about man leaving his parents was *this creator*. This is why, for example, the apostle Paul could use the language of 'creating' about the events of Genesis 2:18-24[11] even though the relevant Hebrew verb is not employed in this pericope. This strengthens our understanding that it was at the same time as Genesis 1:26-27 that the words of Genesis 2:24 were spoken.

---

[10] Note that COD is mistaken in their reading of *Reply 1*, when they comment that it claims, 'the governing pronominal for the whole citation' (sic) is 'the beginning'. *Reply 1* speaks only of the nominal expression being the entire statement, represented above by 'the one who created from (the) beginning'. For the same reason, COD's 'correction' of their misreading by stating, 'The critical expression is not "the beginning" but rather "FROM or AT the beginning"' is, likewise, a mistake.

[11] "Neither was man *created* for woman, but woman for man" (1 Cor. 11:9).

Genesis 1-2

A second reinforcement of the case arises from consideration of the syntax of Matthew 19:4-5. At the intersection of the two verses, we find the Greek syntax is, "he made them and he said". This highlights several features of Matthew's gospel record:

- The nominal expression, 'the one who created from (the) beginning', as seen from the above tabulation of the Greek text, is syntactically separated from both of the verbs, 'making' and 'saying'. This illustrates the need for participant reference analysis for both verbs, not just the verb at the opening of verse 5.

- This syntax closely ties together the acts of 'making' and 'saying' and adds to the force of the chronological element of the nominal expression having a bearing across both acts.

- Finally, this syntax shows that the 'making' clause in Matthew 19:4 and the 'saying' clause in verse 5 are not 'independent', as claimed by COD, since both rely on the same nominal expression earlier in verse 4 for determination of reference.

Critique 8

COD claim that *Cascadia Syntax Graphs*, *Lexham Clausal Outline* and *Lexham Sentence Analysis* evidence that the analysis revisited above is wrong.

Reply 8

This is a case of 'horses for courses'.

Both *Cascadia Syntax Graphs* and *Lexham Sentence Analysis* perform parsing at the sentence level. As valuable as this is for basic grammar, it has nothing to do with the application of grammatical analysis within fuller discourse analysis. *Lexham Sentence Analysis* includes some hierarchical analysis but again with a principal focus on sentences and this per se prevents any fuller discourse analysis.

While *Lexham Clausal Outline* appears to perform some discourse analysis, its main purpose seems to be on identifying what Deppe calls the 'main verb' in a pericope. It does not appear to perform any participant reference analysis, which is the relevant focus for identifying the subject of the 'making' and 'saying' verbs in Matthew 19:4-5.

A final couple of points. It is a well-established fact that the minimum unit of meaning in any language is the sentence. It is also the case that for a variety of reasons, including the issue of participant reference analysis where pronouns and nouns (as opposed to names or proper nouns) are involved, discernment of specific meaning in such sentences often requires multiple sentences to be considered. When these things are contemplated it is obvious that parsing of lexical units within a sentence (per *Cascadia* and *Lexham Sentence Analysis*) is only a part of sentence meaning determination. These considerations also remind us of the need to follow the oft rehearsed maxim of not letting chapter or verse divisions get in the way of understanding scripture's meaning.

Chronological precedence and priority

Critique 9

COD concur that the expression 'from the beginning' is about reinforcing chronological precedence – as stated in *Reply 1*. But COD claim that Jesus was only arguing in the same way as the apostle Paul in Galatians 3:15-18, where Paul reasoned that later revelation cannot annul the earlier scripture but does so without specifying a chronological locus for the earlier revelation. On this basis, COD then proceed to state that Jesus was not making a chronological claim but that the Lord was (only) making a priority claim.

Reply 9

From one perspective, it is clear that Jesus was not making a chronological claim about Genesis 1 and 2; rather, the Lord was arguing the priority of the Genesis law over the teaching in Deuteronomy *on the basis of* an earlier and contemporaneous chronology for the records of creation laid out in Genesis 1 and 2. The chronological locus of Genesis

Genesis 1-2

1 and 2 was a premise in his argument, not a conclusion he set out to prove. See also *Reply 10* below under the heading 'Jesus' argument in Matthew 19:4-5'.

Certainly, there is a structural similarity of primacy between the Lord's argument and the apostle's in Galatians. But to leave the matter at recognising this similarity ignores a fundamental difference in the way each primacy was established. The apostle did so by stating that the covenant which could not be annulled was "previously ratified by God" (Gal. 3:17; cf. v15, "once it has been ratified"). On the other hand, the way the Lord established primacy was to employ a nominal expression – 'he who created them from the beginning' – which, as shown in *Replies 1 and 7*, is the subject of both 'he made' and 'he said'. Furthermore, Christ unequivocally alluded to Genesis 1:1 in his use of 'the beginning' where it is clearly used of a point in time when God performed his creative acts. Thus, Jesus established the primacy of the Genesis law by speaking of the actual chronological locus of God's acts of 'making' and 'speaking' – 'the beginning'. The Lord could have used the same language as the apostle Paul, but he did not.

Jesus' argument in Matthew 19:4-5

Critique 10

COD twice object to the *Replies* to the *Original Post* – and to *Genesis 1-2* before that – on the basis that 'Jesus is not arguing the unity of Genesis 1 & 2' and that Jesus was not commenting on whether these two chapters are the same event.

Reply 10

Nowhere do either *Genesis 1-2* or the original *Replies* claim that Jesus argued the unity of Genesis 1 and 2 or that he was commenting on whether these two chapters speak of the same event. Rather, they present an argument about what Jesus believed regarding the timing of Genesis 1 and 2; it is shown in this argument that what the Lord believed about this timing was adopted as a premise in his dialogue with the Pharisees about the chronological precedence, and therefore primacy, of the Genesis law over that in Deuteronomy.

Structurally, the argument presented in *Genesis 1-2* and the original *Replies* corresponds to the Lord's reasoning from Exodus 3:6 that God is the God of the living and not the dead (Mt. 22:32; Mk. 12:27; Lk. 20:38) – Exodus does not argue that God is the God of the living, but it follows from what is said there that this is true. Likewise, Jesus did not argue that Genesis 1 and 2 speak of the same event at the beginning, but it follows from the structure of the Lord's argument that this is what he believed.

The records in Matthew and Mark

Critique 11

Alongside stating that the original *Replies* show a preference for Matthew rather than 'addressing the significance of the variation between the parallel accounts', COD query whether it is a little dangerous to read significant meaning into Matthew's grammatical construction. COD further urge caution about detailed handling of Matthew's and Mark's records by commenting that the two gospels have a different order in the conversation Jesus had with the Pharisees – this is based on their suggested harmonisation of the two records which shows that Mark mentions Moses' commandment in Deuteronomy 24 at the beginning while Matthew has it at the end – and COD conclude that we do not know whether Jesus introduced Deuteronomy at the beginning or end of the dialogue.[12] Finally, COD comment, 'The point of each record might be in larger details than grammar.'

---

[12] For reasons that are not clearly laid out, COD connects these comments with the view that 'both gospel writers have Jesus quoting the Greek Old Testament.' While this is not the place to address the issue of the role of the LXX in the apostolic writings (assuming this is what is meant by 'Greek Old Testament'), it is important to point out that both Matthew and Mark have syntactical differences with Genesis 2:24 (LXX) and that Matthew also has lexical differences. Such differences introduce a challenge to the view expressed about the Greek Old Testament.

Genesis 1-2

Reply 11

COD's suggested harmonisation of the records in Matthew and Mark can be characterised as 'compressed'. But the fact that this harmonisation yields the dilemma over whether Jesus introduced Deuteronomy at the beginning or end of the dialogue actually argues for a different kind of harmonisation. The proposal here is that the best-fit harmonisation is an expanded dialogue with Jesus mentioning Deuteronomy (and other features) more than once.

However, the greatest concern with COD's handling of the two records lies in an unresolved tension and it is this that is the focus in this *Reply*. On the one hand, COD seem to argue that whatever the grammar of Matthew, the fact that Mark's record differs means we ought not to read too much into the grammar of the first gospel. The effect of such an argument carries two related problems. The first is that it sets aside any differences between the gospels as though they have no purpose. The second is that it pursues a singular message that merges any intentional gospel variances into oblivion. Yet, on the other hand and herein lies the unresolved tension, COD do write of each record having its own point and of there being significance in the variances between gospel records.

Differing and purposeful perspectives between two parallel records is something that *Genesis 1-2* addresses a great deal when examining supposed items of disharmony between Genesis 1 and 2. Likewise, Chapter 2 of the book summarily states, 'There are differences in the way Jesus' teaching is portrayed in Matthew and Mark, peculiar to each gospel's purpose and these differences, when read together, coherently fill out the picture of Jesus' teaching and his discussion with the Pharisees.' It emerges clearly in *Genesis 1-2* that we learn much more about events and God's purpose within them from such differing perspectives. We perform a disservice to scripture if we discard differences between records in an attempt to make the records say the same thing.[13]

---

[13] This was a problem that arose in the early church through misuse of the *Diatessaron*.

And so, it is plainly a mistake to set aside the grammar of Matthew 19:4-5 on the basis that Mark's record differs. For sure, the perspectives in the different gospels are larger than grammar *but* the unique perspectives will not be discovered by ignoring grammar. Furthermore, it is misplaced to interpret the original *Replies* as having a preference for Matthew as though this gospel, on its own, cannot or does not communicate its own unique message. In any case, this is not accurate: the treatment of Matthew 19 on its own runs to one and a half pages in *Genesis 1-2*, while that for Mark 10 runs to two pages. The perspective presented in the original *Replies* focuses on Matthew 19 because it is that viewpoint which was challenged and rejected by COD.

Second Follow-up Post

This post criticised claims about the use of the Hebrew scriptures in the apostolic writings and can be summarised under the following headings:[14] claims about OT use in the apostolic writings; claims about things said in the original *Replies*; and chronology.

The further *Replies* to COD are laid out under these headings.

Claims about OT use in the apostolic writings

Critique 12

COD claim to have demonstrated – through their reference to Mark 1:2 and Acts 13:22 – that 'Old Testament uses are thematic.'

Reply 12

This is an overly bold claim from two perspectives:

---

[14] This *Post* can be accessed here:

https://christadelphiansoriginsdiscussion.wordpress.com/2020/01/07/how-do-ot-citations-work-in-the-nt-responding-to-bro-heavyside/.

Genesis 1-2

a. While it is accurate that COD has asserted that Mark 1:2 and Acts 13:22 are thematic, rather more analysis of the spirit's purpose in these scriptures is needed before it can be affirmed that thematic linkages are the (sole) purpose of these composites. This is not a denial that thematic linkages play a part in composites – they necessarily do since sources are being pulled together to teach something, and this entails that they speak of the same kind of thing. Rather, the observation here is that the analysis which is currently missing could either confirm thematic linkages are the sole or principal purpose, or that they are secondary to some other purpose.[15]

b. Even if thematic linkages were shown to be the primary purpose of apostolic use of the Hebrew scriptures in Mark 1:2 and Acts 13:22, a sample of two is not sufficient, by any stretch of the imagination, to demonstrate this is the way that all such apostolic instances work.

Critique 13

COD add that it has been claimed in the original *Replies* that Matthew 19 and Mark 10 are a different type of citation because they are introduced slightly differently to Mark and Acts.

Reply 13

The way that the Hebrew scriptures are referenced in the four apostolic passages differ:

- In Mark 1:2, it is "As it is written in Isaiah the prophet ...".

---

[15] For an illustration of composite use of the Hebrew scriptures having much larger purpose than thematic linkages, see Peter Heavyside, *The Use of the Hebrew Scriptures in Apostolic Writings* (https://tinyurl.com/yb7c2n36). A shortened version of this article was published under the title, 'Understanding the language and thinking of the Bible: The Hebrew Scriptures in Apostolic Writings', *Testimony*, May-June 2016, 183.

- The apostle Paul's introduction is, "of whom he testified and said ..." (Acts 13:22).

- In Matthew 19, it is more nuanced:

  o "He who created them from the beginning made them male and female" (Mt. 19:4) is formally classified in scholarship as 'allusion', not 'citation' or 'quotation'.[16]

  o "And said, 'Therefore a man shall leave his father and his mother ...'" (Mt. 19:5) is possibly something that would be formally classified as 'citation' but that depends on whether we read, 'and said', as Jesus referencing the scripture in Genesis 2:24 by this expression or whether this expression is part of Jesus' report of what God said at the time of Eve's creation.

- Mark 10 has no candidate expressions that could be interpreted as a way of referencing Genesis 1 and 2 by quotation. "From the beginning of creation ..." and "Therefore a man shall leave ..." (Mk. 10:6-8) have no citation referencing terms. From this perspective, they would formally be classified as 'allusion'.

Reply 2 observes these differences and states that they obviate *equating* what happens in Mark 1:2 and Acts 13:22 with Matthew 19 and Mark 10 – at least without further analysis. Even the two ways of referencing the Hebrew scriptures in Mark 1:2 and Acts 13:22 have different semantic values – 'as it is written' ≠ 'he testified and said' – and so it is even a mistake to equate Mark 1:2 and Acts 13:22 without further analysis. Stated otherwise, given this range of differences between these four scriptures, it is incumbent upon COD to demonstrate that these various modes of reference do not have any contribution to understanding distinct purposes for the 'composite quotations' under scrutiny.

---

[16] See, for example, Richard B Hays, *Echoes of Scripture in the Letters of Paul*, New Haven, CT: Yale University Press, 1989; Graham Allen, *Intertextuality: The New Critical Idiom*, London: Routledge, 2004.

Genesis 1-2

It is now clear on two counts that COD has not presented the analysis necessary to support their claims about the use of the Hebrew scriptures in the apostolic writings. And this is especially noteworthy against a background in which *Genesis 1-2* and the original *Replies* present much more detailed analysis of Matthew 19 and Mark 10 than has COD.

Critique 14

COD claim that Mark 1:2 and Acts 13:22 'use a string of Old Testament quotes which are neither chronological nor tied to the source context' and that this 'demonstrates how Old Testament composite citations work', that they are 'very thematic'.

Reply 14

This is another assertion by COD without supporting, detailed analysis. This is needed, on this third count, because investigation of each source context of the relevant Hebrew scriptures must be undertaken – alongside analysis of the different use of them made by the apostolic prophets – before it can be confidently affirmed that they are not tied to source context. Furthermore, even if Mark 1:2 and Acts 13:22 are not tied to their source context – there are strong reasons to doubt this[17] – this fact would *not* 'demonstrate … composite citations … are "very thematic".' The one does not follow from the other.

The lack of chronological tie between sources in Mark 1:2 and Acts 13:22 is irrelevant as shown in the original *Replies*, and as reinforced by the section 'Chronology' below.

---

[17] For some illustrations of apostolic use being tied to the source context in some way, see: Peter Heavyside, *Hebrews 10v26-27 - A Fury of Fire that will Consume the Adversaries*; *Psalm 19 - A Teacher of the Gentiles*; *Psalm 8 - Perfecting Praise* (https://tinyurl.com/yb7c2n36). A shortened version of *Hebrews 10v26-27* was published in *Testimony*, May-June 2019, 185; *Psalm 19* was published in *The Christadelphian*, 2020; January, 17; February, 66.

Claims about things said in the original *Replies*

Critique 15

Scattered through their reply, COD make a variety of claims about what is said in the original *Replies* regarding the differences between Mark 1:2, Acts 13:22, Matthew 19:4-5 and Mark 10:6-8:

- It is said that a new taxonomy about composite citations has been proposed.

- COD also say the idea is pushed 'that less precisely introduced citations reveal more about the underlying passages than precise citations.'

- They state that it is said that observations about the differences between these four apostolic scriptures means 'we should approach the citations with different expectations.'

- COD add that the original *Replies* indicate that we would 'have us believe we can imply more precision in the OT use with a less precise introduction.'

Reply 15

It is puzzling from which part of the original *Replies* COD have observed these things, because none of them is accurate. In the *Replies*, the sole claim made about these differences is this: 'it is wrong to equate what happens in [Matthew 19 and Mark 10] with the manner of scripture citation in Mark 1 and Acts 13.' It is this same position which is underlined above. Nothing more, nothing less. Nor is there any value judgment made of any kind in the *Replies* about the manner of use of the Hebrew scriptures in these texts.

For the same reasons, it is a mistake to claim that it is said, 'we should approach the citations with different expectations.' Rather, it is only stated, and this is also reiterated above, that the differences call for analysis to determine the significance of the differences.

Genesis 1-2

Chronology

<u>Critique 16</u>

COD criticise the claim in the original *Replies* that Matthew 19 and Mark 10 contain a chronological marker absent from Mark 1 and Acts 13 on the basis that it is not 'perfectly accurate' since Acts 13 talks about a time period. COD also state that this claim ignores the point that 'Jesus saying "from/at the beginning" is not the chronology of Genesis 1 and 2 but that these events proceed [sic] the Mosaic laws on divorce and hence take precedence.'

<u>Reply 16</u>

The only chronological term found in major English language versions of Acts 13:22 is "when" (ASV, ESV, KJV) or "after" (NASB, NET). And, strictly speaking, this does not correspond to any chronological term in the Greek text. Rather, it is inferred as part of the sense of an aorist conditional participle (*metastēsas*, 'having removed'). This cannot in any way be likened to the nominal expression in Matthew 19 which includes the clear chronological term to which the *Replies* referred, 'the one who created from (the) beginning' (AT).

For COD's repetition of the point that Jesus' words do not speak of the chronology of Genesis 1 and 2, see the *Replies* to the first of COD's follow-up posts.

Third Follow-up Post

The arguments presented in the third of COD's further posts can be summarised under the following topics:[18] understanding the heart's function; the interpretation of 'heart' in the original *Replies*; and hermeneutics.

---

[18] COD's third of their *Follow-up Posts* can be accessed here:

https://christadelphiansoriginsdiscussion.wordpress.com/2020/01/14/does-the-bible-use-the-heart-figuratively-responding-to-bro-heavyside/.

Understanding the heart's function

<u>Critique 17</u>

COD maintain that their original criticism that *Genesis 1-2* and the original *Replies* fail 'to present a unified framework in which Jesus can make biologically incorrect remarks and yet be historically accurate about another aspect of God's creation' stands. In support of this, they claim that the figurative use of 'heart' in Genesis 6:6 is still rooted in an incorrect understanding of the heart's function. COD state that this is evidenced by the fact that the sole scope of the figurative use here is anthropomorphism, leaving the 'incorrect understanding of the heart's function' as a feature of this scripture. They add that figurative uses of 'heart', such as found in 2 Samuel 17:10 and Genesis 6:6, 'work because of the physiologically incorrect description of the heart consistently conveyed through inspiration.'

<u>Reply 17</u>

The first thing to note about this is COD's concurrence that scripture does in fact include figurative uses of 'heart' since this was the principal focus of the relevant section in the original *Replies*. Given this acknowledgement, the matter raised in that response is reinforced and must be restated, since, by COD's own agreement, it is they who must address the challenge laid out therein. Why do COD insist that when Jesus spoke of man's heart being the origin of evil, his use of 'heart' should be read literally? This is an insistence which serves COD's purpose, but it is one that is not supported by detailed analysis of Jesus' statement in context (more on this below) – in fact no analysis of any kind was offered by COD, it has just been presumed. Some supporting rationale for their claim is provided in this latest reply and that is dealt with separately below.

Furthermore, whether the figurative language of Genesis 6:6 is limited in its scope to anthropomorphism or not is irrelevant to the original point. In this verse we now have agreement that Genesis 6:6 is an instance of a figurative use of 'heart' and this, per se, shows that we must not just presume other uses of heart are literal, or, preferably for specificity, physiological – not without analysis demonstrating that any particular use is literal or physiological.

With COD's concurrence that Genesis 6:6 is a figurative instance of 'heart' we must reinforce, restate and amplify another point that was drawn from the original observation in the *Replies*. This undoubtedly figurative use is preceded by the first use of 'heart' in scripture:

> "The LORD saw that the wickedness of man was great in the earth, and that every intention of the thoughts of his heart was only evil continually" (Gen. 6:5)

In these verses, scripture produces a clear dissonance – the Lord's heart was not as he would have it because the man whom he had created in his image[19] did not have a heart as it ought to have been. Compare this with the later choice of David as king because "the LORD has sought out a man after his own heart" (1 Sam. 13:14). This correspondence between 'heart' in Genesis 6:5 and that in 6:6, albeit to create dissonance, points to its use in the prior verse also being figurative. And then, given the conceptual likeness between Genesis 6:5 and Jesus' statement about the heart (Mt. 15:18,19; Mk. 7:20-23), the earlier figurative use strongly suggests Christ's use, without detailed analysis showing the contrary, was also figurative and not literal or physiological.

When we turn to a more detailed analysis of Jesus' statements about what comes out of the heart, the context renders it unequivocally clear that we are encountering a figurative use of 'heart'. Mark 7: 20-23 reads:

> "What comes out of a person is what defiles them. For it is from within [*esōthen*], out of a person's heart, that evil thoughts

---

[19] Note the dual mention of 'making' and one of 'creating' (Gen. 6:6,7) which alludes to Genesis 1:26-27.

come – sexual immorality, theft, murder, adultery, greed, malice, deceit, lewdness, envy, slander, arrogance and folly. All these evils come from inside [esōthen] and defile a person"

Esōthen is clearly used in scripture of the inner man, of what a man is really like in his wickedness (Mt. 7:15; 23:25,28; Lk. 11:39) or, through a cognate expression (*esō*), of what we should aspire to be as a new creation (Rom. 7:22; 2 Cor. 4:16; Eph. 3:16). The 'inner man' here is clearly employed of one's character and is figurative. Its correspondence with 'heart' in Mark 7 shows that, likewise, the latter is figurative.

COD's unstated premise that scriptural figures have some physical reality lying behind them is something with which we can concur. In the case of 'heart', is this because it rests on 'the physiologically incorrect description of the heart consistently conveyed through inspiration', or on something else? Scripture often describes emotions and thoughts through employment of the language of physiology or physiological experience. A common one is used of compassion, yearning and tenderness – for example:

- Of God:

    o "The stirring of your inner parts and your compassion" (Isa. 63:15); "the sounding of thy bowels and of thy mercies" (KJV).

- Of the apostle Paul:

    o "I yearn for you all with the affection of Christ Jesus" (Phil 1:8); "I long after you all in the bowels of Jesus Christ" (KJV).

- Of the expectation on all saints:

  o "any affection and sympathy" (Phil. 2:1); "if any bowels and mercies" (KJV).

  o "yet closes his heart against him" (1 John 3:17); "and shutteth up his bowels of compassion from him" (KJV)

It is a rare person who does not recognise the physiological experience in their bodies which accompanies such feelings and thoughts of compassion, yearning and tenderness. Modern psychology, and related disciplines, recognise the reality of these things. Indeed, modern scientific research has gone further than this to the point, for example, of identifying personality changes after heart transplant through attribution of this to cell memory theory.[20] Science evidently does not limit its own understanding of the heart to a physical pump, as suggested by COD.

Clearly also, scripture recognises such things in its use of figurative language about the heart and other organs. And, plainly, there is no need to invoke 'the physiologically incorrect description of the heart consistently conveyed through inspiration' as the physical reality behind scripture's figure – especially when the evidence proffered by COD in support of a physiological reading of Jesus' words is seen to be faulty (on which, see below).

Finally, before turning our attention to COD's representation of the reasoning offered on this topic in the original *Replies*, we will revisit COD's assertion that there has been an omission 'to present a unified framework in which Jesus can make biologically incorrect remarks and yet be historically accurate about another aspect of God's creation.' Even if we were to accept that Jesus made biologically incorrect remarks, why would it follow from this that Christ could not, at the same time, be historically accurate? Jesus' teaching that shows the historicity of the creation record is confirmed in *Genesis 1-2* by detailed analysis

---

[20] See, for example, https://www.medicaldaily.com/can-organ-transplant-change-recipients-personality-cell-memory-theory-affirms-yes-247498 [accessed March 27, 2020].

of other scriptures (cf. Acts 17:11). Since biology and history are two different disciplines, and Christ's historical position on the creation record is confirmed by searching other scriptures, why would supposed erroneous thinking in the biological domain render his teaching on creation as lacking historical integrity? And so, COD's demand for this unified framework is not even a pertinent requirement.

The interpretation of 'heart' in the original *Replies*

Critique 18

COD represent the argument on this topic in the original *Replies* in a couple of ways:

- They claim that the argument laid out is that the single figurative use of 'heart' in Genesis 6:6 means that 'ALL uses are figurative' and observes either that 'claiming "because one therefore all" isn't proof' or that it is 'highly suspect.'

- COD also state 'actually', that 'such physiological misstatements' are classified 'as figurative because of science' and they seem to support this representation by connecting it with the statement that, 'Jesus was not teaching physiology.'

Reply 18

The argument presented in the original *Replies* nowhere employs the (false) logic that a single instance of a figurative use of 'heart' proves that all other uses of this term are likewise figurative. In fact, the expression 'all' does not feature in the relevant reply. It is bewildering whence COD have mined this representation of the argument.

Rather, as originally stated, and as restated above, the figurative use of 'heart' in Genesis 6:6 has been employed to illustrate that it is wrong of COD to presume, without any substantiating analysis, that Jesus' use of 'heart' was 'literal' (or, for a reason already stated, physiological).

To argue that a single instance of a linguistic usage has a particular feature is proof that all other instances have the same feature is not 'highly suspect' it is just plainly false. And it is an irony that it is necessary to point out that COD need to heed their own counsel. As mentioned in *Reply 12*, 'Even if thematic linkages were shown to be the primary purpose of apostolic use of the Hebrew scriptures in Mark 1:2 and Acts 13:22, a sample of two is not sufficient, by any stretch of the imagination, to demonstrate this is the way that all such apostolic instances work.'

The argument that is laid out in the original *Replies*, and as summarised above twice, is this: when it is shown clearly that scripture employs 'heart' figuratively in, for example, Genesis 6:6, it is wrong for COD to default to a literal reading of 'heart' in order to declare scripture and Jesus as displaying an incorrect understanding of the heart's function without the required analysis to show scripture and Jesus employed 'heart' in the relevant contexts literally. This has nothing to do with arguing this 'because of science.' Furthermore, the comment in the original *Replies* about Jesus not teaching physiology occurs in its context, as follows:

> 'Given this plain figurative use, why would anybody insist that when, for example, Jesus spoke of man's heart being the origin of evil, this should be read literally and draw the conclusion that Jesus made "biologically incorrect remarks"? Jesus was not teaching physiology'

It is clear from this that the mention of Jesus not teaching physiology was set in opposition to COD's insistence on reading Jesus' use of 'heart' literally. Rather, it is evident from the context that this observation relates to the fact that Christ was teaching something about personal morality, not physiology, and that this, of itself, contributes to a figurative reading of his use of 'heart' (see more on this above).

Hermeneutics

<u>Critique 19</u>

As noted above, COD do, this time, proffer some support for a literal or physiological reading of Jesus' words. This is expressed in terms of needing to read scripture in the context of 'the known common beliefs of the times.' In this context, COD mention that 'The Bible was not unique in using the heart as a place of thought', advancing in support of this that Egyptians portrayed 'the same idea in the Book of the Dead' and the fact that in 'their complicated burial processes the heart was treated carefully whereas the brain was perceived as worthless.' They also mention the fact that 'Aristotle (4th century BC) thought the brain was just a cooling device for the heart where all the real action was.'

Also relevant to this theme is that COD claim the original *Replies* argue that all should believe that 'the Jews knew better and [that] Scripture was using the heart figuratively only.' And COD add that clear figurative uses of 'heart' in scripture 'does not prove the audience (or inspired writers) knew the heart was a pump.'

<u>Reply 19</u>

In support of their insistence that Jesus and scripture employed 'heart' literally, and that this evidences that they incorrectly described the heart's function, COD arraign support from within the discipline of liberal comparative studies. Yet *Genesis 1-2*, Chapters 13 and 14 lay out fundamental reasons why comparative analysis of any kind – conservative or liberal – needs to take a distant second place to contextual, intratextual and intertextual handling of scripture. In the absence of demonstrating the argument laid out in those chapters to be faulty, COD's liberal comparative evidence carries no weight.

In any case, COD's evidence suffers from anachronism in relation to, at least, Jesus' time, and from unsubstantiated presumptions about cross-cultural commonality. Furthermore, the only data COD have arraigned in support Jewish incorrect beliefs about the function of the heart is the data under dispute and this, consequently, cannot be treated as testimony which is independent of this data.

From the point of view that God is the author of scripture, it is irrelevant what the Jews believed. And so, it is not the case that it has been argued that 'the Jews knew better'. Rather, it has been argued that we should believe that God knows better, and we need to follow God's lead – through contextual, intratextual and intertextual analysis – in order to understand, in any particular context, whether 'heart' is used figuratively or physiologically. It is also irrelevant what the Jews believed since, even if they did not know that the heart is a pump (which is likely, but not proven), that would not prevent them from discerning, from a literary point of view, distinctions between figurative and physiological uses by God.

Fourth Follow-up Post

This post can be summarised under the following topics: a claim that the context has not been respected in *Reply 6*; and rejection of the evidence laid out in that *Reply*.[21] As before, replies to this fourth post are laid out under these headings. But before proceeding with that, it is important to make some preliminary remarks about the discussion over Adam's role.

Preliminary remarks

The principal focus of *Genesis 1-2* is confirmation and defence of the historical integrity of scripture generally, and of Genesis 1 and 2 more particularly. In such an overarching context, the question of whether Adam was the prophetic speaker of the words in Genesis 2:24 is peripheral to this central purpose, since the argument for it in the book was laid out as a preliminary to a later presentation of a 'God-manifestational model' of inspiration, though it is not essential to the model. And, as stated in *Reply 6*, 'even if the criticism offered by COD [about

---

[21] COD's fourth of their *Further Posts* can be accessed here:

https://christadelphiansoriginsdiscussion.wordpress.com/2020/01/21/gen-224-who-is-speaking/.

Genesis 2:24] stands, it does not render faulty *Genesis 1-2*'s exposition which sets out to demonstrate the historical and harmonious nature of the first two chapters of Genesis.' From this perspective, whether to continue this specific discussion has been a matter of debate for the writer, desiring that this should not distract us from the principal purpose of *Genesis 1-2*: the interpretation of Genesis 2:24 is a distant second to the principal objective of promoting right understanding of scripture and of its proper handling.

Furthermore, as COD commented in their latest reply, 'We ultimately agree on the essential issue – v24 is God's opinion (whoever vocalised it).' While it is evident that we disagree on the significance and consequence of Genesis 2:24 being God's word, it is a matter of gladness that we can agree, at least nominally, on this point.[22]

Consequently, the following is only an abbreviated response to COD's reply. And, irrespective of whether COD proffers further critique, or not, this will be the final response on whether Adam was the prophetic speaker of Genesis 2:24.

The context of Genesis 2:24

Critique 20

COD assert about this: 'His counter arguments aren't contextual. In Gen 2:23 Adam is clearly speaking. Gen 2:25 it is clearly God/narrator. Bro Heavyside is claiming v24 is still Adam under inspiration as a prophet. He has the burden of proof yet doesn't attempt to prove his claim, let alone the contrary pointers.'

Reply 20

COD's assertion that the counter arguments are not contextual seems to be a reference to his comment that Adam spoke the words of Genesis 2:23 while God, through his narrator, recorded the words of 2:25. We can agree that there is a transition that takes place somewhere between

---

[22] Cf. *Genesis 1-2*, 9.

v23 and v25, the question is where that boundary lies. COD's claim is that the boundary is at the end of v23, whereas the claim underlying *Reply 6* is that it is at the end of v24. Despite COD's judgment, no one is ignoring context, the context is just being read differently.

The burden of proof that COD seeks was laid out in *Reply 6* with two principal strands:

- The evidence for reading Adam's prophetic role in Genesis 2:24, and that the transition boundary is at the end of v24, has two elements:

  o Intratextual analysis of other uses of 'therefore' which correspond in reported speech to the syntax of Genesis 2:23,24 and which point to the words of v24 being those of the speaker in v23.

  o Intertextual analysis of vv23,24 with the apostolic writings which show that Adam fulfilled a prophetic role in his words at the end of Genesis 2 (more on this below).

- COD's 'contrary pointers' – the evidence for reading 'Therefore' as a narrator's interjection, and that the transition boundary is at the end of v23 – are analysed linguistically and shown to differ in multiple ways from the language and syntax of Genesis 2:23-24.

COD might disagree with this analysis – and they offer reasons why in their reply to which a brief reply is made below – but to characterise this as not attempting to prove the claim about Adam's prophetic role is just plainly wrong.

Furthermore, we can add to the foregoing elements a further contextual point. Both Genesis 2:23 and 24 share, as a principal focus, teaching about the unity of marriage – and this includes some relevant and shared language specific to this unity ("flesh of my flesh" and "one flesh"). Genesis 2:25 has nothing to say about marriage, other than the reference to Adam and Eve through employment of "man" and "his wife"; rather, the principal focus of v25 is the comment about their lack of shame despite their nakedness – a matter which is evidently mentioned at this point to set the scene for Adam and Eve's realisation of their nakedness as a consequence of sin entering the world (Gen. 3:7,10,11). Thus, Genesis 2:25 looks forward in the narrative to Genesis 3 whereas Genesis 2:24 looks back to the previous verse. It follows from these observations that, contextually, there is a stronger argument for Genesis 2:24 being connected with v23 with the transition boundary being read at the end of v24, rather than the boundary being where COD has argued.

COD's reasons for rejecting the evidence offered

Critique 21

There are two elements to COD's rationale in rejecting the evidence laid out in *Reply 6*:

- COD identify that the two examples of 'Therefore' with corresponding syntax to Genesis 2:23-24, which were presented in *Reply 6*, are different to Genesis 2 because 'the conclusions are clearly local ones, conclusions relevant only to the specific parties.' On the other hand, COD identify that the list of instances of 'Therefore' offered in their original critique each contains a conclusion that is 'enduring' in significance. Noting that the words of Genesis 2:24 are clearly of enduring significance, COD then claim that the distinction they have identified demonstrates Genesis 2:24 should, like their original list, be read as a narrator's interjection.

- Against the linguistic and syntactical analysis of *Reply 6* which distinguishes Genesis 2:23-24 from COD's original list of instances of 'Therefore', COD assert this analysis is incorrect because, one of the distinctive pieces of language identified (*'It is called'*) 'stands in the same place as *"a man leaves his father and his mother"*.'

Genesis 1-2

Reply 21

The problem with the first element is that it examines only what COD terms the 'conclusion'. When we examine the two components which COD identify as the 'event' and the 'conclusion', a different picture emerges:

- In Genesis 20:6 and 42:21 – the two instances of speech acts that correspond syntactically with Genesis 2:23-24 – we have a *local* 'event' and a *local* 'conclusion.'

- The three examples drawn from COD's original list (Gen. 10:9; 11:8-9; 19:22) comprise a *local* 'event' and an *enduring* 'conclusion'.

- Genesis 2:23-24 corresponds syntactically with the first two instances but differs from both in terms of its 'event' and 'conclusion'. However, it corresponds to the first two instances in that both the 'event' and 'conclusion' share the same time perspective. We agree that the 'conclusion' in Genesis 2:24 is *enduring*. What of the 'event'? The words of Genesis 2:23 clearly have an *enduring* perspective. There are several ways in which this could be shown, but the briefest and most direct is a reminder of the prophetic significance of these words as evidenced in Ephesians 5:28-30.

- Thus, Genesis 2:23-24's enduring-enduring corresponds more closely to Genesis 20:6 and 42:21's local-local than to Genesis 10:9; 11:8-9; 19:22's local-enduring time perspectives.

Turning our attention to the second element, the first thing to mention is the query that was raised in *Reply 6*:

'is "Therefore" a sufficient criterion on its own to determine the presence of what COD say is a comment of the narrator? We will witness some instances of "Therefore" within Genesis itself where this is not so. Second, are there other features present alongside the use of "Therefore" in the case of clear instances of a prophetic narrator's comment that contribute to the identification of this function, features that are absent from Genesis 2:24?'

The linguistic and syntactical analysis presented in *Reply 6* demonstrates that there is much more language involved than just 'Therefore' when a narrator's interjection occurs. COD has not demonstrated that 'Therefore' is sufficient on its own to fulfil this identifying condition. And they cannot point to the absence of this other language in Genesis 2:23-24 in support of such a claim since this is the passage under dispute.

COD's claim that 'it is called' stands in the same place as 'a man leaves his father and his mother' is bewildering. There is absolutely no obvious functional correspondence between these expressions. Grammatically speaking, 'it is called' is a kind of demonstrative phrase, whereas 'a man leaves his father and his mother' is an active statement. A lot more analysis is needed by COD to substantiate such a claim.

Finally

It is worth repeating something from *Reply 6* in support of reading Genesis 2:24 as the words of Adam, speaking as God's prophet. These points do not appear to have been addressed in COD's reply:

'Strengthening the case for this reading are the following points:

- *Genesis 1-2*, and the additional evidence presented above, shows that God spoke the words of Genesis 2:24 "in the beginning" and this argues against them being read as a narrator's comment when Genesis was later penned. This is further reinforced by noting that Jesus made it clear that "Therefore" was part of what God said at that time, it does not introduce a later comment by the narrator.

- *Genesis 1-2*, Chapter 2, in the context of discussing Adam's prophetic role, briefly mentions that Adam's words recorded in Genesis 2:23 are evidently prophetic (as also confirmed by their use in Ephesians 5:28-30) and this shows that we are to view Adam in a prophetic role in this part of Genesis 2.'

A3: How Long Did It Take God? (Chapter 3)

The second post published by COD criticised the exposition of Genesis 2:4 as laid out in Chapter 3 of *Genesis 1-2*.[1]

There are five major aspects of their criticism: the interpretation of 'these are the generations'; the chiastic structure of Genesis 2:4; ambiguity or vagueness in Genesis 2:4; claims about missteps; and Peter Enns and evolutionary creationists. The *Replies* to COD are laid out under these headings.

The interpretation of 'these are the generations'

Critique 1

COD claim, multiple times, that the review of Genesis 2:4 in *Genesis 1-2* 'conveniently misses a fundamental clue' in this verse which 'points to Gen 2:4 onwards not being the same event as Gen 1.' Mentioning that they have previously explored this matter in more detail, COD affirm that, "These are the generations" (Gen. 2:4) – as in all eleven other instances of the expression in Genesis – speaks of 'a new generation… a new incident, a new story, not additional explanation of the proceeding (sic) story.'

Reply 1

While COD have not specified the piece in which they explored this in more detail, presumably this is a reference to 'Textual evidence distinguishing Genesis 1 & 2'.[2] In this piece, COD extensively quote from

---

[1] The *Second Post* can be accessed here:

https://christadelphiansoriginsdiscussion.wordpress.com/2019/08/27/gen-24-and-bro-heavyside-mind-the-gap/.

[2] Accessible on the COD blog here:

https://christadelphiansoriginsdiscussion.wordpress.com/2017/06/13/textual-evidence-distinguishing-genesis-1-2/.

the NET notes on the phrase under scrutiny and from John H Walton's *The Lost World of Adam and Eve: Genesis 2–3 and the Human Origins Debate*.[3] Apart from prefacing these citations with a comment about the contrasts between Genesis 1 and 2 providing sufficient evidence for Genesis 2:4 onwards being understood as a different record to Genesis 1, COD do not provide any additional analysis of 'These are the generations ...' of their own.

One of John Walton's comments is to point out a difference between Genesis 2:4 and the other instances of "These are the generations" in Genesis. He comments, 'Genesis 2 does not follow the pattern of the recursive examples that follow a genealogy of the unfavored line before returning to the story of the favored line.' The reason for highlighting this is that it forms a suitable introduction for pinpointing the way Genesis 2:4 is distinctively and heavily recapitulative of language from Genesis 1. This evidence is laid out in *Genesis 1-2* in detail. In summary:

> The pairing of 'creation' and 'making' in Genesis 2:4 harks back to the same pair in Genesis 1:26-27.

> The expression "the heavens and the earth" and its chiastic parallel, "the earth and the heavens" (Gen. 2:4), plainly draws on, and repeats, the inclusio found in Genesis 1:1 and 2:1, "the heavens and the earth."

As mentioned in *Genesis 1-2*, this is not trivial language in Genesis 2:4, it is fundamental to its teaching.

It follows from this that Genesis 2:4 differs from the succeeding instances of the expression, 'These are the generations ...', and that, unlike these subsequent Genesis uses, it is heavily recapitulative of the language of the preceding narrative. As argued in *Genesis 1-2*, these distinctive features tie Genesis 2:4ff to Genesis 1, and specifically, the

---

[3] COD also mentions that 'the AMG Word Study Dictionary and TWOT' both support the NET note.

narrative introduced at this verse expands on the creation of man on the sixth day.

COD acknowledge these recapitulative details, labelling them as 'deep ties', but nevertheless conclude that Genesis 2:4 itself demonstrates this is the start of a new event. COD say of these 'deep ties' that they are 'hardly surprising' but does not attempt any explanation of why the ties ought to be there or what their function should be – if this is not as argued in *Genesis 1-2*.

It is one thing to notice the similarity of "These are the generations" (Gen. 2:4) with the remaining uses in Genesis – as acknowledged in the NET notes, in John Walton's book and in *Genesis 1-2* – it is quite another to account for the strong differences displayed in Genesis 2:4. *Genesis 1-2* accounts for the similarities (in a way that is appreciated by COD) *and* for the differences. The NET notes and John Walton account only for the similarities.

There are other features of the NET notes and John Walton's comments that could be critically unpicked (for example, NET's claim that the concept of the expression we are considering is, 'This is what became of ...'; or John Walton's notion of precedence) but this is a response to COD's critique, not an analysis of either of these two sources.

The chiastic structure of Genesis 2:4

Critique 2

COD comment on conclusions about the generational relationship of God to his creation, which is drawn from analysis of the chiastic structure of Genesis 2:4, with, 'Amen. Excellently put.' But follows on immediately that 'this doesn't prove the two chapters are at the same time/same thing.' In the context of COD stating that Peter Enns' point based on 'in the day' is 'unquestionably weak', they also say that *Genesis 1-2* does not demonstrate that Genesis 2:4 'ties the two accounts together as one historical event.'

Genesis 1-2

<u>Reply 2</u>

It is important to review the purpose of Chapter 3 of *Genesis 1-2* and to set this in its literary context.

First, as argued in Chapter 2, Jesus' use of Genesis 1 and 2 in Matthew 19 and Mark 10 confirms to us unequivocally that Genesis 2 deals with the creation of man which is first introduced in Genesis 1.[4] Second, Chapter 3 demonstrates, against evolutionary creationist arguments, that Genesis 2:4 *does not* illustrate that this chapter is disharmonious with Genesis 1 (and therefore unhistorical).

From this perspective, Chapter 3 does not set out to prove what COD claim it fails to accomplish. Nevertheless, as restated above, Chapter 3 does show how Genesis 2:4 picks up multiple language from Genesis 1 – both about the creation of man and about 'the heavens and the earth' – and does so in order to underline that this verse begins another account, from a different perspective, of man's creation on the sixth day. This point builds on the conclusion already reached from examination of Jesus' handling of Genesis 1 and 2 in Chapter 2.

Ambiguity or vagueness in Genesis 2:4

<u>Critique 3</u>

COD assert, without any supporting analysis, that Genesis 2:4 does not indicate much about time nor indicate how the rest of Genesis 2 relates (if at all) to Genesis 1. But, seemingly related to this assertion, while suggesting that *Genesis 1-2* demonstrates that the expression 'in the day' is ambiguous, they state that the book mistakenly provides a 'very concrete meaning asserting it means completion on day 6 of the work started on day 1.' Expanding on this, COD approvingly note *Genesis 1-2*'s dismissal of Peter Enns' reasoning that 'in the day' is contrary to the multiple days of Genesis 1. But then COD aver that *Genesis 1-2* falls into the same error as Peter Enns by interpreting 'in the day' with

---

[4] As also reinforced in Chapter A2.

concrete chronological meaning, and they say such an interpretation reflects prior convictions.

Reply 3

Against COD's suggestion about *Genesis 1-2* that it demonstrates 'in the day' is ambiguous, the book provides evidence of two things:

- First, that the expression does not carry either of the two meanings suggested by evolutionary creationists such as Peter Enns.

- Second, that the expression which should be analysed is not, 'in the day' but 'in [the] day of making'. And then, intertextual analysis of this fuller expression – not 'prior convictions' – shows that it definitively has a concrete meaning of a day in which making was completed.

Neither of these conclusions comes anywhere near demonstrating that this expression is either ambiguous or vague.

This analysis also forms the basis for seeing how Genesis 2:4 indicates a great deal about time and about its relationship with the remainder of Genesis 2. First, *Genesis 1-2* reflects on how 'in [the] day of making' injects a point-in-time perspective into the narrative and that this demonstrates a chronological interest. Second, Chapter 3 shows that the sense in the language of Genesis 2:4 of something being completed calls for an explanation of what that completion was: *Genesis 1-2* references Genesis 2:5,20 to identify those things which were awaited for the completion to be accomplished.

The major recapitulation of language in Genesis 2:4 from Genesis 1 (see above, *Reply 1*) likewise demonstrates that the second chapter of Genesis has a great deal to do with aspects of Genesis 1.

Apart from noting these 'unsurprising deep ties', COD do not address this evidence laid out in *Genesis 1-2* with any attempt to show it is faulty.

Genesis 1-2

Claims about missteps

Critique 4

Classifying some uses of 'proof texts' in *Genesis 1-2* as 'missteps', COD state these are 'pitfalls literalists are prone to.' They also suggest that the misused 'proof texts' contrarily prove 'the point made by Evolutionary Creationists that Scripture uses "creation" spiritually at times.'

Reply 4

The two scriptures to which COD refer are Malachi 2:10 and James 1:17-18.

Regarding the first, *Genesis 1-2* does not, contrary to COD's reading, claim that Malachi 2:10 demonstrates we are all descended from Adam. Rather, both Malachi and James are employed to demonstrate that scripture speaks of the 'relationship of the Lord's fatherhood to his creative works.' There is, in fact, reinforcement that this is the purpose of this section of Chapter 3 by the preceding reference to Deuteronomy 32:6 to demonstrate the 'association of fatherhood towards that which has been made' and says of this scripture that it is 'about another creation.' This prior illustration indicates unequivocally that, in this section of Chapter 3, *Genesis 1-2* has turned our attention to God's creative acts in domains other than the one portrayed in Genesis 1 and 2. Rather than the use of Malachi 2:10 demonstrating that *Genesis 1-2* displays the pitfalls to which 'literalists' are prone, it appears that the shoe is on the other foot.

COD's claim that James 1:17-18 proves the point made by Evolutionary Creationists is a false categorisation. Scripture does indeed speak of multiple creative events performed by God and *all of them*, since God is the creator and he is "spirit" (John 4:24), are 'spiritual', including the one recorded in Genesis 1 and 2. Furthermore, recognition of multiple creations by God is not the preserve of Evolutionary Creationists, as sugggested in COD's critique; multiple creative events performed by God are referred to in Chapters 3, 7, 8 and 10 of *Genesis 1-2*.

Peter Enns and evolutionary creationists

Critique 5

COD characterise *Genesis 1-2* as predominantly endeavouring to counter a book by Peter Enns, adding that they are not in accord with this writer.

Reply 5

This is a mischaracterisation. As stated in *Genesis 1-2*, Peter Enns' writings, across multiple documents, are taken as typical of arguments laid out by Evolutionary Creationists. That Peter Enns' arguments are representative of many Evolutionary Creationists is demonstrated by reference to other writers of this ilk throughout the book – including to a more conservative writer, Denis Alexander.

While it is good to hear that COD are not in accord with Peter Enns, we cannot ignore the fact that they share many of the traits exhibited by Peter Enns in his handling of scripture – and it is the proper handling of scripture that lies at the heart of *Genesis 1-2*'s purpose. Furthermore, it is evident that COD do share with Peter Enns some of his arguments about differences between Genesis 1 and 2 as evidence that they are two distinct stories.[5] And regarding these differences, COD aver in another place that they 'ought to be enough' as 'evidence for Genesis 2v4 onwards being a different record to Gen 1'[6] – something which Peter Enns, himself, argues. Regarding these matters, at least, COD are in accord with Peter Enns.

---

[5] See https://christadelphiansoriginsdiscussion.wordpress.com/2017/06/13/genesis-1-is-not-the-same-as-genesis-2/.

[6] See https://christadelphiansoriginsdiscussion.wordpress.com/2017/06/13/textual-evidence-distinguishing-genesis-1-2/.

A4: Different Depictions of the Beginning? (Chapter 4)

The third post published by COD criticised the way *Genesis 1-2*, Chapter 4 addresses what are claimed by evolutionary creationists to be significantly different depictions of the beginning in Genesis 1 and 2.[1]

COD's criticism is focused principally on what they claim is the inconsistent approach of literalists. While the charge of literalism against *Genesis 1-2* pervades most of COD's critiques, and is dealt with in aggregate in Chapter A6, COD identify *Genesis 1-2*'s use of Psalms 104 and 147 in Chapter 4 for specific criticism. It is this which is addressed in the current chapter.

Psalms 104 and 147

Critique

COD criticise the references to Psalms 104 and 147 in *Genesis 1-2* – and then focus on reasons for doing so by reference to the first of these. Rhetorically asking if God makes grass grow today (cf. Ps. 104:14), the basis of COD's criticism is that 'literalists', for consistency's sake, 'should decry any "theistic grass grower" who claims that grass grows by natural processes established by God.' In addition, arguing that Psalm 104 provides insight into how scripture talks about creation, COD assert that this psalm talks about creation in terms that 'we would [not] recognise as literal' – whereas, they say, that is how the first audience thought. Finally, referencing Psalm 104:30, and stating that 'ongoing natural processes are spoken of as direct Divine action,' COD

---

[1] The *Third Post* can be accessed here:

https://christadelphiansoriginsdiscussion.wordpress.com/2019/09/03/bro-heavyside-demonstrating-the-inconsistent-approach-of-literalists/.

conclude that, 'You can't reject God using evolution if you reject the literal meaning' of this verse.

Reply

Before examining some of the things stated by COD about these two psalms and the conclusions which they draw from these things, we will reflect on whether any rebuttal of *Genesis 1-2* has been accomplished by this post.

The thrust of the argument in the book where reference is made to Psalms 104 and 147[2] is that in these two psalms, both of which speak of God's creation, the language of Genesis 2:5 (the verb 'to spring up [*ṣmḥ*]') is specifically employed and this demonstrates these two later scriptures handle Genesis 2:5 as historical. *Genesis 1-2* adds that the historicity of Genesis 2:5 is further underlined by two other principal features of the psalms: (a) both psalms call for praise and thanksgiving to God because of his creative acts – an empty call if these acts are not historically true; and (b) Psalm 147 comprises several other descriptions of God's acts throughout history showing that what this psalm does, in referring to Genesis 2:5, is to place this verse on historical parity with these other acts.[3] This argument is laid out in a section headed 'Historicity', a heading which sets the argument in this section against the claim of evolutionary creationists that Genesis 2:5 is not historical, something they do on the basis of their analysis that it is disharmonious with Genesis 1 (the harmony of Genesis 2:5 with the previous chapter is dealt with earlier in the same Chapter of the book). The question is, does COD's post about this part of the book invalidate the argument? Unequivocally, the answer is no because they have again been distracted by a misplaced focus on labelling the book as 'literalist'.

The only comments made in the book about the meanings of Psalms 104 and 147 are that they 'speak of the ongoing sustenance of creation

---

[2] *Genesis 1-2*, 43-46.

[3] *Genesis 1-2* adds further evidence for Genesis 2:5's historicity from a couple of other features in Psalms 104 and 147 but these do not need to be included within this particular discussion.

by God and declare the continuation of that which he commenced in Genesis 2:5' (a sentence quoted by COD). *Genesis 1-2* does not attempt a detailed exposition of these psalms nor any analysis of whether they use figurative or literal language. Consequently, COD's focus on the second of these categories means they end up wrestling with a 'straw man' – COD's demand for consistency of treatment of these psalms by literalists entirely misses their target.

While this is not the place to engage in a detailed exposition of either of these psalms, it is important that a few comments are made which illustrate the vacuity of COD's 'straw man' argument:

- *Genesis 1-2* speaks of the psalms dealing with God's ongoing sustenance of creation based on the statements of a couple of verses in Psalm 104 (one of these verses is cited by COD). Psalm 104:29-30 reads:

    "When you hide your face, they are dismayed; when you take away their breath, they die and return to the dust. When you send forth your Spirit, they are created, and you renew the face of the ground"

    A plain aspect of these verses is their teaching that the natural world is sustained by God; without such sustenance it would perish. As stated in the book, the use of language from Genesis 2:5 in Psalm 104 reinforces this meaning by indicating that God's sustenance is a continuation of that which he commenced in Genesis 1 and 2. These things are uncontroversial. And therefore, given this is the only comment about the meaning of Psalms 104 and 147 in *Genesis 1-2*, it is evident how much of COD's post wrestles with a 'straw man'.

- Nevertheless, there are several features of Psalms 104 and 147 which should be noted, and which adversely bear upon some of COD's comments and presumptions:

    o There is a great deal of figurative language employed in Psalm 104 (v1b-4, 5-9,19) and in Psalm 147 (v15-18).

o There are indications in Psalm 104 of God setting things in motion in his creative acts of Genesis 1 and 2 and of the 'natural outcomes' of this initiation being ascribed to God's creative work. For example:

> "He made the moon to mark the seasons; the sun knows its time for setting. You make darkness, and it is night" (Ps. 104:19-20)

> The opening sentence is a specific allusion to Genesis 1:14-15 (and yet another clear reference to Genesis 1 and 2's historicity – as argued in the book). The sentences that follow, especially the figurative expression about the sun 'knowing its time', evidently speak of the ongoing outcome of that which God set in motion in Genesis 1 and 2.

• Another feature of both Psalms 104 and 147 is the way they speak of God performing certain works, while it is clear that these works were performed through agents. For example:

o human agents were involved in building Jerusalem (Ps. 147:2)

o prophets were involved in God's word being declared to Jacob (Ps. 147:19)

o God's spirit sent forth to effect creative works (Ps. 104:30) is associated with the work of his majestic agents – the angels who are described as "spirits" (Ps. 104:4, KJV; cf. Heb. 1:14 where "ministering spirits" alludes to Ps. 104:4 and where "sent out" alludes to Ps. 104:30, thus connecting these two verses of Psalm 104)

The relevance of this picture of agency is that in at least one instance, Psalm 104 speaks of those things which God created performing the work of God's caring sustenance. It is the gushing springs that are said to give drink to all the beasts (Ps.

104:11); it is evident in this case that the things God set in motion when he made "springs gush forth in the valleys" (Ps. 104:10) continue to act as his agents in his creative work (cf. the manner in which the effects of the moon and the sun are spoken of as God making darkness and night, Ps. 104:19-20).

The collective effect of these points are several. First, Psalm 104 *does not* demand that those whom COD categorises as 'literalists' ought to decry others who recognise that natural processes set in motion by God are included in the underlying meaning of this psalm. Second, it is obvious that since both Psalms 104 and 147 contain significant amounts of figurative language, anyone who insists on a 'literal' reading will fail to discern their true meaning. Third, the first audience would have been able to discern any of the features of these psalms which have been noted, and from that to have drawn similar conclusions; it is not at all obvious that a literal reading of these psalms is how the first audience thought.

In any case, what the first audience thought about these psalms does not have supervening relevance. While Roland Barthes' 'death of the author' has made a significant impact on modern literary criticism, we ought not to allow such methodologies to influence our handling of scripture. God is scripture's author, and, unlike human authors, he is perfectly and comprehensively in control of his literary production and its intended meaning. Audiences can read scripture accurately and discover its true meaning or they can misread it and fail to understand God's message; in neither case is the meaning determined by the audience.

Finally, COD'S comment about not being able to reject God using evolution if one rejects the literal meaning of Psalm 104:30, quite apart from laying out a 'straw man', betrays another misreading of *Genesis 1-2*. Nowhere does the book reject that God could use evolution should he so choose. Rather, *Genesis 1-2* examines typical handling by evolutionary creationists of Genesis 1 and 2, a handling which attempts accommodation of these chapters to evolutionary processes. Such handling can generally be characterised as treating these chapters as unhistorical and disharmonious. The book demonstrates that this approach amounts to a gross mishandling of scripture and that it is one which exhibits a denial of scripture's status as the word of God. This is not a rejection of God being able to use evolution if he so wishes, it is a rejection of an evolutionary creationist mishandling of Genesis 1 and 2.

A5: Different Order of Events? (Chapter 5)

The fourth post published by COD criticised *Genesis 1-2*, Chapter 5's grammatical analysis of Genesis 2:19.[1]

COD's criticism falls into two main areas: grammar and grammarians; and identifying the animals of Genesis 2:19. The *Replies* to COD are laid out under these headings.

Grammar and grammarians

Critique 1

There are two aspects to COD's principal criticism – a supposed failure of grammatical analysis – in this blog post:

- First, COD list a range of Hebrew scholars (NET translators, Michael S. Heiser and Vincent M. Setterholm, Gesenius, Driver and Buth), citing some of them, against the scholar who is referenced in *Genesis 1-2* to support the grammatical analysis of Genesis 2:19 proposed in the book.

- Second, COD claims that the reference to the scholar in the book – John Collins in a Tyndale Bulletin article – is an appeal to a single scholar that suits the preferences of the author.

---

[1] The *Fourth Post* can be accessed here:

https://christadelphiansoriginsdiscussion.wordpress.com/2019/09/10/heavysides-interpretation-exposed-by-grammar/.

Reply 1

John Collins specifically reviews the work of all the scholars listed by COD – except the NET and Michael S Heiser and Vincent M Setterholm[2] – plus other scholars not mentioned by COD. But COD seem to have missed the point of John Collins' review which is to lay out the progression of Hebrew scholarship on the topic of the pluperfect tense in the Hebrew scriptures.

John Collins' review can be summarised as follows:

S R Driver disagreed with the earlier work of Gesenius and Jouon who had precluded the possibility of *wayyiqtol*[3] denoting a pluperfect event – Driver allowed for an epexegetical interpretation of *wayyiqtol*. Later, Waltke and O'Connor, referring to the work of other scholars, disagreed with Driver, faulting him for inconsistency and affirming instances of *wayyiqtol* that require a pluperfect sense. The scholars to whom Waltke and O'Connor referred are W J Martin and D W Baker, the latter building on the work of the former; this work identified numerous examples of the *wayyiqtol* form which expressed the pluperfect sense. Based on analysis of numerous identifications of the *wayyiqtol* form expressing the pluperfect sense, R Buth progressed scholarship further by positing the conditions that help us recognise what he coined as the 'unmarked temporal overlay'.

Having presented this review in his Tyndale Bulletin article, John Collins explicitly states that he builds on R Buth's analysis by applying it

---

[2] The NET was released in an original beta in 2001, followed by a second beta in 2003 and the first edition in 2006. Michael S. Heiser and Vincent M. Setterholm, *Glossary of Morpho-Syntactic Database Terminology*, was published in 2013. Thus, both these references postdate John Collins' article dated 1995. More on this in the body of the *Reply*.

[3] *Wayyiqtol* is a scholarly reference to a particular construction of Hebrew imperfect verbs. It is this form of verb which opens both Genesis 2:19 (*wyṣr*) and Genesis 12:1 (*wy'mr*) and which are examined in Chapter 5 of *Genesis 1-2*.

to the data set found in the work of D W Baker. In doing so, he finds that Buth's criteria are too restrictive to cover all the data.

This brief outline of John Collins' review of scholarship, from which he then presents his own academic findings, demonstrates three things:

- Contrary to the posture which seems to be adopted by COD, there is no uniform consensus which can be lined up against the conclusions laid out by John Collins. Indeed, some of the scholars reviewed by the latter – particularly more recent scholars, including R Buth (cited by COD) – are clearly closer to John Collins in thought than to those more remote in time whom COD has listed as opposing scholarship.

- The trajectory of scholarship is clearly away from denial of the possibility of *wayyiqtol* denoting a pluperfect event to a recognition of a growing range of instances of such grammar.

- It is inaccurate for COD to take R Buth as 'the norm' rendering John Collins' conclusion about Genesis 2:19 as 'an exception'; it is clear from the scholarship review presented by John Collins that R Buth is not 'the final word' on the matter of the pluperfect tense in Hebrew.

Thus, it is not the case, as portrayed by COD, that John Collins is a sole scholar against which is ranged a solid consensus. There are several scholars – notably more recent in the trajectory of scholarship – who agree with him. Furthermore, John Collins does not position Genesis 2:19 as 'an exception to the norm' as suggested by COD; rather, it is presented as an example, within his refinement of R Buth's criteria, of a *wayyiqtol* denoting a pluperfect event.

Before moving on to address other elements of COD's criticism, a few comments about the NET and Michael S. Heiser and Vincent M. Setterholm's *Glossary of Morpho-Syntactic Database Terminology* which are cited by COD.

- The NET translation note which COD quotes includes the following reference to scholarship in support of their conclusion:

'See S. R. Driver, *A Treatise on the Use of the Tenses in Hebrew*, 84–88, and especially R. Buth, "Methodological Collision between Source Criticism and Discourse Analysis," *Biblical Hebrew and Discourse Linguistics*, 138–54.'

But the NET note does not end there, it continues:

'For a contrary viewpoint see *IBHS* 552–53 §33.2.3 and C. J. Collins, "The Wayyiqtol as 'Pluperfect': When and Why," *TynBul* 46 (1995): 117-40.'

IBHS is Bruce K. Waltke and Michael Patrick O'Connor's *Introduction to Biblical Hebrew Syntax*, scholars who, you will recall, disagreed with S R Driver, faulting him for inconsistency and affirming instances of *wayyiqtol* that require a pluperfect sense (for proof of which they referred to W J Martin and D W Baker). And, as already noted, John Collins faulted R Buth's criteria for an 'unmarked temporal overlay' as being too restrictive.

These aspects of the NET translation note are an unfortunate omission by COD, yet it is an omission that clearly suits their preferences. They also highlight the fact that, contrary to COD's position, John Collins is not a single scholar who has set himself apart from a uniform consensus.

- It has not been possible to access a copy of Michael S. Heiser and Vincent M. Setterholm's *Glossary of Morpho-Syntactic Database Terminology* to review their full entry or any references. However, at the general grammatical level, the extract quoted by COD is accurate. But it is an entry which, as quoted, does not even purport to address the pluperfect tense in the Hebrew scriptures. From this perspective, the citation offers no support for COD's claims.

Genesis 1-2

Identifying the animals of Genesis 2:19

Critique 2

COD asserts, 'Heavyside's approach to cut the meaning of every animal in Gen 2:19-20 down to just domestic animals is incorrect.' In support of this rebuttal, they claim to have touched on this matter previously and refer to an earlier blog post.[4]

Reply 2

The earlier blog post to which COD have referred is entirely focused on rejecting several christadelphian authors that they label as 'Literalist creationists.' The only evidence briefly offered in the post for rejecting a 'domesticated animal' reading of Genesis 2:19 is the use of what they term the 'global' language of verses 19-20: "every ... every ... every ... all ..." (KJV). There is no analysis presented by COD for reading these expressions in a global sense as opposed to expressions that refer to *all in a delimited context* – analysis which is a well-established requirement.

Consequently, the detailed analysis presented in *Genesis 1-2*, Chapter 5, 'Domesticated animals' still stands without any pertinent rebuttal from COD. Indeed, the evidence laid out in the book for reading Genesis 2:19-20 within that chapter's 'garden' context and not the Genesis 1 'earth' context is underlined by the presence of the anaphoric, "And the LORD God formed [*wyṣr yhwh 'lhym*]" (Gen. 2: 19) – a straight lift from the 'garden' context of Genesis 2:7.

---

[4] 'Literalist creationists become non-literal when it suits them', https://christadelphi-ansoriginsdiscussion.wordpress.com/2018/11/30/literalist-creationists-become-non-literal-when-it-suits-them/.

A6: The Charge of Literalism

Critique

COD pervasively characterise *Genesis 1-2* as 'literalist'.

Reply

The first matter to note is how much at odds this characterisation is with an entire chapter of *Genesis 1-2* which is devoted to examining the *figurative language* of scripture, including of Genesis 1 and 2 (Chapter 7, 'Figurative Language and Historicity'). In addition, throughout the book there is frequent insistence on the need to discern literary features of scripture, such as metaphorical language, as fundamental to proper analysis and exposition. These features unequivocally demonstrate that a 'literalist' approach to Genesis 1 and 2 is certainly not adopted in *Genesis 1-2*. Contrarily, COD have never in any of their posts pinpointed any specific aspect of *Genesis 1-2* to show that it has mistakenly adopted a 'literalist' approach.

Several times during their posts, COD seem to adopt a stance that for something to be historical it must be literal, whereas if the language is figurative, it cannot be historical. As a way of establishing such a position, COD employ expressions such as 'historical literal' and ask how we can know whether the language of Genesis 1 and 2 is figurative or literal. This is a stance shared with many evolutionary creationists as illustrated in *Genesis 1-2*. And yet, the whole of Chapter 7 of *Genesis 1-2* is devoted to showing two principal things:

- Scripture frequently employs figurative language to describe historical events.

- More particularly, figurative language is used in Genesis 1 and 2 and so, given the first point, its use there does not mean we should handle Genesis 1 and 2 as not historical.

Genesis 1-2

In the absence of any analysis from COD that the reasoning in Chapter 7 is in error, we can set aside any implication they might have in mind from querying how anybody can know whether creation statements are figurative or not. Some of them clearly are and yet they are demonstrably historical. Alongside this absence of any demonstration that the reasoning in Chapter 7 is faulty, COD defines 'historical literal' as '24 hour creation from nothing style.' Anyone will search in vain for any claims or statements in *Genesis 1-2* that either, (a) the days of creation in Genesis 1 were 24 hours, or (b) that creation was from nothing. The book has nothing to say about either of these things and so such a judgment cannot truly be reached, and this further illustrates the lack of proper analysis of the arguments in *Genesis 1-2* by COD.

Finally, it is strange that COD persistently charge *Genesis 1-2* with being 'literalist', despite the presence of Chapter 7 and the above objections having been presented to them. It is even stranger that in their opening post COD quote from Chapter 1, 'Preliminary Remarks' as follows:

"there must first be right interpretation of scriptures through discerning their various literary features"

This statement from the opening chapter of the book makes it clear that the approach adopted in *Genesis 1-2* is one of sensitivity to the literary features manifest in any specific scripture under scrutiny, and certainly not 'literalist'. It is puzzling how COD can quote this from the book, a clear statement that we should expect more than 'literality' from scripture, and yet still persist with the charge of literalism. It is noteworthy that this extract is closely followed by an example in the book which highlights this meaning:

"In the case of a metaphorical scripture, for example, the meaning of the metaphor must first be discerned before we are in a position to determine what the event is that is being described and which we are then obliged to take, since scripture is 'sure' and 'true', as having actually happened"[1]

Consequently, COD's continuing mischaracterisation of *Genesis 1-2* as 'literalist' is seen to be pejoratively programmatic. Had COD characterized *Genesis 1-2* as 'historicist', there would not be any objection.

---

[1] *Genesis 1-2*, 13.

Scripture Index

Genesis 1-2

Genesis 1-2

Genesis 1-2

Genesis 1-2

Scripture Index

Matthew			Matthew		
1		67	19:5		18, 19, 24, 26, 179, 189, 194
2:15		75	19:6		24, 191
3:17		57	19:8		23
5:22, 28, 32, 34, 39, 44		152	21:16		14
7:15		209	21:33		119
7:18		121	21:42		14
7:20		128	22:31		14
7:28		152	22:32		199
12:3,5		14	22:43-45		102
15:13		119	23:25		209
15:18-19		208	23:28		209
16:18		120	24:29		76
18:16		172	26:39-44		129
19:1		194	**Mark**		
19:3-6		Chapters 2; A2; 86, 113, 194	1:2		180, 181, 201, 202, 204, 205, 212
19:4-5		17, 26, 191, 192, 193, 195, 196, 197, 198, 201, 203, 205	1:11		57
			7:20-23		208
19:4		14, 15, 19, 180, 181, 195	10:2-9		Chapters 2; A2; 23, 26, 86

251

Genesis 1-2

John		Acts	
12:46	66	17:11	211
12:49	153	17:26	140
17:3	66	20:32	120
17:14	153	**Romans**	
17:16	153	3:5	128, 140
17:17	12, 153, 165	3:25	85
Acts		4:6-8	102
1:16	102	5	5, 89, 97, 116
1:20	102	6:5	119
2:25-28	102	7:22	209
2:34-35	102	8:29	37
4:25-26	102	9:6-8	106
7:2-3	53	11:9-10	102
13:22	180, 181, 201, 202, 203, 204, 205, 206, 212	**1 Corinthians**	
		2:10-13	167, 174
14	86	3:6-8	119
14:15	78	5:7	85
14:17	78, 79	9:7	119
15:1	107	10:1-6	75
15:14-15	107	10:11	75

Genesis 1-2

Scripture Index

1 Timothy

1:4	158
2	86
2:13	58, 113
4:7	158

2 Timothy

2:15	13, 167, 171
3:7-8	10
3:14-15	10
3:16-17	2, 10, 120, 165, 168
4:4	158

Titus

1:2	133
1:14	158

Hebrews

1:1-2	69
1:13	129
1:14	231
2	122, 130
2:6-10	97
2:8	130

Hebrews

3-5	75, 105
3:1	101
3:7-11	102, 110
4:7	102, 110
5-7	131
5:6	129
6:18	133
6:20	129
7:2-3	25
7:17	129
7:21	129
7:24	133
8-9	75
9:5	85
9:24	46, 84
10:1	84
10:7	129
10:11-12	129

James

1:17-18	36, 68, 226

Genesis 1-2

www.ingramcontent.com/pod-product-compliance
Lightning Source LLC
Chambersburg PA
CBHW071412090426
42737CB00011B/1443